# Key Essentials of International Trade and Business Law

Harald J. Jauk

Scriptum

International Law

International Investment Law

WTO Law

EU Competition Law

Private International Law

International Commercial Practices

Harald J. Jauk

# Key Essentials of International Trade and Business Law

2024/25

Key Essentials of International Trade and Business Law
Harald J. Jauk
Scriptum / Textbook / Course reader
Vienna, 2024/25
Publisher: BoD · Books on Demand GmbH, In de Tarpen 42, 22848 Norderstedt
Printed by: Libri Plureos GmbH, Friedensallee 273, 22763 Hamburg
Cover: Karoline Schreiber
ISBN: 978-3-7693-0083-3

# Contents

# List of abbreviations

| | |
|---|---|
| ABGB | Allgemeines Bürgerliches Gesetzbuch (Austrian Civil Code) |
| ADR | alternative dispute resolution |
| ALI | American Law Institute |
| BER | block exemption regulation(s) |
| BGB | Bürgerliches Gesetzbuch (German Civil Code) |
| Brussels Ia | Regulation (EU) No 1215/2012 on jurisdiction and the recognition and enforcement of judgments in civil and commercial matters (recast) |
| CoC | choice of court |
| CoL | choice of law |
| COTIF | Convention concerning International Carriage by Rail |
| CJEC | Court of Justice of the European Communities |
| CJEU | Court of Justice of the European Union |
| CIP | Carriage and Insurance Paid To (INCOTERMS clause) |
| CISG | United Nations Convention on Contracts for the International Sale of Goods |
| CIV | Uniform Rules concerning the Contract for International Carriage of Passengers and Luggage by Rail (appendix to Montreal Convention for International Carriage by Air) |
| CMR | Convention on the Contract for the International Carriage of Goods by Road |
| COM | European Commission |
| CPT | Carriage Paid To (INCOTERMS clause) |
| DAP | Delivered at Place (INCOTERMS clause) |
| DDP | Delivered Duty Paid (INCOTERMS clause) |
| DPU | Delivered at Place Unloaded (INCOTERMS clause) |
| DSB | Dispute Settlement Body of the World Trade Organization |
| DSU | Dispute Settlement Understanding (WTO) |
| EC | European Community / Communities |
| ECHR | European Convention on Human Rights |
| EO | Exekutionsordnung (Austrian Enforcement Code) |
| EU | European Union |
| EXW | Ex Works (INCOTERMS clause) |

| | |
|---|---|
| FCA | Free Carrier (INCOTERMS clause) |
| FDI | foreign direct investment |
| GATT | General Agreement on Tariffs and Trade |
| GATS | General Agreement on Trade in Services |
| GTC | General Terms and Conditions |
| HJC | Convention on the Recognition and Enforcement of Foreign Judgments in Civil or Commercial Matters |
| ICC | International Chamber of Commerce |
| ICCt | International Criminal Court |
| ICJ | International Court of Justice |
| ICSID | International Centre for Settlement of Investment Disputes |
| IDI | Institut de Droit International |
| IIOO | International Organizations |
| ILA | International Law Association |
| ILC | International Law Commission (UN) |
| ILO | International Labour Organization |
| IMF | International Monetary Fund |
| INCOTERMS | International Commercial Terms (ICC) |
| IP | intellectual property |
| IPRG | Bundesgesetz über das internationale Privatrecht (Austrian Federal Law on Private International Law) |
| ITLOS | International Tribunal for the Law of the Sea |
| JN | Jurisdiktionsnorm (Austrian Law on Jurisdiction) |
| KSchG | Konsumentenschutzgesetz (Austrian Consumer Protection Act) |
| LDCs | Least Developed Countries |
| LoN | League of Nations |
| Lugano | Convention on jurisdiction and the recognition and enforcement of judgments in civil and commercial matters |
| MC | WTO Ministerial Conference |
| MFN | most favored nation |
| MIGA | Multilateral Investment Guarantee Agency |
| MS | member state(s) |
| NATO | North Atlantic Treaty Organization |
| NT | national treatment |

| | |
|---|---|
| NTBs | non-tariff barriers |
| NYC | New York Convention on the Recognition and Enforcement of Foreign Arbitral Awards |
| OECD | Organisation for Economic Co-operation and Development |
| PICC | UNIDROIT Principles of International Commercial Contracts |
| PIL | Private International Law |
| Rome I | Regulation (EC) No 593/2008 on the law applicable to contractual obligations |
| S&D | Special & Differential (Treatment) |
| SWIFT | Society for Worldwide Interbank Financial Telecommunication |
| TFEU | Treaty on the Functioning of the European Union |
| TiG | Trade in goods |
| TiS | Trade in services |
| TRIPS | Agreement on Trade-Related Aspects of Intellectual Property Rights |
| UCC | Uniform Commercial Code (USA) |
| UCP | Uniform Customs and Practice for Documentary Credits (ICC) |
| UGB | Unternehmensgesetzbuch (Austrian Companies Code) |
| UN | United Nations (Organization) |
| UNCITRAL | United Nations Commission on International Trade Law |
| UNCLOS | United Nations Convention on the Law of the Sea |
| UNCTAD | UN Trade and Development |
| UNGA | United Nations General Assembly |
| UNIDROIT | International Institute for the Unification of Private Law |
| URC | Uniform Rules for Collections (ICC) |
| VCLT | Vienna Convention on the Law of Treaties (between States) |
| WB | World Bank |
| WCO | World Customs Organization |
| WIPO | World Intellectual Property Organization |
| WTO | World Trade Organization |

# Foreword

It is my pleasure to offer a few introductory words for this handbook on international trade and business law. I strongly support this intentionally concise publication, which aims to provide essential knowledge on critical subjects in international trade and business law. While law and regulations can often be highly technical, frequently left to the domain of legal professionals, their significance extends far beyond the legal community. These laws and rules shape how we collaborate, uphold standards, and ensure prosperity not just for a select few but for society as a whole.

In specific, I want to emphasize the political importance of these subjects. Competitiveness is the central issue that we as the European Union must address. There are two key points I would like to highlight.

First, the positive one: Trade within and outside the EU is a success story. With a total of 74 countries, the EU has the world's largest network of trade agreements. The value of EU trade through trade agreements with global partners now exceeds 2 trillion euros.

Second, the slightly more critical reflection: The pressure of competition is mounting. Thirty years ago, Europe accounted for 25% of global wealth. By 2040, it is projected to shrink to just 11%, placing us well behind China and the United States, and on par with India.

One often-overlooked aspect is the significance of the EU internal market, our most critical trade agreement. The EU internal market has developed into the strongest economic area in the world, from which Austria and all EU member states benefit significantly. According to the European Commission, EU export companies save around 2,2 to 5,5 billion euros per year thanks to the elimination of the EU's internal borders. Competition law plays a crucial role in this by promoting fair business practices and ensuring effective competition within the internal market, as thoroughly presented in this book.

The figures are clear: Austrian exports to other EU member states have more than tripled from 33 to 112 billion euros since joining the EU – in 2021, almost 70% of Austrian goods exports were destined for the EU. Thanks to the harmonization of standards and norms, domestic companies can now sell their products and services to 448 million people. Investments by foreign companies have also increased more than fivefold from around 1,3 billion euros per year to around 7 billion euros. The EU single market also means that all Austrians have an average annual income of 1 583 euros more in their wallets.

These figures demonstrate the tangible impact of a shared legal and economic framework. Without international trade and a clear legal structure governing our economy, these achievements would not be possible. That said, there is still vast untapped potential. Completing the EU internal market alone could yield efficiency gains of up to 829 billion euros annually. The possibilities for growth and further integration are immense.

I am excited that this handbook will guide you through the opportunities, challenges, and legal nuances of international trade and business law. May your exploration of these topics inspire new insights and innovations in the future of global commerce.

**Othmar Karas**
former First Vice-President of the European Parliament
25 years member of the European Parliament's ECON Committee

# Preface

After university or some national experience, most people are directly "thrown" into international business activity without knowing in detail how the international system works. That is ok.

We do not have to know how International Law and its trade and business related specialized regimes work *in detail*.

What we do have to know though is – for competence reasons, for not embarrassing ourselves and, finally, for performing most efficiently – how it works in *very general terms*.

This is what this book does – it provides shortest summaries.

While most books provide broad information of which you only remember 10%, this book displays exactly those 10% you should remember. With practical examples it makes remembering easier. (Often we remember theory thanks to an example that stays in our memory from which we then deduce theory.)

So instead of investing 100% for remembering 10%, you save 90% and directly focus on those 10% worth investing your time in and remembering.

This book is a practical handbook that summarizes and simplifies often dry and hard to handle theory.

In fact, the topics here displayed are very diverse and range from general International Law to WTO Law, EU Competition Law and Private International Law. It further includes common practices in international business, uniform law like the UN Sales Convention and widespread contract clauses like the INCOTERMS.

Normally you would need to buy a separate book for each of them because very rarely all of them are included in *one* book. If they are, those books usually do not have less than 1000 pages. So you save time and money.

It is a book for non-lawyers, especially students and businesspeople, and lawyers specialized in something else who want to get a glance of a substantial yet thrilling area of law.

Nobody implicated in international business and trade on a higher level should and properly can do without the basic knowledge provided in this book. It is general knowledge every international trader, consultant, accountant, sales manager, trade official and business analyst should have.

Getting a birds-eye view of the topics is ensured not only by conciseness but also by the choice of language made for this book:

The language used in it is kept as simple as possible and includes as few complex vocabulary as possible.

In addition, orientation is facilitated by symbols and graphics as well as **bold print** and *italics* in between for highlighting specifically important points or words.

This preface being as succinct as this book, it's necessary to calling it a day now.

I wish you not to enjoy your reading (who actually *enjoys* reading textbooks?) but to get the most out of it.

Harald J. Jauk

# A International Economic? Business? Trade? Law

The first challenge one encounters when dealing with international economic law is the diversity of terminology used for the subject itself. International Economic Law, International Business Law, International Trade Law... To most, that sounds very similar but – like basically always in law – there is a (possible) distinction between these terms and other related ones.[1]

Let us start with the first one – *International Economic Law*. What is often seen as a specialized legal regime of International Law (and in many general International Law books has its own chapter) can be seen as the broadest one of the mentioned notions. That is why – also due to its ambiguity (in application too) – it does not surprise that Andreas Lowenfeld said

> It is not inappropriate to begin by asking whether there is such a thing as international economic law, a body of law that can be subjected to systematic treatment between the covers of a book.[2]

While to some it might seem too broad and vague to be covered between the covers of a book, Lowenfeld answers his own question by writing exactly such a book and naming it "International Economic Law".

**So what does International Economic Law cover?**

Areas generally included in literature about this topic are **International Trade Law** (see below), **International Investment Law** (investment

---

[1] Also take into account that in law (doctrine), in many cases there is no such thing as unanimity of opinions, but instead there is a *prevailing* view and there are other views of the same subject matter.

[2] Lowenfeld, Andreas F., 2008: *International Economic Law*[2], Oxford University Press, New York, preface.

protection etc.) and **International Monetary Law** (providing liquidity, exchange rate stability, etc.).

Sometimes international economic sanctions (such as those mandated by the UN) and International Competition Law (anti-competitive acts by enterprises or states etc.) are also included in such books. The bulkier books[3] sometimes also comprise International Capital Markets Law (which state's capital markets law should be applied) and additionally focus on specific areas such as telecommunication, transport, financing and international payments.

Some of the literature that refers to itself as *International Economic Law* also includes private law aspects[4], such as factual international trading practices between private parties (incl. model laws and contractual clauses) and *uniform law* (see chapter *Uniform Law*). Sometimes also International Corporate (or Company) Law (see below), Private International Law (PIL, see below) and other areas of (partly) internationally regulated matters are covered in such books.

In other words, the scope of International Economic Law – also due to its inclusion in its broadest sense of both public and private law[5] matters – is indeed very broad, maybe even confusingly broad to be seen (and studied) as *one* area of law.

---

[3] Such as Kronke, Herbert et al., 2017: *Handbuch Internationales Wirtschaftsrecht*[2], Linde, Vienna.

[4] Some authors clearly distinguish between International Economic Law as exclusively *public* law regulating international economic matters and, on the other hand, International Business Law as exclusively *private* law and practices in the international economic sphere. See e.g. Fernández Rozas et al., 2013: 37, 43 et seq.

[5] According to the subject theory, Public and Private Law can be distinguished by the parties taking part at a legal action. If at least one of the parties acts with *imperium* (state power), we talk about Public Law. If none of the concerned parties acts with *imperium* (there are only private persons or entities), we talk about Private Law.
See e.g. Bydlinski, Franz, 1994: „Kriterien und Sinn der Unterscheidung von Privatrecht und öffentlichem Recht", in *Archiv für die civilistische Praxis*, vol. 194, 329 et seq.

Therefore, other terms provide a more reduced scope but are often also only imprecisely delimited.

### *What about International Business Law?*

There are several books, courses of study and university subjects/courses that bear this name, but this label does not clearly define what they actually comprise either.

What seems certain though is that it comprises some private law areas[6], like **International Corporate (or Company) Law** (international M&A, corporations' legal forms and transformations, international transfer of shares, etc.) or **Private International Law** (Where is the dispute being heard, which rules govern it and is the decision recognized and enforced?) and arbitration (see *Arbitration*). Generally, also **International Trade Law** (see next paragraph) is included here.
In Europe, International Business Law courses[7] (of study) often also cover European Union (EU) Law, especially EU Competition Law.

Since the term International Business Law (such as International Economic Law), thanks to its imprecision, leaves space for other subjects it can also cover other areas of (international) law.[8]

Comparing both concepts, International Economic Law is mostly understood as the broader concept with a clear public law focus (but some possible private law aspects), whereas International Business Law is narrower and generally tends to have a stronger private law emphasis and include only core principles of public International Law, such as

---

[6] Some authors even consider that International Business Law exclusively deals with "international transactions performed by private individuals" (Fernández Rozas et al., 2013: 37, translated), i.e. private law issues.
[7] Some university etc. courses avoid the ambiguity of the terminology and instead opt for course names like "Law *for* International Business", which opens the concept to *any* legal matter of interest for international business relations.
[8] Like this book, which also quickly outlines some key concepts of International Law in general.

International Trade Law.[9] What they both have in common is their imprecise definition, which leaves lots of space for flexible focus placing as well as expanding or narrowing down the covered matters.

### At last, is the concept of International Trade Law sharper?

After having seen the imprecisely delimited concepts of International Economic Law and International Business Law, it nearly surprises that there is more consensus (and therefore clarity) on the term International (or World) Trade Law. This goes back to the centrality of *one* International Organization in this sphere: the World Trade Organization (WTO).

> the term 'World Trade Law' (…) emphasises the central role of the World Trade Organization (WTO) in regulating the rules of world trade. The WTO is not the only relevant legal instrument or international organization, but it is the broadest and most comprehensive in its coverage.[10]

In other words, International Trade Law in most cases is understood as the legal system and framework of the WTO, including both its international treaties and its "case law". In short, it focuses on trade barriers both in goods and services (including quotas and tariffs) and partly also on the harmonization of regulation in its member states (e.g. regarding intellectual property rights[11]).

Hence, in comparison to the meanings of *International Economic Law* and *International Business Law*, *International Trade Law* is the "narrowest" term (despite being itself a big and substantive legal area) and, at the same time, integrates itself in the former two concepts as a part of them.

---

[9] To make it clear that this book about International Business Law focuses, among other subjects, also on International Trade Law, it was named "… International *Trade and* Business Law".

[10] Lester, 2018: 3.

[11] For more information, see *TRIPS*.

22

Since we now understand what might[12] await us in this book, we can proceed to the general setting in which *International Trade and Business Law* is embedded – *International Law* itself.

---

[12] "Might", since, as we know now, the term International Business Law is imprecise.

# B International Law

Before having a closer look at specific areas of International Law[13], such as International Investment Law and International Trade Law, it is worth getting a basic understanding of International Law as such.

Due to the broad material scope the term (public) *International Law* covers, there are numerous definitions of it (definitions by sources of law, by legal sanctions, by topics covered, etc.). In short and simplified, it can be defined as follows:

*Legal provisions of not exclusively national belonging that regulate the relations between subjects of International Law.*

 Subjects of International Law are, primarily, **states** and **International Organizations**, i.e. entities with legal personality created (mainly) by states by means of international treaties.

Notably *not* included in this concept is the in the later chapters of this book also covered Private International Law (PIL), which refers to the relations not between states/International Organizations but between *private persons or entities*.[14] Due to its completely different nature, PIL is not discussed in this chapter but in the second part of this book.

---

[13] General International Law, which is covered in this first chapter, refers to the international legal order as such, its actors, rules and breaches thereof. But International Law also covers special disciplines focusing on specific material areas, which are called *specialized regimes* (e.g. International Criminal Law, International Humanitarian Law, International Sea Law and International Economic Law, part of which are International Investment Law and International Trade Law).

[14] Although some of the relevant laws in PIL are indeed International Law, it is also and primarily (!) composed by national law.

The *legal provisions* mentioned in the expounded International Law definition are law and should have the enforcement power of law but, in many cases, are broken with no consequences.

If *national* law is violated (**A** drives too fast), a superordinated entity (the state) – with its coercive power – will sanction the violation and/or take care of compliance (**A** will get a fine or loose his/her license).

In *International* Law there is no superordinated entity (all states are equal). Therefore, it is unclear from where this sanctioning and enforcing coercive power should come from. In fact, apart from special cases like the UN Security Council or the European Union, there is no central entity that makes International Law subjects (and others) comply with International Law (!).

States and International Organizations (IIOO) comply with International Law due to other negative consequences if not (political, economic, etc.) which have their origin in their peers – other states. Nevertheless, if these disadvantageous consequences are considered less important by the infringing state than the advantages of the violation, it most likely will not comply with International Law.

> Due to this often politically dominated voluntariness in implementation (…), which results from the non-obligatory enforcement (…), the term "soft law" regularly appears to be somewhat accurate for International Law.[15]

**Example**

When the Russian Federation invaded Ukraine in 2022, it did not comply with the UN Charter's *prohibition of use of force*-rule (Art. 2) and the UN

---

[15] Jauk, 2023: 22, translated.

General Assembly's Resolution on the end of the Russian Federation's illegal use of force against Ukraine.[16]

Although many states (and the EU) imposed political and economic sanctions and it had severe diplomatic consequences, to date, the illegal use of force in Ukraine is still ongoing.

Nevertheless, most of International Law is complied with anyway and a story of success.[17]

***Why do states generally honor their international obligations if there is no enforcement?***

Due to the many benefits it has, e.g.

- the long-term benefit of a well-functioning international legal system,
- the good reputation of a state, which would be lost if it stopped following international rules,
- the many benefits of IIOO (political, economic, etc.), such as the EU.

But also due to the negative consequences non-compliance with International Law can have, e.g.

- the threatening retorsion or even countermeasures by other states,
- the threatening sentences (and punishments) of international (or national) courts,

---

[16] Resolution adopted by the General Assembly on 23 February 2023 (02.03.22), A/RES/ES-11/6, UNGA, https://documents-dds-ny.un.org/doc/UNDOC/GEN/N23/063/07/PDF/N2306307.pdf?OpenElement.
[17] Especially International Law of the Sea, WTO Law and some international conventions like the NYC on the Recognition and Enforcement of Foreign Arbitral Awards.

- the negative precedence-effect a breach can have, with a possible chain reaction of many states not complying with an international rule,
- the possible loss of international goodwill and negative effects on future cooperations with other states and IIOO.

# I. Origins of International Law

In the Late Middle Age and the beginning Modern Age the pope had some *international* influence over emperors and there were *transnational* networks of knights and merchants (incl. private transnational contracts with some kind of private international rules[18]), but there was no public international legal structure yet.

The **17th century** can be considered as the beginning of the modern international legal thinking:

- The Dutchman **Hugo Grotius** suggested to apply *natural law* (*all is predetermined*-law based on common ethical principles) to international relations.
- The **Peace of Westphalia** (1648) marked the birth of the international state system by reducing the powers of transnational forces like empire and religion and compartmentalizing territory into sovereign states.
  Against the background of the raging wars in Europe (Thirty Years' War etc.), an international order with agreed rules and limits and a clear source of authority (*sovereignty*) was created. It spread to the rest of the world.

 From that moment on up until the 20th century the international order was made by the **West** and is based on western values (individual rights, open economic markets, democracy, etc.).

In the **19th century** further steps were made:

- **Positivism** and statutory law ("*all law must be man-made and man-legitimized*") came to the fore and international consensual theory

---

[18] See *Lex Mercatoria*.

28

was established: unless a state consents to be bound, there is no international obligation.
- The **first formal institutions** of International Law appeared: the *International Telegraph Union* (1865)[19] and the *Universal Postal Union* (1874), that both still exist and are UN Specialized Agencies.
- The **first modern multilateral treaties** were concluded: the *Hague Conventions* (1899, 1907) regulating responsibility of individuals in armed conflict (International Criminal Law) and establishing the Permanent Court of Arbitration.

The **20th century** marked the final step in the creation of the international system as we now know it, with the following "highlights" (selection):

- Until the 20th century war was the standard means for settling international disputes (!).
  The foundation of the **League of Nations** (LoN, 1919, incl. Permanent Court of International Justice) was the first step to change that: It certainly did *not* prohibit war, but it required states to submit their disputes to a settlement mechanism (and wait three months after its decision) before resorting to war.
- Another step for outlawing war was the **Kellog-Briand-Pact** (Treaty of Paris, 1928) concluded between the foreign ministers of the US and France to refrain from resorting to war as means for settlement of international controversies.
- Finally, in 1945 the **United Nations Organization** (UN) was founded in San Francisco, which was from its beginning equipped with a Security Council as the worldwide only organ to authorize the use of force. The UN General Assembly (UNGA) played a key role in decolonialization (e.g. *Declaration on Self-Determination*, 1960) and the advancement of International Law (with the International Law Commission [ILC]).

---

[19] Now *International Tele**communication** Union*.

- In 1944, the world's key international **finance/monetary and trade institutions** were created in Bretton Woods/USA (World Bank, 1947 GATT and 1995 WTO).
- While the **Nuremberg Tribunal** (1945) set an important precedent in International Criminal Law addressing war crimes, the **Geneva Conventions** (1949) advanced International Humanitarian Law regulating the conduct of war in order to avoid e.g. civilian victims.
- In 1949, the US-European military alliance **North Atlantic Treaty Organization** (NATO) and the **Council of Europe** with its main goal to protect human rights were founded.
- **European integration** commenced with the creation of the European Coal and Steel Community (1951) as well as the European Economic Community and Euratom (1957).
- In the 2000s, the **African Union** (2001) was established and emerging economies founded the intergovernmental cooperation platform **BRICS** (2009).

# II. Sources of International Law

On the *national* level lawmaking is generally centralized with laws deriving from *one* origin, which is often the *parliament*, i.e. in states with a separation of state powers, the legislation (which is separate from execution).

*International* lawmaking[20] is decentralized with its rules deriving from *various* origins. This has to do with the different constellations in which e.g. international treaties are concluded, i.e. between varying states and IIOO at varying locations. Another difference to national laws is that international legal rules do not emanate from the *legislative* power[21] but from the same power they are executed by: the *executive*.

That being said, what kind of legal rules does International Law have, or better:

*What are the sources of International Law?*

This question is easy to answer thanks to the Statue of the (UN) International Court of Justice (ICJ), which contains the classical list of International Law sources:

    a.  **international conventions**, whether general or particular, establishing rules expressly recognized by the contesting states;

    b.  **international custom**, as evidence of a general practice accepted as law;

    c.  the **general principles of law** recognized by civilized nations;

    d.  subject to the provisions of Article 59 [*individual decisions are only binding for the specific case they refer to*], **judicial decisions** and the

---

[20] Except e.g. in the EU, where it is centralized in Brussels and Strasbourg.
[21] Although frequently the national parliament is also required by law to agree on international treaties.

**teachings** of the most highly qualified publicists of the various nations, as subsidiary means for the determination of rules of law.
(ICJ Statute Art. 38, bold print added)

International conventions, international custom and general principles of law[22] are the so-called *primary* sources of law and are law *creating*.

Judicial decisions and scholarly contributions are the secondary sources of law because they are only law *identifying*, i.e. they are not International Law in a strict sense (but only help detecting and delimiting it).

Apart from that, in practice **unilateral statements** of persons (organs) with sufficient official power are another source of International Law. These can be both law creating and identifying.

## 1. Treaties

States and IIOO[23], as International Law subjects, are free to conclude international treaties (=conventions =covenants =agreements[24]) *when, with which other state(s) or International Organization(s) and on what*[25] they like.

The legal basis for their conclusion is *state consent*, which means that an international treaty only creates legal obligations for the states consenting to it, but not for other states (no rules by **A** and **B** for **C**). These treaties can be "simple" treaties or establish an institutional framework like an International Organization.

---

[22] The reference to "civilized nations" referring to *developed national legal systems* and being with no meaning anymore.
[23] And some also other entities such as the *Sovereign Military Order of Malta*, the Holy See or even some NGOs.
[24] Although *agreements* can also be of a non-legal nature.
[25] For that, there are certain limits though, see below.

Apart from *creating* an International Organization, states can also transfer some of their competences to an International Organization and, by that, give it the competence to adopt legally binding acts (e.g. the *EU* as a prime example). If states do so, we have somewhat of a new source of law, which is called *treaty based* (but does not constitute an independent sources of law-category).

International treaties can be oral or written, the latter being the regular case though (this being understandable for evidence purposes).

They can be concluded between two states/IIOO (*bilateral*) or more states/IIOO (*multilateral*[26]).

More information on international treaties can be found in the chapter *Law of Treaties*.

## 2. Custom

Law (of international or national nature) cannot only be made *consciously/actively*, but also *uncounsiously/passively*.

 In fact, law adapts according to the *factual* interaction between states (and IIOO) under certain circumstances.

For international custom (= *international customary law*) to emerge, two factors are necessary: international/state *practice* and *legal belief*.

**State practice** (*consuetudo*) is the (more) objective element of these two and refers to all state acts, e.g. physical acts (military operations, seizure

---

[26] In WTO Law, *multilateral* refers to treaties between all of the WTO's members and *plurilateral* to those between only some of its members.
Generally, the term *multilateral* refers though to any international treaty with more than two parties.

33

of foreign vessels) and public verbal acts (diplomatic statements, press releases, national judgments, resolutions&declarations of IIOO in which the state participated).

This practice must be *generally consistent* with the supposed rule (see below) that will become customary law.

Usually also a rather *long duration* of this practice is necessary, except – according to some – in situations of rapid change, where so-called *instant custom* can appear.

An **example** for instant custom is the international state practice reaction to 9/11, according to which armed attacks can allow self-defense also if these are committed by a *non-state* actor (and not only a *state*, as was the situation before).

The practice must be performed by the *majority* (not necessarily all) of the existing states whose interests are specifically affected.

**Legal belief** (*opinio iuris*) is the subjective element in the assessment if international custom exists and refers to the state practice being *regarded and accepted as legally binding* by the participating states. This is certainly difficult to demonstrate[27].

Also for this reason, some consider that *opinio iuris* must only be looked for when there is reason to believe that the state practice goes back to *non-legal* motivations (political expediency, good neighbor relations, etc.).[28]

---

[27] It often can be determined by state practice itself (laws, judgments, protest notes, countermeasures, etc.).
[28] See e.g. Henricksen, 2019: 27.

34

Once emerged, international custom binds all implicated states except the so-called *persistent objectors*, which are (existing) states that regularly explicitly contradict to it. New states are bound by existing customary law and cannot object against it.

It must be noted that international customary law does not have to be universal. It can also emerge e.g. between only two states or a geographic area (e.g. in Europe *democratic governance* and the *non-refoulement* principle[29]).

Other examples for international custom are the sovereign equality of states, the existence of peremptory International Law (*ius cogens*, see below) as well as the *pacta sunt servanda* (agreements must be kept), *(clausula) rebus sic stantibus*[30] and *estoppel*[31] principles. These three principles are also part of the *general principles of law*, which sometimes overlap with international custom. Often international custom is also codified (see now), by an *international treaty*, which shows the often close connection between these three sources of International Law.

### What happens when a matter is found in both a treaty and customary law?

If they are *identical*, they reinforce each other and states are bound by both. In fact, it is not so rare that treaties "codify" international customary law, i.e. systematically put custom into writing. The UN International Law Commission (ILC, Geneva)[32] is specifically tasked with this job of codifying international (customary) law.

If they are *conflicting*, the treaty prevails unless a customary rule has developed subsequently to the treaty (and therefore is the later or more

---

[29] According to which people (e.g. refugees) cannot be returned to countries where they risk grave human rights violations (e.g. torture).

[30] Possibility to adjust (or terminate) contracts if fundamental circumstances change.

[31] Prohibition of contravening one's own former actions if the other party counted on these and would be harmed by a change in behavior.

[32] And also some private organizations, such as the Institut de Droit International (IDI) and the International Law Association (ILA).

specific rule [*lex posterior, lex specialis*]), and in case of ius cogens (see below).

The reason why usually the treaty prevails is that it constitutes *a* more deliberate act of law-creation.

The other way around, international treaties can (and sometime do[33]) with the time also develop into customary law so that, in the end, if they were conflicting before, they are not anymore.

## 3. General principles of law

The *general principles of law* refer to the principles that are common to a representative majority of national[34] legal systems. They are construed as gap fillers in case treaties and custom are unable to resolve a matter.

Apart from those mentioned which also became international custom thanks to a coinciding state practice (see above), typical examples for general principles of law are

- equity: fairness e.g. regarding maritime delimitations
- no harm/due diligence: e.g. the obligation of states to not allow their territory to be used for acts that damage other states significantly (e.g. cyberspace or international environmental law)
- res iudicata: *final* judgments cannot be relitigated
- obligation of paying default interest in case of late payments
- *good faith* in the performance of contracts (*pacta sunt servanda*[35]) and their interpretation
- duty or obligation to mitigate damages

---

[33] E.g. the *Hague Conventions* of 1899 and 1907 regulating responsibility of individuals in armed conflict.
[34] But they can also stem from *international* law.
[35] Agreements must be kept.

36

# 4. Judicial decisions

Judicial decisions are, as mentioned, a secondary source of law, i.e. only used for *identifying* other (primary) International Law sources.

These judicial decisions can have their origin in both an international and a national court.

To be mentioned specifically are the

- ICJ's decisions and advisory opinions,
- awards from international arbitral tribunals,
- decisions of specialized international courts, such as the Nuremberg Military Tribunal (1945/46) and the International Tribunal for the former Yugoslavia,
  the DSB (WTO), the ITLOS (sea law), the ECHR (human rights), the CJEU (EU), and the International Criminal Court (ICCt) and
- decisions of last instance national courts.

Judicial decisions are not case law in the sense that courts applying International Law must stick to them in any case.
Quite the contrary holds true (at least in theory): Individual decisions are only considered binding *for the specific case they refer to*. Nonetheless, specifically ICJ decisions that represent settled jurisprudence are seldom departed from by the ICJ.


# 5. Scholarly contributions

Another secondary source of law are scholarly contributions, although – for determining International Law – rarely the contributions of individual scholars are made reference to. Courts determining and applying International Law tend to use and cite primarily the contributions of organizations.

Examples are the draft articles and commentaries by the International Law Commission (or the IDI and the ILA) on its international codifications; the commentaries to the Geneva Conventions (1949) by the International Committee of the Red Cross or writings by the American Society of International Law or the European Society of International Law, which publish prestigious International Law journals.

## 6. Unilateral statements

Although unilateral statements by high state representatives are not an official source of International Law, they certainly are *de facto* due to their often legally binding function.

They must be brought by heads of state, heads of government and ministers for foreign affairs and, although there are no form requirements, must be clear and specific. If the freedom of action of their own country was limited by the statement, they must be interpreted restrictively.

**Example**

A (long) while ago, the Norwegian foreign minister stated that, regarding the Danish claims to Greenland (which is part of Denmark), his country "would not make any difficulties". When Danish sovereignty was later contested by Norway, the PCIJ (the "predecessor" of the ICJ at the LoN) found the earlier statement legally binding.[36]

---

[36] *Legal Status of Eastern Greenland*, PCJI Judgment, 1933, A/B Series No. 53.

# 7. Soft law instruments

Apart from the sources of law just mentioned, which, at least in theory, have the binding force of law, there are other instruments of international nature concluded between states that are not meant to be binding. These instruments are often referred to as "soft law" because they have the goal to make their parties do something (like *law*) but are specifically not enforceable (and therefore *soft*).

### What is the advantage of soft law? Why do states "adopt" it?

Key advantages of international soft law instruments are that they are frequently faster in their conclusion and more flexible (easily and at any time modifiable and withdrawable). However, despite their not legally binding "softness", states in many cases anyway comply with them due to the political price they often pay if they do not stick to an officially and publicly concluded (soft) agreement.

At last, such soft law agreements can (and sometimes do) become legally binding.

### How?

 By way of a long and continuous state practice soft law may become customary international law (!).

Apart from that, soft law may serve as evidence for *consuetudo* or *opinio iuris* emanating from other acts and assist in interpreting international custom.

Examples for soft law are the famous Universal Declaration of Human Rights (1948), the UN Global Compacts on Migration / on Refugees (both 2018, focusing on international cooperation and burden sharing) and some resolutions and declarations of the UNGA, e.g. the Self-Determination Declaration for Colonies of 1960 (UNGA Resolution 1514 (XV)).

# 8. Hierarchy of sources and *ius cogens*

All the (primary) sources of International Law have the same hierarchy.[37] Nevertheless, there are some rules that are "above" these. These are the so-called **a)** international peremptory norms (*ius cogens*)[38], **b)** international obligations *erga omnes* and **c)** obligations under the UN Charter.

International **ius cogens** is defined in the *Vienna Convention on the Law of Treaties* (1969), which regulates international treaties between states, as

> a norm accepted and **recognized by the international community** of States as a whole **as a norm from which no derogation is permitted** and which can be modified only by a subsequent norm of general international law having the same character. (VCLT Art. 53, bold print added)

The result of the conclusion of a treaty conflicting with such a norm, is *voidness*, which is also the case for other sources of International Law that contradict *ius cogens*.

The most prominent examples for peremptory international norms are the crimes of International Criminal Law (e.g. *Genocide, War crimes* or *Crimes against humanity*, which refers to large-scale attacks on civilians), torture and slavery. Also the general prohibition of the use of force, which is also an obligation under the UN Charter (see below), has been referred to as *ius cogens*.

Apart from voidness, acts against *ius cogens* have another consequence. If a state breaches it, all other states must not render assistance to it and refrain from recognizing the breach as lawful.

---

[37] And the *lex posterior/lex specialis* – rule applies, which means that a newer treaty (provision) replaces an earlier one and a more specific one a more general one.
[38] Not to be confused with *national* ius cogens that in Private International Law can play a role.

40

In other words, *ius cogens* sets basic substantive rules determining which material content any source of International Law cannot have, otherwise it being both void and not recognized by the international community.

The second "superior" norms category are **obligations erga omnes**, i.e. obligations owed by a state to the international community *as a whole*.

While *ius cogens* refers to *substantive* no-gos, obligations *erga omnes* do not refer primarily to illegal substantive contents but to an important procedural question:

*If an obligation is owed to nobody in specific (but all states together) who in specific can invoke this obligation if it is breached?*

Obligations *erga omnes* create a *procedural* possibility for states: The breach of such an obligation can be **invoked by *any* state**, even though it is not specifically affected.

These obligations are often referred to for invoking International Environmental Law provisions. Apart from that, all *ius cogens* has *erga omnes*-effect, meaning that a breach of international peremptory norms can always be invoked by *any* state. In addition, human rights (also those that are not *ius cogens*) generally have *erga omnes*-character.

The third category of "superior" international rules are **obligations under the UN Charter** including Security Council Resolutions.

Just like peremptory norms, the rules established in these prevail if a source of International Law is not in line with them. The only condition is that (the Charter and) Resolutions do not violate *ius cogens*.

The most prominent example is, of course, the prohibition of the use of force (excluding limited cases where it is allowed).

# III. Law of Treaties

Rules for international treaties between states[39] are contained in the Vienna Convention on the Law of Treaties (VCLT, 1969, 1980 in force), in which customary practices were codified.

It covers **a)** *written* treaties between **b)** states (not IIOO) irrespective of their material content. (VCLT Art. 1, 3)

 *Written* does not mean that it must officially be named *treaty*, *convention* or *covenant* – minutes/protocols, exchanges of notes, memoranda of understanding etc. suffice, if there is an intention to create rights and obligations under International Law.

The **c)** intention to create international rights and obligations (not given in soft law) can, in fact, be seen as a general requirement for international treaties.

### How can we know about the state parties' intention?

Important clues can be found in the terminology and form of the agreement as well as the precision in language, the circumstances of its conclusion and the manner in which parties have dealt with the agreement after its conclusion (e.g. submitted to the national parliament according to the country's national laws or not).

Treaties are based on **d)** consent, which is why **A** and **B** can determine legal obligations between themselves in a treaty but not (also) for **C**. (VCLT Art. 34) Even (seemingly) unequal or unreasonable treaties are possible if consent is given.

---

[39] As for IIOO, the *Vienna Convention on the Law of Treaties Between States and International Organizations or Between International Organizations* (1986) was created, which is not (yet) in force though.

*Who can conclude a treaty (representing the state)?*

Heads of state, heads of government and ministers for foreign affairs have the power to conclude international treaties. Apart from that, heads of diplomatic missions (permanent representatives/ambassadors), depending on the act and circumstances, may also conclude certain treaties.
Other persons can be authorized to negotiate and conclude a treaty, if a *full power* is issued to them.

*How to conclude a treaty?*

One of the mentioned persons must *sign* the treaty, which expresses the state's consent. In many cases, the treaty must also be *ratified*[40] though to be binding, which is done according to the respective national law of the state parties to a treaty (e.g. confirmation by the national parliament). There are also other forms for becoming "part" of an international treaty (e.g. accession, where a *signature* is regularly not necessary).

If the treaty allows[41] **reservations**, i.e. unilateral statements excluding or modifying the legal effect of one or more treaty provisions, states can also exclude parts of a treaty to be applied to them. Apart from reservations being permitted, they must be compatible with the object and the purpose of the treaty and made at the beginning (at signature/ratification/accession etc. of the reserving state).[42]

---

[40] The *ratification* is the formal declaration by a state to be legally bound by the treaty.
[41] E.g. the Rome Statute of the ICC, the UNCLOS and the ILO-Conventions do not.
[42] If not done at the beginning but a later moment, the other state parties must all accept it.

**Example**

Regarding the UN Sales Convention (CISG), e.g.

Denmark, Finland, Iceland, Norway and Sweden declared that the Convention would not apply to contracts of sale where the parties have their places of business in these countries and the US declared that, if the Conflict-of-Laws rules of a state lead to the law a CISG party, that not the CISG should be applied but this state's *internal laws*. (see *UN Sales Convention (CISG)*)

Authorization or no objection within 12 months by an other contracting state usually leads to the effectiveness of the objection in relation to this state.

If a state objects to an other state's reservation, generally only the by the reservation affected provisions do not apply between those two states (but the remaining treaty does).

**Example**

*State **A** does not want Art. 10 of treaty **X** to be applied to it, for which it makes a reservation. The other state parties to **X** are **B**, **C** and **D**. **B** expressly authorizes the objection, **C** does not react at all to the reservation and **D** objects to **A**'s reservation.*

**A**'s reservation is applied in relation to **B** and **C** but not to **D**.

Last but not least, international treaties must be **e)** registered with UN Secretariat. (UN Charter Art. 102)

**Example**

In 2017, the ICJ decided that a Memorandum of Understanding between Kenya and Somalia on maritime delimitation was an international treaty because, among other reasons, it contained a provision on its "entry into force" and Kenya requested its registration at the UN and Somalia did not protest.[43]

The *interpretation* of an international treaty must be done according to

- the ordinary *meaning of the* treaty's *terms* and
- the *context* of the provision as well as its purpose and objective (determined e.g. by the treaty's preamble, annexes or connected agreements; agreements and practice established afterwards and other relevant international rules applying between the parties).

As a *supplementary* means of interpretation also the *preparatory works* (e.g. drafts of treaties, conference records, explanatory statements) may be used, especially for confirmation or when the meaning stays ambiguous or unreasonable after looking at the terms and context.

Some international treaties also provide for interpretation according to the effectiveness/functionality (e.g. constitutive treaties of IIOO). This means that a treaty's terms must be interpreted so they provide for the highest level of effectiveness and functionality (e.g. in the EU according to the *Van Gend en Loos* judgment[44]).

---

[43] *Maritime Delimitation in the Indian Ocean*, ICJ Judgment / Preliminary Objections, 2 February 2017.
[44] *Van Gend en Loos vs. Netherlands Inland Revenue Administration*, CJEC Judgment 26-62, 5 February 1963.

Some of the *consequences* of a valid international treaty are, apart from its provisions applying in the state parties, that

- parties may not invoke national laws as a justification for non-performance of an obligation stipulated in the treaty – generally even if that means that it has to breach its own national laws. (VCLT Art. 27)
- if an other party breaches the treaty, the parties can unanimously suspend the treaty in part or in whole, only in relation to defaulting state or between all state parties. (VCLT Art. 60)

*Suspension* of the treaty by one of its members is e.g. possible if a fundamental circumstance for consent changed, this was unforeseen and it led to a radical transformation of the extent of its obligations (*rebus sic stantibus*, which is also international custom, VCLT Art. 62).

*Modifications* of international treaties (often called "protocols") generally require the same procedure as the conclusion of the treaty, unless it provides for other provisions on its own amendment. (VCLT Art. 39, 41)

*Withdrawal* of an international treaty is possible with 12 months' notice, if it is compatible with the nature of treaty (and not prohibited[45]). (VCLT Art. 56)

An international treaty *terminates* if its purpose is fulfilled, it is limited in time (like e.g. the Treaty of Paris creating the European Coal and Steel Community 1952-2002) or with the consent of all parties. (VCLT Art. 54, 57)

---

[45] It the treaty prohibits withdrawal, this does not mean that a state cannot at all withdraw itself but that the treaty (if multilateral) also between other states would not be valid any more.

# IV. Violation and enforcement of International Law

*What happens when one state harms another by breaching International Law?*

States must fulfil their international obligations. If they do not do so,

> in most cases (…) **an aggrieved state** is left with no choice but to **adopt its own measures in response to another state's violation of** international law. International law is thus first and foremost a system of self-help.[46]

This has to do with the already mentioned in International Law missing (central) compulsory execution of law.

## 1. Countermeasures and retorsion

*What can the aggrieved state do?*

First of all, it must be checked if another state is **responsible**[47] for the breach of International Law. This is, in short, the case when the perpetrator's acts are attributable to this state, e.g. if it was a state organ or officially empowered to commit the act.

If the act is attributable to a state, there also must be **no exceptions** legitimizing the act. These are, amongst others,

---

[46] Henriksen, 2019: 16, bold print added.

[47] This is most prominently regulated in the *Articles on Responsibility of States for International Wrongful Acts* (2001) and the *Draft Articles on Responsibility of IIOO* by the ILC (2011), which reflect international customary law.

- *Consent* given by the affected state, e.g. UN peacekeeping operations or NATO operations (e.g. Afghanistan 2001-2021),
- *Force majeure*, i.e. an irresistible force beyond the control of a state that makes it impossible to comply,
- *State of necessity*, i.e. the breach being necessary for safeguarding an essential state interest which is of more weight or urgency than the effect of the breach,
- *Distress*, i.e. necessary for saving a state agent's life,
- Countermeasures (formerly "reprisals "), i.e. actions as a reaction to a breach of another state. These must fulfil certain requirements (see below).

Generally speaking, if the other state is **1. responsible** and there are also **2. no exceptions** for this breach, the state that is **3. affected**, i.e. whose rights are violated or denied by the other state[48], can resort to *countermeasures*.

Countermeasures are actions that are in principle *against* International Law but can be taken under the mentioned circumstances and if

**4.** the other state was **called upon to fulfil** its international obligations before.

**5.** the other state was **notified** about them before (unless in urgent cases). In case of *military* self-defense (see below), it must also be reported to the Security Council.

**6.** the countermeasure is **temporary**.

**7.** the countermeasure is **proportional**, which must be assessed according to the pursued aim (generally halting and repelling the attack, not punitive retaliation).

---

[48] Or every state in case of *erga omnes* obligations.

48

**8.** the countermeasure is **not against *ius cogens*** (see above) and taken in a way that permits the resumption of the performance of the obligations.

If all these conditions are given, a state is entitled to countermeasures of a ***non-violent*** nature.

If these conditions are *not* (all) fulfilled, countermeasures are unavailable to the affected state. However, it has another option, which is always available – no matter whether the conditions for countermeasures are given or not: *retorsion*.

In contrast to countermeasures, **retorsion** is *not* in principle against International Law. It refers to (only) "unfriendly" actions on a political, diplomatic or economic (or possibly other) level that may though be of severe consequences for the other state subject to them.

They range from cancelling state visits, downgrading or breaking off diplomatic contact to halting foreign aid, suspending trade, financial sanctions and severing non legally binding agreements (and many more).

Also the UN Security Council can call on (and this way legitimate) states to implement **sanctions** against another member, which may even be against International Law[49]. For that, it must determine though that there is a threat to or breach of the peace or an act of aggression. (UN Charter Art. 39, see also *Use of force*)

---

[49] But not *ius cogens*.

## 2. Use of force

As mentioned, the creation of the United Nations was the final step of outlawing the use of force as a means for the settlement of international conflicts. The UN Charter stipulates as follows:

> All Members shall **refrain** in their international relations **from the threat or use of force against the territorial integrity or political independence of any state**, or in any other manner inconsistent with the Purposes of the United Nations. (UN Charter Art. 2, bold print added)

The term *force* does not only refer to armed measures but also to cyber operations, when their scale and effects are comparable to armed operations.[50]

The prohibition comprises both the *exercise of physical power* of one state on the territory of another state (***territorial sovereignty***) and the *intervention in internal affairs*, i.e. inducing policy changes of a political, economic, social, cultural, environmental, etc. nature or supporting the political (or other) opposition or group in an other state. (***non-intervention***)

Nevertheless, the UN Charter does not *entirely* outlaw the use of force. In very limited cases, in order to keep or restore international peace and security, the use of force is (still) permitted.

In fact, there are two important exceptions of the prohibition of the use of force:

I.    **self-defense,** which is a countermeasure using force

II.   the **authorization of the UN Security Council**

---

[50] See e.g. the *Tallinn Manual 2.0 on Int Law applicable to Cyber Operations* (2017) of scholarly origin, which is used by the NATO.

50

Nothing in the present Charter shall impair the inherent **right of individual or collective**[51] **self-defence if an armed attack occurs** against a Member of the United Nations, until the Security Council has taken measures necessary to maintain international peace and security. (…) (UN Charter Art. 51, bold print added)

Should the Security Council consider that measures provided for in Article 41 [measures not involving force] would be inadequate or have proved to be inadequate, it may take **such action by air, sea, or land forces as may be necessary to maintain or restore international peace and security**. (…) (UN Charter Art. 42, bold print added)

In addition to the requirements mentioned above for countermeasures, a state may exercise **self-defense** if:

9. it is **subjected to** or **under the imminent threat of force of a certain intensity**, i.e. not just small-scale attacks but such with e.g. massive property destruction, territorial invasion, several human fatalities, killings of diplomatic representatives or military officials (also abroad);

10. self-defense is **necessary**, i.e. the harmed state has **a)** no choice of means because there are no other (more) peaceful means of redress available (*last resort*) and **b)** no choice of time because it cannot wait any longer.
Therefore, self-defense must generally be immediate to an attack (or during the attack in progress), but the harmed state has reasonable time to explore peaceful resolution means before.

11. it is **reported immediately to the Security Council**. (UN Charter Art. 51)

---

[51] Collective self-defense refers to the situation in which an attacked state requests for support of other states and these assist in self-defense.

Then, and *only* then, armed self-defense is in accordance with International Law.

By contrast, the **Security Council** can **authorize the use of force** also when these elements are not given (or not *all* of them).

For that it needs two things though:

**a)** the **necessary majority**, i.e. nine affirmative votes, consisting of the votes of the five permanent Security Council members (although abstentions do not bock Resolutions) and four additional votes of whichever of the other 10 non-permanent members.

**b)** "coalitions of the willing" that voluntarily execute the mandate of the use of force, since there are no UN forces for that aim. Therefore, the Security Council must rely e.g. on IIOO (e.g. African Union missions, NATO forces) or individual states.

Apart from the authorization of the use of force, the Security Council has also other measures of a forcible (i.e. using force) or a non-focible nature at hand. These can be legally binding or non-binding.

It can e.g. determine, with considerable discretion, a *threat to the peace* (internal conflict, terrorism, piracy, democracy violation, arms control, etc.), and *non-forcible measures* (countermeasures/retorsion), e.g. the interruption of economic relations, rail/sea/air and postal/radio communications, the severance of diplomatic relations and the creation of *ad hoc* courts. (UN Charter Art. 39, 41)

Apart from that, it can adopt temporary *provisional measures* to prevent the aggravation of a conflict situation (e.g. ceasefire/humanitarian pause, withdrawal of troops) and establish peacekeeping operations.[52] (UN Charter Art. 40; Chapters VI-VIII[53])

Legal limits to the actions of the Security Council are *ius cogens* (see *Hierachy of sources and ius cogens*) and partly human rights.

---

[52] But also the UN General Assembly can establish peacekeeping operations on the basis of consent of the concerned state(s).

[53] The UN Charter does not explicitly provide for peacekeeping, instead peacekeeping operations are somewhat based on the sum of the articles in Chapters VI, VII and VIII of the Charter.

# V. International Investment Law

Apart from the mentioned general International Law referring to the international legal order as such, its actors, rules[54] and breaches thereof, International Law also covers special disciplines. These focus on specific material areas and are called *Specialized Regimes*, being e.g. International Human Rights Law, International Criminal Law, International Humanitarian Law, International Sea Law, International Environmental Law and International Economic Law.

As mentioned initially, the term *International Economic Law* is relatively vague and brings some complexities (see first chapter). Areas it certainly covers though are International Monetary Law (IMF, World Bank etc.), International Investment Law and International Trade Law (WTO).

While the International Monetary Law is left out in this book for reasons of conciseness, the key essentials of International Investment Law and International Trade Law are displayed in the following.

**International Investment Law** is an area of public International Law with no central lawmaking and ruling institution.[55]

Instead, it is governed by a huge number of different international treaties concluded in different constellations of states (and IIOO) and, supplementarily and subsidiarily, by customary international law.

In contrast to general International Law and International Trade Law, which regulate the legal relations primarily between *states*, and to Private International Law, which regulates legal relationships between

---

[54] Including *immunity* from national jurisdiction and diplomatic rights, which are not covered in this book though.
[55] Unlike International Trade Law, which counts with the WTO as central institution.

*private persons/entities*, International Investment Law refers primarily to the legal relationships between *states and private persons/entities*.

Before looking at the rules of International Investment Law, the term "foreign/international investment" *itself* must be determined though.

# 1. Foreign (Direct) Investment

*What is a foreign investment?*

*Foreign investment* can be defined as the "movement of assets or business operations from an investor's home country"[56] to another country.

This includes both passive and active investments.

When an investor buys shares of stock in a foreign company, this is a passive *portfolio* investment.

Whereas when the investor buys or sets up a company or a part of it in another country, it is an active *direct* investment, e.g. a factory, distribution or sales center or an infrastructure or natural resources extraction project.
This is also called **Foreign Direct Investment (FDI)** and what International Investment Law (mainly) deals with.

Possible reasons for FDIs are **a) reduction of transport and customs costs** (compared to export) if e.g. the product is sold in the (region of) the foreign country, **b) reduction of production costs** thanks to cheaper production conditions (local resources, labor) in this country than in the home country or **c) legal reasons**, e.g. the foreign state's laws requiring the actual national presence of a company for producing a certain good.

Often FDIs follow a successful period of export to the country in question or of licensing of intellectual property to a foreign company.[57]

FDIs are frequently done through a *subsidiary*, i.e. a separate company fully or partly in the other country owned by the investing company, or a

---

[56] Folsom et al., 2016: 305.
[57] Or, the other way around, establishing a subsidiary is necessary because a foreign company cannot be trusted regarding intellectual property or commercially valuable knowhow.

56

*branch*, i.e. a non-separate part of the investing company in the other company.

In many cases, for tax and liability reasons, subsidiaries are preferred to branches in international investment.

Furthermore, FDI is often realized in the form of a joint venture, term which refers to (usually) subsidiaries whose ownership is shared between a foreign investor and a local investor.[58] In some cases, this is required by the national law of the state the investment is done in.

 If a joint venture is created, it is recommended that a foreign investor owns a *majority of the voting equity* of the subsidiary to have sufficient control over the investment (or any other effective assurance of control).

As for the place where to invest, several not only legal and financial factors are to be considered:

> Different legal systems may be involved, as may different languages, currencies, cultures, forms of doing business, concepts of legal practice, forms of labor participation and workers' rights, levels and forms of officer compensation, risks of expropriation, intrusiveness of government participation (…).[59]

*What laws apply to foreign investment?*

States are free to decide whether to accept foreign investment and under which conditions. Thus, FDIs are governed primarily by **1. the *national law of the state in which they are made***.

While most states generally permit foreign investment, many of them restrict it. This is often done by provisions restricting control, ownership

---

[58] But also between two *foreign* investors.
[59] Folsom, 2016: 312.

and financial flexibility, e.g. mandatory subsidies (i.e. branches being forbidden), mandatory joint ventures, foreign employee limits, limits on profit transfers, withdrawal restrictions (including difficulties to repatriate capital or at insolvency proceedings).[60]

! Apart from restricting laws, often also unwritten or unpublished policies[61] are applied by foreign authorities.
Therefore, an experienced *local counsel* is highly recommended for anybody planning FDIs.

In addition, it must be taken into account that factual policies but also laws, especially over the usually several years (or even decades) a FDI is ongoing, may – and *do* – change.

Apart from the national rules of the host country, also some **2. *laws of the home country of the investor*** can apply, e.g. export restrictions, antitrust rules and regulations for securities.

Last but not least, once an investment is permitted in a country (according to its national laws), it can be and is[62] *protected* by **3. *international law***.

Both international customary law and international treaties provide for investor protection, although the existence of the former is harder to demonstrate (in court or arbitration) than the latter.

---

[60] Most countries though do permit total foreign ownership of investments, and provide for *voluntary* joint ventures (although they might be encouraged).

[61] A so-called "operational code of the way things work"(Folsom et al., 2016: 318), which may be factual rules applied to everybody or even distinguishing in their application between nationals and foreigners.

[62] *"Can be"* referring to the possibility of international investment treaties. *"Is"* referring to the fact that international customary law always protects investments though (but is harder to prove).

58

Therefore, international custom is mainly only of importance in international investment protection when the home state of the investor and the host state of the investment have not concluded an international treaty covering investment protection.[63]

International treaties in this area of law are mainly bilateral and have a clear *investment* focus, so-called Bilateral Investment Treaties (BITs). However, investment protection clauses sometimes are also included in bi- or multilateral treaties with a trade[64] focus (Free Trade Agreements, FTAs).[65]

Worldwide, there are currently more than 2500 BITs and other treaties with investment provisions in force (!).[66]

These BITs (and other treaties regulating the area) are, as all international treaties, concluded *between states* (or IIOO).

 However, they normally do not provide for one state suing the other because its investors were not correctly treated but for *private persons or companies* suing the state.

In other words, by the conclusion of BITs, International Law gives non-subjects of International Law rights. These usually include the possibility of such *non-subjects* of International Law to sue International Law *subjects* other than the state whose nationals they are. This is indeed very special. (see below)

---

[63]Apart from international custom and treaties, sometimes also the national law of the host country provides for protection of foreign investments targeted at it.

[64] I.e. focused mainly on the elimination of tariffs and non-tariff barriers.

[65] E.g. the United States-Mexico-Canada Agreement (USMCA), the Energy Charter Treaty and also the EU-Canada Comprehensive Economic and Trade Agreement (CETA), most parts of which are provisionally in force (although ratification process is still ongoing).

[66] UNCTAD, IIA Navigator update, 13 April 2023, https://investmentpolicy.unctad.org/.

Among the member states (MS) of the **EU**, "the world's main provider and the top global destination of foreign investment"[67], investment is regulated differently.

Investments between the EU MS are covered not only by national law but also by *EU-law*, eliminating investment restrictions and protecting investments (non-discrimination).[68] This is due to the fact that investments are included in two of the *four freedoms of the EU single market* –the **free movement of capital** and the free movement of persons (of which the **freedom of establishment** is part).

Investments with a *controlling influence* by the investor over the foreign company etc. are regularly attributed to the freedom of *establishment* (TFEU Art. 49); other investments, i.e. those where this control is not given[69], to the free *movement of capital* (TFEU Art. 63).[70] In contrast to the other freedoms, movement of capital also covers nationals from non-EU states.[71]

The EU, as part of its exclusive competence in the area of common commercial policy, also has the *exclusive* competence to conclude foreign investment treaties with third countries. Nevertheless, it allows its MS to maintain bilateral investment treaties from before.[72] BITs *between EU MS* are considered incompatible with EU Law though.[73] Furthermore, ISDS

---

[67] European Commission, 2024: *Investment*, https://policy.trade.ec.europa.eu/help-exporters-and-importers/accessing-markets/investment_en.

[68] Investments in the EU are further – indirectly through the right to property – protected by two legally binding international fundamental rights documents, the EU Fundamental Rights Charter (FRC Art. 17) and the European Convention on Human Rights (ECHR Prot. 1 Art. 1).

[69] And e.g. entry into the foreign company's business segment or market is not (primarily) intended.

[70] See e.g. CJEU *Baars* judgment (C-251/98) and Council Directive 88/361/EEC (1988) for the implementation of Article 67 TFEU.

[71] See e.g. Kronke et al., 2017: 1202.

[72] Regulation (EU) No 1219/2012 establishing transitional arrangements for bilateral investment agreements between Member States and third countries.

[73] See e.g. Kronke et al., 2017: 1207.

procedures involving arbitration are prohibited against EU MS if the investor is from (another) EU MS.[74]

In summary, international investments are a matter regulated by a *multiplicity of legal sources*, comprising the national legal orders of the host states and possibly also those of the home states, as well as investment treaties, EU Law and international custom.

---

[74] Since the CJEU *Achmea* judgment in 2018 (*Slovak Republic v Achmea BV,* C-284/16).

## 2. Investment protection

### What must investments be protected from?

Investments, especially those in a foreign country, of course have a certain economic risk. No other than if we open an ice cream shop in our home country, certain risk of losing all or part of our investment this entailed is inherent in the concept as such (the ice cream shop may not have enough customers).
This risk remains also in foreign investment.

If the ice cream shop is taken from us by the state, e.g. because it is in the way of a highway to be built there, national law protects us and we will be compensated.
If we instead opt for an investment in a foreign country, which – as we saw – is governed by this foreign country's national law, it can happen that our investment is illegally taken by the host state or legally but without us being compensated.

The main goal of BITs (and international custom) therefore is to **protect investors from illegal expropriation**[75], i.e. the illegal taking of private property for public purposes. *Illegality* is determined according to the requirements stipulated in the BIT (and/or international custom) for expropriations (see *Investor-State Dispute Settlement*).

Expropriation can be done in a *direct/explicit* way, i.e. when the investor is formally (by an act of expropriation) deprived of the power to control and dispose of his/her business operation.

It can also be done *indirectly/de facto* though, i.e. when the investor is not formally (not by an act of expropriation) deprived of his/her investment but by other means equivalent to expropriation in their effect.

---

[75] And nationalization, where entire sectors (e.g. the oil sector) are "taken" from private persons/entities.

62

No matter whether the investor is expropriated directly or *de facto*, he/she loses control of the business operation and its value.

This is what international investment treaties (and international customary law) try to avoid, creating a *win-win situation* of investor protection where investors feel save and states benefit from the resulting increased number of investments.

Most of the world's **BITs** have a **standardized format and structure** including all or most of the following provisions (which mostly represent also international custom):

1.  *Fair and equitable treatment*, i.e. protection of legitimate expectations, due process and prohibition of arbitrary treatment.

2.  *Non-discrimination*, i.e. *national treatment* – the same treatment of foreign and national investors (e.g. regarding the investment itself, court and administrative access, taxes, etc.) – and, in principle, *most favored nation treatment* – conceding the best treatment given to a foreign investor also to all other foreign investors.

3.  *Full protection and security*, i.e. the host state's (intent of) protection of the investment from non-state actors (e.g. rebel groups).

4.  *Expropriation limits*, an expropriation only being allowed if it is

    a) realized for *public purposes*,

    b) *non-discriminatory*, i.e. applicable in the same way to foreign investments as to investments of a national of the host state,

    c) accompanied by full, prompt and utilizable *compensation*,

    - *full* referring to the *market value* of the investment, i.e. the price an informed willing buyer would pay to an informed willing seller if both want to maximize their financial gain,

    -*prompt* meaning without undue delay,

    -*utilizable* meaning that compensation must be provided in a usable currency (e.g. not in a non-convertible national currency).

5. *Investor-State Dispute Settlement* (ISDS), i.e. the possibility of legal actions of an investor against an (infringing) host state (e.g. arbitration pursuant to the ICSID, see below).

6. *Extraordinary circumstances*, e.g. how to deal with the foreign investment during economic crises.

Apart from international investment treaties concluded between states that make investments between these safer, an investor can also *insure* him/herself.

**Investment insurances** are often offered by the home state[76] of the person/entity that plans a foreign investment.[77] Risks insured must not be commercial but (only) political, e.g. expropriation, armed conflicts and non-convertibility of the host country's currency.

For foreign investments in one of its developing member countries, also the Multilateral Investment Guarantee Agency (MIGA)[78] offers insurance against non-commercial risks for persons/companies based in another member. The insurable risks are those just mentioned plus contract breach by the host state. (MIGA Convention Art. 11-14)

The basis condition for a MIGA insurance/guarantee is that the investment insured is economically sound and contributes to the development goals (and complies with the laws) of the host country. (MIGA Convention Art. 12)

---

[76] States are often only willing to offer foreign investment insurances if there is a BIT in place between the insuring state and the state where the investment takes place, which gives the insuring state some security.

[77] E.g. in Austria the *Österreichische Kontrollbank,* which offers participation guarantees protecting investments.

[78] An International Organization founded in 1988 and based in Washington D.C. as part of the World Bank Group with currently 182 member states.

# 3. Investor-State Dispute Settlement

As mentioned, foreign investment treaties regularly include a provision establishing the possibility of *Investor-State Dispute Settlement* (ISDS).

These provisions are special in International Law because, as mentioned, the rights conferred to investors by investment treaties between states give them – as *private* persons/companies – the possibility to claim these rights against a *public* foreign entity – the host state.

This is mainly done by arbitration (see *Arbitration*) and mostly in the scope of the International Centre for Settlement of Investment Disputes (ICSID) in Washington D.C., which was founded in 1966 and is part of the World Bank Group.

 ISDS has often been criticized in the last years, which has especially to do with the fear that especially big enterprises profit from this possibility of suing states in non-transparent proceedings with potentially biased arbitrators.

Also the fact that investment treaty provisions are often vague and far-reaching could lead to both misuse and legal uncertainty.

On the upside, ISDS clauses in investment treaties provide the security for investors that – in case of illegal expropriations, discrimination, etc. – they can claim their legitimate rights. This way, they encourage foreign investment.

While there are also other procedural rules for investment (and other) arbitration such as the UNCITRAL Arbitration Rules[79], the ICSID provides for its own procedural rules in the ICSID Convention.[80]

> **!** The ICSID is (only) an arbitration *institution* administering and supporting proceedings but not the arbitral *tribunal* itself. Arbitral tribunals are established *separately* and act using the framework provided by institutions like the ICSID (see also *Arbitration*).

The ICSID is competent for acting as arbitral institution in investment disputes where

1. **both states**, i.e. the state whose national investor initiates the dispute and the respondent state, are **contracting parties** to the ICSID-Convention and

2. the **parties** (investor and host state) **consent to submit the dispute to ICSID arbitration.**

   (ICSID Convention Art. 25, 26)

This consent to submission usually exists automatically:
The consent by the *investor* is given because he/she is the complainant at ICSID. The consent by the *respondent state* has regularly already been given upfront by the inclusion of ICSID's competence for ISDS proceedings in a BIT between the two states.

The decisions of arbitral tribunals acting in the framework of ICSID are legally binding and generally not appealable. (ICSID Convention Art. 53, 54)

---

[79] Parties opting for the ICSID as arbitral institution can choose e.g. the UNCITRAL Arbitration Rules to be applied to their proceedings instead of the ICSID Arbitration Rules.
[80] The ICSID Convention is "both" an international treaty ratified by 158 states creating the International Organization ICSID and a set of procedural rules for the proceedings in its framework.

For assessing if an investor can initiate proceedings before an arbitral tribunal in the framework of ICSID because of a potentially violated standard BIT[81] due to expropriation, the following steps should be taken into account (if the answer is *yes*, the respectively next point applies):

**I. Is a BIT applicable?**

1. Are the two affected states (**A** and **B**) contracting parties to a BIT?

2. Is the in **A** / **B** investing claimant a national/enterprise of **B** / **A**?

3. Is the investment included in the BIT's scope (e.g. no portfolio investment)?

**II. Was the BIT violated due to an illegal expropriation?**

1. Was there an expropriation (direct or *de facto*) by **A** / **B**? (see *Investment protection*)

2. Was the expropriation not justified? (see *Investment protection 4. a)-c)*)

**III. Is an arbitral tribunal acting in the ICSID framework competent?**

1. Are **A** and **B** members of the ICSID Convention?

2. Is there party consent to conduct arbitration under the ICSID Convention?

---

[81] Containing all the BIT standard elements mentioned in *Investment protection*.

# C International Trade Law

The concept of *International Trade Law* is terminologically clearer and narrower than the ones of *International Economic Law* or *International Business Law* (see *International Economic? Business? Trade? Law*). This has to do with the fact that it is mostly understood as only or mainly the law of the World Trade Organization (WTO) whereas the other two concepts cover several areas of law.

Behind the WTO and its treaties are basic notions of the functioning and benefits of international trade, i.e. trade crossing the borders of a state.

Before having a look at International Trade/WTO Law, let us have a look at the reason why people and companies (or other legal persons) trade internationally.

## I. Free trade theory

### (Why) Does international trade make sense?

The idea of the economic advantages of international trade is far older than the WTO (1995) or its preceding and "main" treaty, the General Agreement on Tariffs and Trade (GATT, 1947), with some of its main theoretical inputs dating back to the $18^{th}$ century.

This theory is often designated as *Free Trade Theory*; "free trade" referring to an (as much as possible) unlimited international exchange of goods and services.

In *The Wealth of Nations* (1776) Adam Smith explained that the gains from specialization of economic activity (and labor division) within one state can be extended to economic activity between states:

> The tailor does not attempt to make his own shoes, but buys them of the shoemaker. The shoemaker does not attempt to make his own clothes, but employs a tailor (...) What is prudence in the conduct of every private family, can scarce be folly in that of a great kingdom [or *internationally*]. If a foreign country can supply us with a commodity cheaper than we ourselves can make it, better buy it of them with some part of the produce of our own industry employed in a way in which we have some advantage.[82]

Each country should focus economically on where it is "best", i.e. where its production (or service) conditions are most advantageous. This is conditioned by the *factors of production*[83] land, labor, capital and knowledge. Where these most advantageous conditions are given, a so-called *absolute advantage* exists.

Countries with tropical climates might have an absolute advantage (e.g. the appropriate amount of sun, moisture and rain) for cultivating bananas or pineapples. Quality will be best and effort and prices low. Countries with industrialized economies, in contrast, might have an absolute advantage (e.g. the necessary knowhow and machines) regarding the conceptualization and production of wind plants and IT systems. Also here quality, effort and prices will normally be lower than in not-industrialized countries.

*What if one country focusses on (production according to) the absolute advantage, but others do not?*

That is not perfect[84] but better than none specializing on its absolute advantage. This one country will have no problems finding foreign buyers

---

[82] Smith, 1776: 364.

[83] Or "component parts of price" in the words of Adam Smith. (Smith, 1976: 53)

[84] If, in theory, "everybody" specialized on its comparative advantage–product, prices would even be lower and quality better.

for its cheap and high-quality products. Therefore, exporting this product and, with the revenue created, importing all other necessary products where it has no advantage from the country which produces them the cheapest would be a solution.

*What if one country has no absolute advantage (because it is not the best in producing anything)?*

This question is best answered by having a look at the following fictitious examples:

Let us suppose there are only three products in the world (bananas, pineapples and oranges) and three states (Pinora, Banpin and Onlyora). The total costs based for producing one piece of product are as follows in these states (*the less units of labor costing production, the better*):

|  | Pinora | Banpin | Onlyora |
|---|---|---|---|
| **1 banana** | 1 unit of labor | 3 units of labor | ½ unit of labor |
| **1 pineapple** | 2 units of labor | 3 units of labor | 1 ½ units of labor |
| **1 orange** | 2 units of labor | 1 unit of labor | 3 units of labor |

As we can see, Pinora in not best in producing any product and, therefore, has *no absolute advantage*.

*Is that a problem?*

No. According to the famous classical economist David Ricardo and his book *The Principles of Political Economy* (1817), what matters is the so-called **comparative** *advantage*, i.e. the advantage *compared* to other countries.

If Pinora exports bananas to Banpin (e.g. because Onlyora, where bananas are even cheaper does not have any left because everybody wants to buy its cheap bananas from it) in exchange for oranges from

70

Banpin, it is still a win-win: Pinora saves 1 unit of labor thanks to the cheaper oranges and Banpin saves 2 units of labor thanks to the cheaper bananas.

The comparative advantage also works when one country has better production conditions in *everything* than another country.

The two states Lowcos and Winclo both produce wine and T-shirts.
In Lowcos producing one liter of wine costs 8 units of labor and one T-shirt costs 9 units of labor.
In contrast, in Winclo producing one liter of wine costs 12 units of labor and one T-shirt 10 units of labor.[85]

If Lowcos, due to having limited labor, resources, space etc.[86], focusses only on producing wine and exports it to Winclo in exchange for T-shirts, Lowcos gets T-shirts for 8 units of labor (instead of 9) and Winclo gets wine for 10 units of labor (instead of 12).

In other words, if there is no absolute advantage and even if there is, it is usually worth focusing on the *comparative* advantage, i.e. specializing in producing and exporting goods (and services) where the comparative advantage is greatest and the comparative disadvantage is smallest.

Nowadays products often undergo several steps in their life cycle (inventing, producing and assembling many different product parts), i.e. not one country producing only final products but only parts of it.

---

[85] See similar (and more) examples in Trebilcock, 2020: 2 et seq.
[86] Keeping in mind that any country has e.g. an in size limited territory and an in number limited population, Lowcos might not have enough of them for producing both wine and T-shirts in extremely high quantities.

Also in this case specialization makes sense, namely on the part(s) and processes where the comparative advantage is most pronounced.[87]

In addition, specialization on a certain stage of a product's life cycle[88] may make sense:

> Highly developed economies will tend to specialize in the manufacture of products in the early stages of development, where financial capital, specialized human capital and innovation are at a premium. In the later stages of the product cycle, as production technology becomes standardized, it is adopted by producers in other countries, typically countries with lower labour costs. At this point in the product cycle, comparative advantage shifts to these countries.[89]

The mentioned theory of the (absolute and) comparative advantage would, with some fine tuning, most likely function relatively well if the world's states and companies would "stick to" it:

> If economists ruled the world, there would be no need for a World Trade Organization. The economist's case for free trade is essentially a unilateral case – that is, it says that a country serves its own interests by pursuing free trade regardless of what other countries may do.[90]

Economic liberalism – as perfect as it may seem – is often thwarted by governments interests (and resulting policies). These often depend on electors requiring economic protection(ism) and therefore (and for many other internal reasons) often do not strive for international economic perfectionism.

Apart from that, international trade was discovered to be a well-functioning vehicle in foreign policy for showing political affection or

---

[87] E.g. lots of know-how for the invention of the product itself and the first-time production of machines than can manufacture the product; natural/mineral resources for producing chips, batteries or steel elements.

[88] See e.g. the *Product Cycle Theory* by Raymond Vernon.

[89] Trebilcock, 2020: 4

[90] Krugman, 1997: 113.

72

disaffection to another state. Arbitrary "trade punishments" by one state against another have been, at least to some extent, reduced in the last decades thanks to the WTO.

# II. How tariffs work

The key instrument used in international trade to protect national economies (among other things) are *tariffs*. Together with *quotas* limiting the quantity of imported products (and complete import *bans*), they are an easy tool applied regularly at a country's border to limit imports[91]. They can be considered as the most typical (and still very common) trade barriers.

### What are (import) tariffs? How are they calculated?

A tariff (often referred to also as *customs duty*) is an amount of money that must be paid so a product can cross the border. The amount to be paid is calculated mostly *ad valorem*, referring to the so-called "transaction value".
The transaction value is the price that the importer pays for the imported goods, including packaging and free "goodies" connected to the sale. Of this transaction value normally a certain percentage must be paid (e.g. a tariff of "15% *ad valorem*") by the importer.

In some cases though, the transaction value is an inappropriate basis for calculating the tariff. This can be e.g. because the parties are related (same parent enterprise) or they agreed on an artificially lower price to reduce import duty payments (*transfer pricing*). For such cases, alternative methods are available to the authorities, e.g. a (product) specific tariff on milk or cheese types according to which a certain price must be paid per imported kilo.
Tariffs for certain products can also be mixed, for instance 50% ad valorem and 50% specific.[92]

---

[91] Although there can be also export tariffs, which are much rarer though.
[92] The multilateral Agreement on the Implementation of Article VII (Customs Valuation Agreement) provides for rules regarding customs valuation.

74

We know now on which value the tariff must be applied.

*But how do we know which tariff (percentage) is applicable?*

We have to look into the *Tariff* or *Goods Schedule*, formally "Schedule of Concessions", of the state applying the tariff. These Goods Schedules contain so-called *tariff bindings* or *concessions*, i.e. maximum tariffs imposed in principle to all WTO members. These tariff concessions are the result of negotiations of this state with other states.
*But where to look with thousands of existing products?*

The World Customs Organization (WCO) has established a *Harmonized System* categorizing products. Based on the *Convention on the Harmonized Commodity Description and Coding System* ("HS Convention"), which is in force since 1988, it provides a worldwide (incl. also non-WTO states[93]) nomenclature. This nomenclature is a system of numbers periodically updated, the most current edition being from 2022. Based on 21 sections, it classifies goods in product categories using a six-digit code.

| SECTION II | VEGETABLE PRODUCTS |
| --- | --- |
| Chapter 10 | Cereals |
| Heading 10.06 | Rice |
| Subheading 1006.30 | Semi-milled or wholly milled rice, whether or not polished or glazed. |

*Image: Hsmind, creative commons.*

After the six digits level, countries are free to add national (or EU-specific) distinctions, e.g. additional numbers for further product specification.

---

[93] Currently 161 contracting states but being used in more than 200 countries around the globe.

Every three years WTO members can withdraw or modify tariff concessions but must offer other concessions so that the total level of concessions is (at least) as favorable (for the other WTO members) as before. (GATT Art. 27)

Apart from tariffs, states can impose administrative fees, which are limited though to the approximate cost of the services rendered by the authorities. (GATT Art. 8)[94]

### What is the reason for imposing tariffs?

Tariffs were originally created to raise revenue for the government: with every imported product the state earns money. Some states even decided to (and in rare cases still do) impose *export* tariffs for that reason, requiring everybody to pay money so a product could leave a country. For this product then usually again an import tariff had to be paid to the destination country. This, of course, makes exports and international trade twice as unattractive.

Nowadays, thanks to the invention of income taxes, tariffs are a comparably less important source of government revenue. In the EU, furthermore, most of the customs duties collected are transferred not to the member states' budgets but the EU budget.

This is why the main purpose of tariffs in the last decades shifted to their second important role – protection of national (or EU) products and services against foreign competition. Seen on a global scale, this is welfare reducing though and contradicts the theory on the comparative advantage (see *Free trade theory*).

---

[94] Both the Revised Kyoto Convention on Simplification & Harmonization of Customs Procedures (WCO, in force since 2006) and the Trade Facilitation Agreement (WTO, in force since 2017), among other things, aim to harmonize, simplify and expedite administrative border processes.

Currently, tariffs on **services** are very rare. This has to do with the fact that electronic transmissions or digital products, which in principle could be subject to tariffs, are covered by the so-called "**E-Commerce Moratorium**". This moratorium focusing on electronic transmission tariffs was originally agreed on in 1998 and has been prolonged repeatedly, lastly at MC13 (extending it until March 2026 at latest).

### *Who carries the final burden of a tariff?*

Even though a former US president insinuated that (import) tariffs are paid by exporting countries[95], this is not the case. The importer has to pay the tariff and, by adjusting the sales price according to the level of the tariff, he/she transmits it to the final customer. Therefore, in the end it is the customers who normally (indirectly) carry the burden of tariffs and pay more for a product/service[96]. Only in special situations of market power or demand it sometimes happens that foreign producers carry some of the tariff-costs.

Apart from the mentioned higher prices for consumers tariffs (and quotas, see below) lead to, they regularly *do* have the secondary consequence that the country or countries on whose products they are imposed export less to the country imposing the tariffs.

### *What are quotas and non-tariff barriers*

While tariffs, depending on their level, usually lead to moderate to high price increases, quotas normally lead to *skyrocketing* prices. This has to do with the nature of a quota (or *quantitative restriction*):

---

[95] See e.g. De la Garza, Alejandro, 2019: *White House Economic Advisor Contradicts President Trump on Who Actually Pays for the Tariffs on China*, Time, 12/05/2019, https://time.com/5587848/kudlow-trump-china-tariffs-fox-news-sunday-interview/.
[96] As mentioned, tariffs on **services** are (still) very rare.

A *quota* fixes the maximum limit of imports of a certain product and, after this limit is reached, does not allow any more imports.

If national demand is high and domestic production of this product not given or insufficient, prices soar. While quotas at least allow some imports, import *bans* do not allow *any* imports and therefore have even more extreme trade effects. That is why quantitative restrictions are generally prohibited in WTO members.

After two countries aiming for trade liberalization have eliminated all quotas, bans and tariffs between themselves, there still may be obstacles on trade. These remaining obstacles are designated *non-tariff barriers* (NTBs) and refer to regulations, standards and procedures products (or services) are subject to for their import or sale in the importing country. NTBs are often related to safety (food safety, product dangers, occupational safety etc.), nature/environment (ecological production, animal health, nature conservation labels and requirements etc.), consumer rights (type of and information on packaging etc.), labor, sanitary and health standards, technical requirements etc.
In addition, NTBs can also exist due to intellectual property laws or due to administrative and bureaucratic (customs) rules, e.g. for (pre-)shipment inspections, goods valuation and for determining where goods come from (rules of origin).

In comparison with quotas, bans and tariffs, NTBs are often harder to eliminate because of the huge variety of standards, regulations and procedures the world's states have developed.
Creating uniformity has been aimed for by the big players EU[97], USA, China and others by adopting norms that serve as an example for the other states.

---

[97] E.g. by the General Data Protection Regulation (GDPR), Green Deal-measures etc.

### Does every country impose different tariffs?

Usually, every country decides (or, in the WTO, *negotiates*) for itself which import duties it imposes, resulting regularly in a high diversity of different levels of tariffs among countries.

Nevertheless, in some cases states decide to unify part of their trade policies and create *customs unions*. This means that all states which are part of such a customs union impose the same level of customs duties to imports from states that are *not* part of this union – they have common external tariffs. Apart from that, trade among the member states of a customs union is liberalized and customs duties among each other regularly eliminated.
In short: free trade *within* the customs union and same customs duties for third country importers.

Prominent examples for customs unions are e.g. MERCOSUR in Latin America and the European customs union (including Türkiye (!)). So, in principle, e.g. Spain, Sweden, Poland, Türkiye and Austria[98] impose the same external customs duties.

---

[98] States not having an external customs union border being normally only affected by shipment.

# III. Economic integration and Free Trade Agreements

In principle, countries can freely decide for themselves which level of trade barriers (tariffs, quotas, NTBs, etc.) they impose.

Most of the world's countries have however decided to reduce this total liberty and negotiated maximum levels of trade barriers at the WTO; e.g. a tariff of one WTO member of max. 3% ad valorem for a certain product for all other WTO members, which in exchange also offer maximum levels of barriers.

In other words, every WTO member offers special tariffs ("most-favored nation [MFN]-terms"[99]) to all other members. If the WTO members trade with other states that are not members of the WTO, they have all liberty to impose higher tariffs (exceeding the limits offered to WTO members).

The WTO therefore liberalizes trade nearly worldwide (in its 166 members). If states want to go further and liberalize trade even more, they can conclude a so called *Free* (or synonymic *Preferential* or *Regional*) *Trade Agreement* (FTA / PTA / RTA). This FTA allows the participating states to reduce their tariffs and other trade barriers among themselves to even lower maximum levels than those of the WTO or to completely eliminate them.

The geographical area covered by such an FTA and constituted by the FTA's state parties is called **Free Trade Area** and represents the first type or **stage of economic integration**.[100] (e.g. CETA [EU-Canada])

The second stage is the **customs union**, where trade is not only liberalized between its members but also the *same* level of customs

---

[99] If a WTO member offers a certain low level of tariff to one WTO member, it has to offer the same (low) tariff to all WTO members (MFN-Principle). See *Most Favored Nation (MFN)*.
[100] See e.g. Balassa, 1962 and Balassa, 1976.

duties is imposed by each of these members towards third states. (e.g. Mercosur)

Next is the single or **common market**, where not only trade in goods (and services) is liberalized but also e.g. people and capital can move (and work) freely within this market. (e.g. EU)

The fourth stage is the **economic and monetary union**, where – in addition to the mentioned elements that characterize the former stages – the economic policy is unified and there is a common currency (e.g. Eurozone).

The fifth and last stage is the total or **complete economic integration**, where not only all elements of the other stages are clearly given but there is also a common fiscal policy (e.g. limited areas of the EU: partly EU own resources).

**Stages of economic integration**

1. **Free Trade Area**          preferential trade among members
2. **Customs Union**            + same tariffs for third countries
3. **Common Market**            + additional freedoms (persons, capital/assets, etc.)
4. **Econ. / Monet. Union**     + common economic policy / currency
5. **Complete Econ. Integr.**   + common fiscal policy

Up until now, in terms of numbers, the by far most successful of these stages is stage **2** – Free Trade Areas.

Whereas in the 1990ies there were only about 100 FTAs in place, this number has risen to far more than $300^{101}$ FTAs currently in force. Of these, ⅔ were concluded between developing countries. Most FTAs include only

---

[101] According to M. Trebilcock even 460. (Trebilcock, 2020: 48)

goods, lately there has been an increase of FTAs covering both trade in goods and services.

 Nevertheless, about ¾ of the world trade in goods still occurs on the WTO's MFN terms (!).[102]

The average number of FTAs a WTO member has is 12, while some have considerably more (e.g. the EU has more than 40).[103]

---

[102] Van den Bossche/Prévost, 2021: 60.
[103] Trebilcock, 2020: 48; https://trade.ec.europa.eu/access-to-markets/en/content/trade-agreements.

82

# IV. WTO history, agreements and structure

The World Trade Organization (WTO) is one of the biggest, most important and most effective International Organizations ever created. Currently, it has 166 members, with several additional states currently negotiating accession to the WTO.

In total, the WTO's members account for 99,5% of the world's population, and 98% of the world's trade. ¾ of its members are developing countries (based on self-selection, see *Developing countries exception*) and ⅕ are so-called *Least Developed Countries* (LDCs, based on UN classification).[104]

The law of the WTO, its agreements and decisions[105] has reached paramount importance for international exports and imports of goods and (partly) services as well as many other matters (such as subsidies, dumping and intellectual property), which is why International Trade Law, in its core, is nothing else than WTO Law.

That was not always the case though and it was a rather long way until this most important trade organization of the world was created.

---

[104] Van den Bossche/Prévost, 2021: 21, 22.
[105] And partly also of the decisions of the WTO Dispute Settlement Body.

83

# 1. Long way to the WTO

Even before the Second World War was over and before the United Nations were founded, the allied nations held a big conference in order to regulate the post-war monetary, finance and trade world order. This conference took place in Bretton Woods (USA, 1944) and, apart from the International Monetary Fund (IMF) and the World Bank (WB), planned an organization for global trade – the *International* Trade Organization.

While the IMF and WB were established in 1944/45, the International Trade Organization never came into existence due to opposition in the US Congress (because of national sovereignty concerns).

Instead, a few years later, a *provisional agreement* and not an organization was created – the General Agreement on Tariffs and Trade (GATT). The GATT was concluded in 1947 between 23 major trading countries (China, USA, UK, France, India, South Africa, etc.) and entered (provisionally) into force in 1948.

This is how – by default, due to failure – the GATT became the basis for the world's new trade regime. Finally, it took the GATT nearly 40 years to become (part of) an International Organization, the WTO (1994).

Since the creation of the GATT, nine rounds of negotiations took place, extending its regime. While the first six focused on reduction of tariffs on manufactured (*not agricultural*) goods, the last three, among other things, focused on NTBs[106] and trade in services.

The last GATT based negotiation round, called the *Uruguay round* (1986–1993) for having started in this country, finished with its last meeting in Marrakesh. There the Marrakesh Agreement (1994) "establishing the World Trade Organization" (WTO Agreement) was concluded.

---

[106] WTO members' domestic regulatory policies, i.e. technical, health/food & safety standards, intellectual property, foreign direct investment; as well as dumping, subsidization and government procurement.

Finally, in 1995, the WTO commenced its operations in Geneva (where it is still headquartered) giving the GATT an organizational "home". Apart from the GATT, the WTO "hosts" several other agreements the negotiations led to – most importantly the General Agreement on Trade in Services (GATS) and the Agreement on Trade-Related Aspects of Intellectual Property Rights (TRIPS Agreement).

# 2. WTO agreements

Whereas the general international terminology uses the word "multilateral" for all international agreements, organizations etc. having more than two state parties, the WTO Agreement distinguishes between multilateral and plurilateral agreements: Whereas, under WTO terminology, the former ones refer to agreements (international treaties) that have *all* WTO members as parties, the latter ones are agreements between only *some* WTO members.

The mentioned three agreements (GATT, GATS and TRIPS[107]) are multilateral agreements and therefore binding for all WTO members. Other such *multilateral* agreements (which can be found in Annex 1 to the WTO Agreement) are the

Agreement on Agriculture,
Agreement on the Application of Sanitary and Phytosanitary Measures,
Agreement on Technical Barriers to Trade,
Agreement on Trade-Related Investment Measures (TRIMs),
Agreement on Implementation of Article VI of the GATT (Anti-dumping),
Agreement on Implementation of Article VII of the GATT (Customs valuation),
Agreement on Preshipment Inspection,
Agreement on Rules of Origin,
Agreement on Import Licensing Procedures,
Agreement on Subsidies and Countervailing Measures,
Agreement on Safeguards and the
Agreement on Trade Facilitation (TFA), which entered into force in 2017.[108]

---

[107] The TRIPS was amended in 2017 so WTO members could grant special compulsory licenses for the production and export of medicines to other members that do not have sufficient domestic production possibilities.

[108] The also in GATT Annex 1 included Agreement on Textiles and Clothing terminated in 2005. In 2022, another multilateral agreement was negotiated, the Agreement on Fisheries Subsidies, which is not in force yet.

In addition, there are the multilateral Understanding on Rules and Procedures Governing the Settlement of Disputes (Dispute Settlement Understanding [DSU], Annex 2) and the multilateral Trade Policy Review Mechanism (Annex 3).

The *plurilateral* agreements (see GATT Annex 4) only binding for some WTO members are the

> Agreement on Trade in Civil Aircraft,
> Agreement on Government Procurement (amended in 2012) and the
> Information Technology Agreement (1996, expanded in 2015).[109]

The WTO serves as a **a) common administrative body** for these agreements, as a **b) forum for negotiation** of new treaties and treaty revision and as a **c) platform for dispute settlement** in the scope of these treaties.

Apart from that, the multilateral and plurilateral agreements are self-reliant/independent and stand for themselves in their legal effects.

---

[109] The in GATT Annex 4 also included International Dairy Agreement and International Bovine Meat Agreement terminated in 1997. Not included in the GATT Annex 4 is the Information Technology Agreement concluded in 1996.

# 3. WTO negotiations

After some years pause following the Uruguay negotiation round leading to the creation of the WTO in 1994/95, in 2001 WTO members initiated another round of negotiations in Doha/Qatar. The **Doha round** is the $9^{th}$ negotiation round since the conclusion of the GATT in 1947 and the first one realized in the scope of the WTO.

The conferences realized within this round are called "Ministerial Conferences" (MC, see *WTO institutional structure*), the most current one realized being MC13 in Abu Dhabi (2024).

The Doha round has not yet finished and – despite rather difficult negotiations until now – has led to some **outcomes**:

- Two additional multilateral agreements were successfully negotiated:
  - the Trade Facilitation Agreement (2013, in force since 2017) aiming for simpler and faster customs procedures and cooperation between customs authorities, and
  - the Fisheries Subsidies Agreement (2022, not yet in force), with the goal to protect marine life by prohibiting subsidies for overfishing.[110]
- The plurilateral Agreement on Government Procurement was renewed in 2012.
- In 2015, it was decided to expand the plurilateral Information Technology Agreement (ITA), now covering a series of additional tariff-free products. Membership of the ITA further increased, now covering about 97% of the world's trade in IT.[111]

---

[110] Subsidies **a)** contributing to illegal, unreported and unregulated fishing, **b)** regarding overfished stocks and **c)** in the High Seas. (Fisheries Subsidies Agreement Art. 3-5)
[111] https://www.wto.org/english/tratop_e/inftec_e/itaintro_e.htm. Duty-free access to ITA's members resulting from ITA tariff eliminations must be granted to *all* WTO members and therefore benefit not only ITA members.

- The TRIPS was amended in 2017 (new Art. 31*bis*) so special compulsory licenses could be granted for the production and export of medicines to WTO members that are not able to domestically produce enough of them.
- In 2022, a TRIPS waiver was agreed on to limit the exclusivity of patent rights to support worldwide access to Covid 19-vaccines.
- Agricultural export subsidies were prohibited (Ministerial Decision on Export Competition 2015), with most exceptions having phased out between 2020 and 2023.
- Trade conditions for Least Developed Countries (LDCs) were improved by enhancing preferential treatment of LDCs' services providers (Ministerial Decisions 2011, 2015 – "LDC (Services) Waiver"[112]) and preferential Rules of Origin for LDCs (Ministerial Decisions 2013, 2015).

### *How do trade negotiations work?*

According to the WTO-Agreement, decision-making should, if possible, be done by *consensus* (Art. 9). If consensus (no formal objection by any member) cannot be reached, generally the simple majority of the votes cast suffices. Each WTO member has one vote except for the EU, which has 27.[113]

**Amendment proposals** to any WTO agreement must be tabled at least 90 days so that the WTO members have enough time to have a look at it. After discussions, the Ministerial Conference (MC) has a vote, which in this case mostly requires a two-thirds majority of the members (the decision then being binding only for members that have voted in favor). However,

---

[112] The *LDC Waiver* permits WTO members to concede preferential treatment to services and service suppliers from LDC members.
[113] If the EU as a whole participates in a decision, its MS do not also participate (individually).

the MC, supported by the WTO Secretariat, always strives for unanimity. (WTO Agreement Art. 10)

The reason for this is that consensus is regarded as a **a)** democratic guarantee, a **b)** guarantee for implementation as well as **c)** for the protection of smaller (in negotiations often due to their size less "powerful") WTO members. Therefore, voting in the WTO is relatively rare.

In view of the large number of WTO members, negotiations in general are frequently done in so-called *green room-meetings*, in which the most important members (e.g. EU, USA, China, India, Brazil) as well as the member states groups'[114] representatives and the members that have a specific interest (e.g. for being especially affected) negotiate *first* among themselves. Then, based on the outcome of these green room-negotiations, negotiations with the remaining WTO members take place.

**Tariff negotiations** can e.g. be done

*product by product* (*Which tariff reductions can I offer for which product?*), which has the disadvantage that – due to the huge variety of existent products – not all products are included in the negotiation (outcome) but only the most important ones. Apart from that, this way of negotiating is relatively time ineffective.

and/or

*formula-based*, which is normally preferred. *Formula-based* means that a certain percentage of customs duties reduction ("linear cuts") is conceded to *all* products of a certain kind (e.g. agricultural products) of all WTO members, with (only) some individual products being excepted.

---

[114] WTO members are divided into (geographical, development-based or matter-based) groups for negotiation purposes, e.g. the *African, Caribbean and Pacific States, Asian developing members, Small, vulnerable economies.* (https://www.wto.org/english/tratop_e/dda_e/negotiating_groups_e.htm)

The problem here is that if a **50% linear reduction** was agreed on and one country had a relatively high level of 40% customs duties *ad valorem* in place, the customs duties in this country still remain relatively high after the 50% cut (20% *ad valorem*). This might be considered unfair by another country that initially had a low level of only 4% customs duties *ad valorem* in place for the same product type, for it would have to further reduce it to only 2% *ad valorem*.

Therefore, *non*-linear cuts are usually preferred, meaning that larger cuts are made of higher customs duties than of lower customs duties.

### *How do accession negotiations work?*

WTO accession negotiations are normally done *bilaterally*, meaning that the acceding state negotiates bilaterally with each WTO member requesting that, how it can / should liberalize its trade in relation to (all) WTO members. The outcome of these bilateral negotiations is the so-called "ticket of admission". Apart from this *ticket*, the future member has to bring all its laws and procedures into conformity with WTO standards *before* it can finally accede. This is why the average total duration of accessions is about 10 years (!).[115]

If the WTO members decide so, the future member also has to fulfil additional obligations ("WTO+", e.g. no export duties for China) or has only limited rights ("WTO-", e.g. temporary restrictions on certain Chinese products by some members).

---

[115] Van den Bossche/Prévost, 2021: 23.

# 4. WTO institutional structure

The WTO consists of several bodies, the Ministerial Conference, the General Council and the Secretariat being the most important ones. Apart from these, there are three Councils and several Committees supporting the General Council as well as some *ad hoc* bodies.

The **Ministerial Conference** (MC) consisting of the competent (trade, economy, etc.) ministers of the WTO members is the main decision-making body of the WTO and convenes every two years. Among its competences are

- adopting authoritative interpretations of the WTO agreements (¾ majority, has never happened),
- adopting waivers of WTO obligations (¾ majority), e.g. MC12 TRIPS-waiver (Jul 2022) for the production of Covid-19 vaccines for 5 years,
- adopting amendments of the WTO agreements (⅔ majority)[116],
- deciding on accessions (⅔ majority) and receiving withdrawal notifications (six months waiting period, has never happened) and
- appointing the Director General (consensus by General Council).

The **General Council**, which is composed of ambassador-level delegates of the WTO members, convenes every two months in Geneva. Additionally (and more frequently), it convenes as *Dispute Settlement Body* (DSB, see *WTO Dispute Settlement*) and as *Trade Policy Review Body*.

Supported by three specialized Councils (one each for the GATT, GATS and TRIPS) and subordinate Committees, the General Council exercises the MC's powers between its sessions.[117]

---

[116] Although treaty revision generally requires unanimity; the states that did not vote in favor of an amendment are not bound by it. (Trebilcock, 2020: 23, 24)
[117] Van den Bossche/Prévost, 2021: 18.

Apart from supporting the General Council, the specialized **Councils** and **Committees**, among other things, oversee the functioning and implementation of the WTO agreements.

*Ad hoc* **Panels** are created for dispute settlement, appeals being handled by the permanent **Appellate Body**. *Ad hoc* **Working Groups** and other bodies deal with accessions and the Doha round negotiations.

The **Secretariat** provides information as well as administrative, technical and legal assistance to the WTO's bodies. It further monitors world trade developments and is responsible for media, press and public relations.

The Secretariat is headed by a Director General (appointed by consensus, currently Ngozi Okonjo-Iweala) and has comparably limited staff (only around 700 regular staff; vs. European Commission over 30 000) and limited budget (annually around 200 mill. Swiss Francs; vs. EU 2024 189 000 mill. €). Its budget is established on the basis of the members' trade (imports and exports) in relation to the total WTO trade.

Therefore, the WTO is often referred to as a **member-driven organization**. The EU, by contrast, has some executive competences and organs representing not members' interests but (only) the organization's interests (the European Commission).

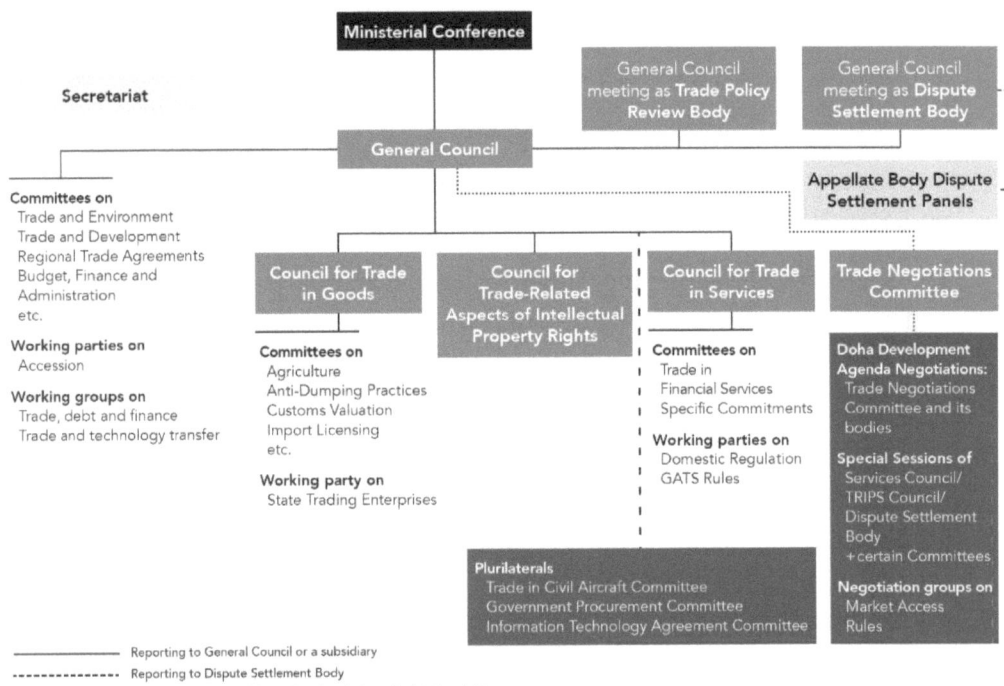

Image: © Karoline Schreiber, based on WTO. All rights reserved.
This image can be found in the Annex in color and bigger size (!).

94

# V. WTO Principles

The WTO and its law is based on some key principles, the most important one being the **non-discrimination** (or *equality/equal treatment*) principle. This fundamental principle has two "faces", the **Most-Favored-Nation (MFN) – Principle** and the **National Treatment – Principle**.

## 1. Most Favored Nation Treatment (MFN)

The Most-Favored-Nation (MFN) – Principle is defined similarly in Article 1 of the GATT (trade in goods) and in Article 2 of the GATS (trade in services):

> With respect to **customs duties and charges of any kind** imposed on or in connection with importation or exportation (…) any **advantage, favour, privilege or immunity** granted by any contracting party [WTO member] to any product originating in or destined for any other country shall be **accorded immediately and unconditionally to the like product** originating in or destined for the territories **of all other contracting parties**. (…) (GATT [1994] Art. 1, bold print added)

> With respect to any measure covered by this Agreement, each Member shall accord immediately and unconditionally **to services and service suppliers of any other Member treatment no less favourable than that it accords to like services and service suppliers of any other country**. (GATS [1994] Art. 2, bold print added)

As we can see, an "advantage, favour, privilege or immunity" or "favourable treatment" given by a WTO member to another WTO member must be *extended to all other WTO members*. This means that, as soon as a preferential treatment is offered to one, it must be offered to all (non-discrimination). This must be the case even if the other members do not have a disadvantage because one member is treated better.

## a. Trade in Goods – MFN

As for trade in goods (TiG), regulated by the GATT, MFN means the following:

**Any advantage granted at the border (and also internally) by any WTO member to a product from any WTO member must be accorded immediately and unconditionally[118] to** *like* **products of all the other WTO members.**

In other words, there must not be accorded trade advantages to any importing country, competitive opportunities must be the same for importers from all WTO countries.
More concretely, if e.g. WTO member **A** offers a tariff reduction to WTO member **B**, it has to offer it also to all other WTO members.

The MFN-Principle primarily applies to **tariffs** and **other import/export charges** as well as **customs formalities**.

MFN Treatment is not primarily applied to quantitative restrictions (bans, quotas) simply because the necessity is not given:

**Quantitative restrictions** among WTO members are **generally prohibited under the GATT.**

> **No** prohibitions or restrictions other than duties, taxes or other charges, whether made effective through **quotas, import or export licences** or other measures, shall be instituted or maintained by any contracting party on the **importation** of any product of the territory of any other contracting party or on the **exportation** or sale for export of any product destined for the territory of any other contracting party.
> (GATT [1994] Art. 11, bold print added)

---

[118] Conditions are generally possible as long as they are applied to all WTO members. "Unconditionally" in this context therefore means *no additional conditions*.

96

*Why is (or – in 1947 – was) MFN Treatment necessary?*

The inter-war years were characterized by so-called economic factionalism, i.e. the creation of economic groups and their clear and partly insuperable divisions, which contributed to the outbreak of the Second World War.

Against this background, the idea of an economic level playing field under a common set of ground rules was conceived. This was put into practice by the GATT in 1947 and later by the WTO and is expressed, among other things, by the MFN-Principle. In other words, International Trade Law has at its core the aim of worldwide economic inclusion and, finally, of peace among nations.

*If A negotiates a tariff reduction with B, what happens with C ?*

Also (WTO member) **C** profits, for the same tariff reduction must be conceded to it. This is called "free riding" and very common in the WTO. It can be avoided though if **A** negotiates a Free Trade Agreement (FTA) with **B**, which allows it to exceptionally treat some WTO members (e.g. **B**) better than others (e.g. **C**). See *Free Trade Agreements exception*.

The MFN-Principle covers both *direct* and *indirect* discrimination.

*What is the difference between direct and indirect discrimination?*

Let us have a look at this example first, which makes it easier to understand.

**Example**

*Variant a)* Country **A** *imposes a customs duty of 5% ad valorem on honey from* **B** *but a 10% duty ad valorem on honey from* **C** *and* **D**.

*Variant b)* *Country A imposes a customs duty of 5% ad valorem on honey coming from bees that spend at least 6 months a year at an altitude of more than 1200m (B's territory being located at an altitude of 1100m-2500m) and a 10% duty ad valorem on honey coming from other bees. C's and D's highest mountain are located at 1000m and 1100m above sea level respectively.*

While *variant a)* represents a *direct* discrimination, *variant b)* represents an *indirect* one (despite the fact that the *altitude*-criterion is seemingly objective and applied to *all* states).

If a rule is based on the illicit criterion itself (*statehood* | **countries** C and D) leading to a certain group (some *states* | countries C and D) being discriminated against, it is *directly* discriminatory with respect to this group.

If a rule is based on an other criterion (any | altitude) but leading to the same group being mainly affected (some *states* | countries C and D and any other country not fulfilling the criterion), it is *indirectly* discriminatory with respect to this group.

It therefore does not matter if a criterion is applied to *all* states without differentiating but if certain/some (potential trade partner) states are in a clear disadvantage because of it while others are not.[119]

In the afore-mentioned example a border measure (tariff) is concerned, which is the regular case when the MFN-Principle is applied. However,

---

[119] If a state implements trade barriers against products made with seal meat but eliminates these barriers (only) for products whose seal meat was hunted/produced by Inuits, countries not having an Inuit population are in a clear trade disadvantage (compared to countries having such a population) and therefore indirectly discriminated. In 2014, a similar case on seals involving the European Communities, Greenland, Canada and Norway was decided by the WTO Appellate Body. (DS400 / DS401)

MFN Treatment must also be conceded after a product has crossed the border of the importing state (internal measures).[120]

*Country **A** exempts honey candy from **B** from its sale prohibition of sweets in college cafeterias but does not exempt honey candy from **C**.*

A direct discrimination against **C** exists.

A (simplified) **assessment for determining if in trade in goods MFN Treatment is duly granted** can be done by asking these three questions:

1. ***Discrimination?*** Are more favorable competitive opportunities[121] given to the product of another importing country?
2. ***Like products?*** Are the compared imported products "like" (see below)?
3. ***No exception?*** Is there no exception applicable that justifies the different treatment? (see below)

For determining if (from different countries) imported products are "***like* products**", an *overall* assessment of the factors determining the competitive relationship must be done. This means that the *sum* of the following factors must lead to the conclusion that the products are like, one factor individually usually does not suffice:

---

[120] The application of MFN to internal measures is less common because internally (inside the destination country of imports) also the National Treatment-Principle applies (see below).

[121] No *actual* trade effects are necessary for that nor must be proven; the (theoretical) *opportunity* suffices.

99

- **physical similarity/identity** – the products should be physically identical, a difference in the production method usually only plays a role if it affects consumer tastes. E.g. fair-trade chocolate, see next point.

- **substitutability for consumers** – the products should be substitutable for consumers (if the one is not available, the other one can be and is used just as readily instead) E.g. GMO-free food might in some markets not be substitutable for consumers by genetically modified food.[122]

A can treat genetically modified corn (mostly done in **B**) less favorably than corn made/cultivated according to standards prohibiting genetical modifications of corn (as offered by **C**) if genetical corn modifications affect consumer tastes and thus constitute a difference in competition.

- **end use** of the products, which should be the same.

- **tariff classification** of the products, which should be the same; e.g. under the *HS Convention* by the World Customs Organization (see *How tariffs work*)

As mentioned, for determining if the MFN-Principle was violated, apart from a 1. discrimination concerning 2. *like* products, there must be 3. **no exceptions**.

These include government procurement (unless the state is a party to the plurilateral Agreement on Government Procurement) but even more importantly the FTA exception (see *Free Trade Agreements exception*), the developing countries / LDCs exception (see *Developing countries exception*) as well as the General Exceptions (see *General Exceptions*).

---

[122] In 2001, the WTO Appellate Body e.g. ruled that health risks (possibly affecting consumer tastes) must be included in the analysis if (possibly carcinogenic) asbestos fibers and PVA/cellulose/glass fibers are *like*. (DS135)

## b. Trade in Services – fundamentals and MFN

### Fundamentals

While trade in goods is a classical area regulated by International Trade Law and finds its home since 1947 in the GATT, the international regulation of trade in services, with the GATS 1994, is comparably new.

An additional challenge to its young age is that services tend to be regulated industry by industry / occupation by occupation, and this often at the sub-national level.

For these reasons, progress in liberalizing services has been rather slow until now and, as we will see, international regulation of trade in services is less far-reaching than of trade in goods. Nonetheless, it has made a huge step forward thanks to the GATS and an increasing number of FTAs covering both trade in goods *and* services.

This makes perfectly sense, since services account for more than 20% of global trade in goods and services combined.[123] In other words, there is a lot of potential waiting to be harnessed by trade policy and regulation.

When speaking about *international trade in services*, usually **4 modes of supply** are referred to[124]:

**1. Cross-border supply**, e.g. IT support by videoconference from a company based in country **A** to a company based in country **B**.

---

[123] https://ec.europa.eu/eurostat/statistics-explained/index.php?title=World_trade_in_services.
[124] The following examples are *from the perspective of B* granting the provision of services in the respective modes.

**2.** (physical) **Consumption abroad**, e.g. an employee of a company based in **B** travels to **A** for having his/her professional laptop repaired.[125]

**3. Commercial presence**, e.g. a service supplier based in **A** establishes a branch office in **B** in order to install new graphics cards and cooling systems in all employees' computers at the offices of a company based in **B**.

**4. Presence of natural persons** (physical supply abroad), e.g. a service provider based in **A** changes the motherboards of a company based in **B**.

## MFN in trade in services

As for trade in services (TiS), regulated by the GATS, MFN Treatment refers to non-discrimination/equality regarding the origin (or destination) of (any) *service itself* and of the nationality of the *service provider*.

Similarly to the MFN-Principle in the GATT, also the GATS MFN-Principle (contained in its Art. 2) covers *direct* and *indirect* discrimination. For more information, see *Trade in Goods – MFN*.

**Example**

*Variant a)* State **A** prohibits the establishment of foreign bars in its territory except for those from nationals of its neighboring state **B**, with which it shares cultural heritage regarding furniture-style and cocktail-making.

*Variant b)* **A** requires all bars established in its territory to offer cocktails made with a traditional juggling method and to have furniture made with

---

[125] Generally, services can *always* be purchased abroad with **B** not being able to limit this. However, they may be practical constraints, e.g. in health services regarding the portability of health insurance. (OECD/EU/WHO, 2017: 510)

local wood in the typical interior design style of **A**. **B** shares this bartending style and interior design culture with **A**, but no other WTO members.

While **variant a)** represents a *direct* discrimination based on the *nationality of the services provider*, **variant b)** represents an *indirect* one (despite the fact that the *bartending style and furniture quality*-criteria are seemingly objective and apply to *all* states). This has to do with the fact that this way especially service providers from (most) other countries are in a disadvantage compared to those from **B**.

As with MFN Treatment in trade in goods, also in trade in services the MFN-Principle in principle applies both at the country's border and *in* the country.

Concerning the border, however, tariffs in services (e.g. on electronic transmissions or digital products) are barely existent thanks to the so-called *E-Commerce Moratorium*, which is in place since 1998 and was extended by the latest Ministerial Conference (MC13) to March 2026. Furthermore, market access of foreign service providers is not granted automatically but only if a commitment exists by the state in question (**opt-in** approach).[126]

Inside the country ("internal" measures) the MFN-Principle coexists with the National Treatment-Principle (see below).

---

[126] **See also** *Trade in Services – NT and Market Access*.

A (simplified) **assessment for determining if in trade in services MFN Treatment is duly granted** can be done by asking these three questions:

1. *Discrimination?* Are more favorable competitive opportunities[127] given to the service or service provider of another importing country?
2. *Like service and service suppliers?* Are the compared services and service suppliers "like" (see below)?
3. *No exception?* Is there no exception applicable that justifies the different treatment? (see below)

Assessing *likeness* in trade in services is done somewhat different than doing so in trade in goods.

For determining if provided services and service providers (from different countries) are *like*, first an analysis in isolation has to be done, i.e. determining if the services are *like* (in a competitive relationship) must be done separately from determining if the service suppliers are *like* (in a competitive relationship). Only then an *overall* assessment should be done.

---

[127] No *actual* trade effects are necessary for that nor must be proven; the (theoretical) *opportunity* suffices.

104

In these assessments the following parameters should be taken into account:

- **characteristics of the services / service suppliers** – factors such as the kind and proceeding of the services (e.g. juggling cocktail mixing in the example above) and
the size, assets and expertise of the suppliers (e.g. certified nursing professionals having to complete university studies and practical training vs. having only to complete a short course and no practical training)

**Example**

*A establishes that foreign IT experts providing services in its territory must have a university degree or a minimum two-years official training certificate.*
*IT experts from B must have a degree or formation for providing IT services (in B) according to B's national laws. IT experts from C, however, do not need such formation for professionally supplying IT services (in C) according to C's national laws.*

IT experts of **B** have an advantage compared to most of **C**'s IT experts that could possibly represent an indirect discrimination (provided that the IT service providers from **B** and **C** are considered *like*).
Since the proven expertise of **B**'s IT service suppliers and of (some/most of) **C**'s IT service suppliers might differ considerably and possibly also the kind and proceeding of their services, *likeness* might not be given though. Therefore, a different treatment (discrimination) might be legal.

- **substitutability for consumers** of the services and service suppliers

- **classification** of the services, which should be the same e.g. under the UN Central Product Classification (CPC). Issued by the UN Statistics Division, the CPC offers a classification structure for data analysis regarding both goods and services and, since its original publication in 1998, is regularly updated.

As mentioned, for determining if the MFN-Principle was violated, apart from a 1. discrimination concerning 2. *like* services and service providers, there must be 3. **no exceptions.**

In contrast to the GATT, where MFN Treatment is construed as *compulsory for all* WTO members, the **GATS**, despite also setting MFN as a general default, **allows WTO members to partly *opt-out* of the MFN Treatment obligation in trade in services** (!).

These opt-out measures must be specific (e.g. not concerning a whole sector) and are, in principle, limited in time (max. 10 years).[128]

For opting out, (future) members have to negotiate *Article II[129] Exemptions* during their accession with the other WTO members (e.g. the protection measures of traditional bar culture from the example above could be exempted).[130] The exemptions are furthermore subject to (re)negotiation in subsequent trade liberalization rounds.

Other **exceptions** refer e.g. to

- services supplied in the exercise of governmental authority (not commercial, not in competition with anyone)[131], e.g. police or prison services,

- granting advantages to adjacent countries for service facilitation between frontier zones (if the service is locally supplied and consumed), e.g. taxi services in the border area,

---

[128] GATS Annex on Article II Exemptions; Lowenfeld, 2008: 125, 130.

[129] The MFN-Principle being regulated in Art. 2 of the GATS.

[130] "Founding" members, i.e. states present at the conclusion of the GATS in 1994, could unilaterally exempt measures from the MFN Treatment obligation, provided that they listed these measures in the Article II Exemptions-Annex before the entry into force of the WTO Agreement (Van den Bossche/Prévost, 2021: 63, Lowenfeld, 2008: 125)

[131] Except in members of the plurilateral Agreement on Government Procurement.

- recognition of foreign qualifications of (the service providers of) one country if (the service providers of) the other countries have been given adequate opportunity to obtain comparable recognition.

Moreover, even more importantly, there exist exceptions regarding FTAs (see *Free Trade Agreements exception*), developing countries and specifically LDCs[132] (see *Developing countries exception*), and General Exceptions (see *General Exceptions*).

---

[132] In 2011, the *LDC (services) waiver* was adopted, which permits WTO members to concede preferential treatment to services and service suppliers from LDC members.

# 2. National Treatment (NT)

The National-Treatment (NT) – Principle is defined in Article 3 of the GATT (trade in goods) and in Article 17 of the GATS (trade in services):

> The products of the territory of any contracting party [WTO member] imported into the territory of any other contracting party shall
>> (2) **not be subject**, directly or indirectly, **to** *internal taxes or other internal charges* of any kind **in excess of those applied**, directly or indirectly, **to like domestic products**.
>> Moreover, **no** contracting party shall otherwise apply **internal taxes or other internal charges** to imported or domestic products[133].
>> (…)
>> (4) be accorded **treatment no less favourable than** (…) **like products of national origin in respect of all** *laws, regulations and requirements* affecting their internal sale, offering for sale, purchase, transportation, distribution or use.
>
> (GATT Art. 3, bold print and italics added)

> In the **sectors inscribed in its Schedule** [(!) see below], and subject to any conditions and qualifications set out therein, **each Member shall accord to services and service suppliers of any other Member**, in respect of *all measures* affecting the supply of services, **treatment no less favourable than that it accords to its own like services and service suppliers**. (…)
>
> (GATS Art. 17, bold print and italics added)

As we can see, "internal taxes, charges, laws, regulations and requirements" applied or "less favourable treatment" given by a WTO member to its own products or services/service suppliers, must be

---

[133] "A tax (…) would be considered to be inconsistent with the provisions of the second sentence [of paragraph 2] only where competition was involved between (…) the taxed product and (…) a *directly competitive or substitutable product* which was not *similarly* taxed." (GATT Annex I: note/supplementary provision on Art. 3, italics added) See *Internal Taxation (GATT Art. 3 (2))*.

*extended to all WTO members.* This means that, as soon as a member offers an internal preferential treatment to its own products/services/service providers, this preferential treatment must be offered also to those from all members (non-discrimination).

National Treatment refers to *internal* measures, which are typically measures *within the territory* of a state. Put differently, the NT-Principle applies to measures directed at a product / service (provider) *after* it has crossed the border to access a country's market (*not* to border measures).

**Example**

*Product X is sent from country A to country B to be sold there.*

When **X** enters **B**, at the border, MFN applies (but not NT). After **X** has paid customs duties etc. and can therefore legally enter **B**'s market, NT (and MFN) must be conceded. I.e. the tax, sales etc. conditions must be as favorable as for **B**'s national products.

*Service provider Ya from country A preforms the service Yb in country B.*

When **Ya** enters **B**, at the border, (in principle) MFN applies (but not NT; furthermore market access may be limited[134]). When **Ya** (and **Yb**) have legally entered **B**'s market, NT must be conceded[135]. I.e. internal conditions for **Ya** and **Yb** must be as favorable as for **B**'s national service providers and services.

---

[134] See below *Market Access.*
[135] If a commitment of **B** exists in its Services Schedule, see below *Trade in Services – NT and Market Access.*

109

## a. Trade in Goods – NT

As for trade in goods (TiG) regulated by the GATT, in short, NT means the following:

**Any tax, charge or regulatory advantage granted in a WTO's member's market to a national product must also be accorded to the imported like products of all WTO members in this market.**

In other words, as soon as a product has crossed the border and entered a state, it has to be given the same treatment as domestic products.

More concretely, if e.g. WTO member **A** imposes a tax (reduction) and certain (facilitated) sales conditions to its own products, **A** must also concede the same tax and sales conditions to WTO member **B**'s (and **C**'s, **D**'s, **E**'s etc.) products.

Similarly to MFN Treatment, also regarding NT both *direct* and *indirect* discrimination (see *MFN in trade in services*) is prohibited. Also like in MFN Treatment, *potential* effects due to different treatment suffice (*actual* negative effects resulting from different taxes, internal regulations, etc. are not necessary).

### Example

*Country **A** applies higher taxes to spirits like whisky, gin and vodka (no matter where they come from) than to pisco, being the mainly produced national spirit. In countries **B**, **C** and **D** only other kinds of spirits than pisco are produced (and exported).*

There is an *indirect* discrimination[136] against states that do not produce pisco but only other distilled types of alcohol ("spirits"): The imported

---

[136] Regarding taxes, an indirect discrimination usually exists when there are a lower tax bracket covering primarily domestic products (e.g. pisco) and a higher tax bracket covering primarily imported products (e.g. other types of spirits).

110

products from these states are in a disadvantage compared to domestic *directly competitive or substitutable* (see below) spirits.

Furthermore, it is not necessary that whisky, gin or vodka are *actually* sold with the higher tax on top in **A**. It suffices that there are higher (discriminatory) taxes *in place* with "no actual harm yet done" (no products yet sold) for affirming a discrimination.

The NT-Principle in trade in goods (TiG) is construed narrower than MFN in TiG, and NT in trade in services[137], because it formally does not cover "all measures" (GATS Art. 17) but only **a) internal taxes and charges** and **b) internal regulatory measures**[138].

**When assessing if a) internal taxes/charges or b) internal regulatory measures comply with the NT-Principle, *different* parameters must be look at respectively.**

---

[137] But certainly, for a NT-obligation in trade in services, a state must commit itself to it. See below *Trade in Services – NT and Market Access*.
[138] Internal laws, regulations and requirements relating to the sale, transportation or distribution of products.

Internal Taxation (GATT Art. 3 (2))

Higher taxes *per se* constitute less favorable competitive opportunities (*discrimination*). That is why the question if discrimination between a higher and a lower taxed product exists usually does not have to be specifically analyzed (in contrast to NT referring to regulation [see below] or MFN).

Taxation (and charges) here refers only to ***product*** **taxes**, i.e. not to corporate taxes, income taxes etc.

*If e.g.* ***A*** *required foreign companies to pay higher corporate taxes than* ***A****'s national companies, this would not be against the NT-Principle.*

A (simplified) **assessment for determining if in trade in goods *NT* *referring to internal taxes and other internal charges* is duly granted** can be done by asking these three (or five) questions referring to domestic and imported products:

| | |
|---|---|
| **1.** Are the products ***like***? (Art. 3 (2) first sentence) | |
| **2.** In case ***yes***, is the imported product taxed <u>higher</u>? | **2.** In case ***no***, are the products ***directly competitive or substitutable***? (Art. 3 (2) second sentence) |
| |    **3.** In case ***yes***, is the imported product taxed <u>considerably higher</u>? |
| |       **4.** In case <u>yes</u>, is it done to afford **domestic protection**? |
| **3.** Is there <u>*no exception*</u> justifying the different treatment? | **5.** Is there <u>*no exception*</u> justifying the different treatment? |

112

As we can see in the diagram above, two scenarios of the *NT-Principle referring to taxation or other charges* are distinguished:

i.    the *higher* taxation of *like* products,[139] and
ii.   the *considerably higher* taxation of *directly competitive or substitutable* products.[140]

This means that for products that are *like* (see below) no tax difference at all (not even 0,01%) is allowed, whereas for products that are (only) *directly competitive or substitutable* a small tax difference *is* permitted.

## ad i. *like* products

*Likeness* of national products and imported products is assessed using the same parameters as for *likeness* in MFN Treatment: *physical identity, substitutability for consumers, end use* and *tariff classification*.

The concept of *like products* in NT referring to taxation/charges is narrower than regarding MFN (!). In NT-taxation a *strong(er)* competitive relationship between the compared products must be given.

 The same products could be considered *like* under the MFN-Principle but *not-like* under the NT-Principle regarding internal taxation/charges.

## Example

Small garden tomatoes and cherry tomatoes may be *like* products according to the GATT's MFN requirements but not to GATT's NT-taxation requirements.

As mentioned, if products are *like* under the *NT-Principle referring to taxation or other charges*, **no tax difference *at all*** is allowed.

---

[139] GATT Art. 3 (2) first sentence.
[140] GATT Art. 3 (2) second sentence.

113

The **reason** why the products are taxed differently (e.g. for protecting national products or other reasons) **does *not* matter.**

### ad ii. *directly competitive or substitutable* products

The parameters used for assessing if an imported product *is directly competitive or substitutable* in relation to a national product, are similar to those regarding *likeness* (*physical identity, substitutability for consumers, end use* and *tariff classification*). However, they are less strict in the sense that not physical *identity* of the products is necessary but *physical **similarity*** suffices. In addition, not *complete* substitutability for consumers must be given but an ***imperfect*** *substitutability* is enough.

This is why the notion *directly competitive or substitutable* products in NT[141] is broader than *like* products in MFN Treatment[142] and *much* broader than *like* products in NT[143].

### Example

Big garden tomatoes and cherry tomatoes may be *directly competitive or substitutable* products in NT but not *like* products (nor according to MFN neither to NT requirements).

Real examples (from WTO dispute settlement) of directly competitive or substitutable products are e.g. domestic cane sugar and imported high fructose cane sirup; or (Japanese) shochu and whisky, brandy, rum, gin and vodka.[144]

---

[141] GATT Art. 3 (2) second sentence.
[142] GATT Art. 1.
[143] GATT Art. 3 (2) first sentence.
[144] WTO Appellate Body DS8, 10, 11 (shochu, 1996) and DS308 (cane sugar, 2006).

114

If products are directly competitive or substitutable, a **small difference in tax is permitted** (in contrast to scenario **i.**, where no tax difference *at all* is allowed).

This small tax difference being permitted is, however, subject to a condition referring to the *reason why it is applied*: **domestic protection**.

 *Directly competitive or substitutable* foreign and domestic products may be taxed slightly differently if it is for protecting national production (!).

## Internal Regulation (GATT Art. 3 (4))

The GATT NT-Principle does not only refer to taxes and other internal charges but also to "laws, regulations and requirements affecting" the "internal sale, offering for sale, purchase, transportation, distribution or use" of imported products (GATT Art. 3). This second area covered by the NT-Principle is succinctly referred to as *internal regulation* in the following.

In contrast to higher *taxes*, which automatically constitute less favorable competitive opportunities, a difference in *internal regulation* for domestic and imported products does *not automatically* signify worse competitive opportunities for imports.

This is why regarding internal regulation (GATT Art. 3 (**4**))[145] it must be assessed if this regulation constitutes a less favorable treatment, i.e. less favorable competitive opportunities for imported products than for domestic products.

 Only different internal regulation (and measures) affecting the sale/purchase, transportation, distribution or use of products *that has a **detrimental effect on competitive opportunities** of* imported products is prohibited by GATT Art. 3 (**4**).

Such *internal regulation* can e.g. be

a minimum price,

a limitation of sales points
e.g. imported beer can only be sold by wholesalers, not by small shops[146],

---

[145] But not taxes, GATT Art. 3 (**2**).
[146] See e.g. GATT Panel DS17/R (Canada-Provincial Liquor Boards, 1992).

116

a ban on advertising
e.g. only for foreign cigarettes or a regulation negatively affecting their sale[147],

special requirements or a higher price for transport or storage
e.g. imported beer and wine have to be transported by *common carrier* (carrier offering its services to the general public) and domestic ones not[148]

for imported products (but not, or to a lesser extent, for domestic products).

A (simplified) **assessment for determining if in trade in goods *NT* referring to internal regulation is duly granted** can be done by asking these three questions:

1. *Discrimination?* Are more favorable competitive opportunities[149] given to a domestic product (than to the imported product) by internal regulation?
2. *Like products?* Are the imported and domestic products "like" (see below)?
3. *No exception?* Is there no exception applicable that justifies the different treatment? (see below)

For determining if an imported and a national product are "***like* products**", the same parameters as in MFN and NT-taxation are applied (*physical identity, substitutability for consumers, end use* and *tariff classification*).

---

[147] See e.g. GATT Panel DS10/R (Thailand-Cigarettes, 1990).
[148] See e.g. GATT Panel DS23/R (USA-Malt Beverages, 1992).
[149] No *actual* trade effects are necessary for that nor must be proven; the (theoretical) *opportunity* suffices.

The scope of *likeness* in NT-internal regulation can be situated somewhere between[150] the scope of NT-taxation's *like products* and *directly competitive or substitutable products*:

| Scope of terminology (from narrower to wider) | |
|---|---|
| **National Treatment** | **Most-Favored-Nation Treatment** |
| Taxation *like* <br> Art. 3 (2) first sentence | |
| Internal regulation *like* <br> Art. 3 (4) | *like* (similarly) <br> Art. 1 |
| Taxation *directly competitive or substitutable* <br> Art. 3 (2) second sentence | |

Beamers with a 3D-function and those without might be *like products* according to Art. 3 (4) and *directly competitive or substitutable products* under Art. 3 (2) second sentence but **not** *like products* according to Art. 3 (2) first sentence.

Nevertheless, the scope of both *like* and *directly competitive or substitutable* on which the comparison of the products is based in NT-taxation does **not** *significantly* differ from the scope of *like* in NT-internal regulation.

### What would happen if the scope was very different?

*WTO member **A** wants to support its domestic production and protect it from competing imports.*

---

[150] What is clear thanks to WTO Appellate Body decisions is that the concept of *like* in taxation is narrower than *like* in internal regulation and that the *combined* scope of *like* **and** *directly competitive or substitutable* in taxation is not *significantly* different to that of *like* in internal regulation. (Van den Bossche/Prévost, 2021: 75)

118

For that it basically has two options: *taxation* and *regulation*.

If the scope of one of them was much narrower than the scope of the other, **A** would of course choose the one with the wider scope (and not the most appropriate one) just to elude the narrower scope of the other (which might be more appropriate) for achieving the same end, i.e. protection of domestic production.

As mentioned, for determining if the NT-Principle was violated, apart from a 1. discrimination concerning 2. *like* products, there must be 3. **no exceptions**.

These exceptions to GATT Art. 3 include

- direct subsidies to domestic producers[151],
- government procurement regulations[152] that regulate the purchase of products for government purposes by governmental agencies, e.g. establishing that government departments must only purchase gas to heat their buildings from domestic gas producers,
- the developing countries and LDCs exception (see *Developing countries exception*) as well as the
- General Exceptions (see chapter below).

---

[151] If subsidies were generally prohibited, there would be no need for the specific rules on subsidies of the (WTO) Agreement on Subsidies and Countervailing Measures.
[152] Unless the state is a party to the plurilateral (WTO) Agreement on Government Procurement.

## b. Trade in Services – NT and Market Access

In trade in *goods*, National Treatment (NT) is a general obligation *all* WTO members must comply with.[153] It is established by the GATT as a general and by default applicable rule.

This is, unfortunately, **not** the case in trade in services and the GATS.

In comparison to *MFN* Treatment in trade in services, which the members generally must concede (with the possibility to initially partly opt-**out**), NT in trade in services is **only exceptionally covered** (if members decide so – opt-**in**).
In other words, in trade in services there is normally an equal treatment *between foreign countries* (MFN) but generally *not between a foreign country and the own country* (NT).

> **!** In services, WTO members are only bound by the NT-Principle (Art. 17 GATS) **if they decide so.**

This is done by a member committing itself to NT in its so-called "**Schedule of Specific Commitments**", also *Services Schedule*.

These *specific commitments* of the respective WTO members are, as their name says, specific and normally members do not decide to liberalize all possible areas the NT-Principle could cover (no *all in* or *all out-* mechanism).

---

[153] Another difference between NT in trade in goods and trade in services is that, *in TiG* NT "only" refers to *internal taxes and internal regulation,* while NT commitments *in TiS* may cover "**all** measures affecting the supply of services". This is only the case though if members committed to it in their Services Schedule (see below).

## Market Access

The *Services Schedules* do not only refer to NT in the above-described sense but also to **market access**, i.e. the basic criteria a service (supplier) must fulfil in order to enter into a market.

Measures impeding market access are **generally permitted** in trade in services, e.g. measures requiring a certain quality of the service or qualifications of the services provider.

Some of them, however, are prohibited. These refer to the following *quantitative restrictions*, restricting

the number of service suppliers;
the value of service transactions or assets;
the total number of operations or quantity of output;
the total number of natural persons supplying a service; (…)
the participation of foreign capital the type of legal entity.[154]

In addition to these quantitative limits, the limitation of the form of legal entity (or joint venture) is forbidden. (GATS Art. 16)

These measures are prohibited in any case, but others are not. If members want to go further and reduce other market access barriers, they can do so by including a commitment in their Services Schedule. As with NT, they have to **opt-in**.


The Services Schedules are divided into two main sections, the

- *horizontal commitments*, i.e. commitments referring to all services sectors, and
- *sector-specific commitments*, i.e. commitments referring (only) to a specific service sector.

---

[154] https://www.wto.org/english/tratop_e/serv_e/cbt_course_e/popup_market_access_e.htm.

121

Services Schedules have three relevant[155] columns, the first one referring to the *sector*, the second one to *market access* (non-discrimination at accessing) and the third one to *national treatment* (non-discrimination *after* accessing / inside the country).

The members
- choose the section, i.e. horizontal commitment or sector-specific commitment; in case of the latter, they name the sector and subsector it concerns,
- *for horizontal commitments*, mention *only* the services mode(s)[156] to which their commitment corresponds (e.g. mode 2), and specify the full or partial existence (or a limitation) of a commitment in this/these mode(s) for all sectors
- *for sector-specific commitments*, mention *all four* services modes (1, 2, 3, 4), and specify whether there is a full or partial commitment or no commitment in the respective mode for the concerned (sub)sector

In the specifications by the states "unbound" means *no commitment* of the member and "none" means no limitation, i.e. *full market access or national treatment* (see table below).

---

[155] In fact, there are *four* columns. Apart from the three mentioned, there is also the column "additional commitments", which often remains empty.
[156] 1 *Cross-border supply*, 2 *Consumption abroad*, 3 *Commercial presence*, 4 *Presence of natural persons*. See *Trade in Services – fundamentals and MFN*.

**Example**

| EXCERPT OF THE SERVICES SCHEDULE OF STATE **A**[157] | | |
|---|---|---|
| (1) cross-border, (2) consumption abroad, (3) commercial presence, (4) natural persons | | |
| **I HORIZONTAL COMMITMENTS** | | |
| Sector or subsector | Limitations on market access | Limitations on national treatment |
| All sectors included in this Schedule | (4) Unbound, except for specialists, being natural persons with essential technical or professional skills assessed in terms of the applicant's employment experience and qualifications, and the scarcity of such skills in **A**. | (3) Eligibility for subsidies may be limited to legal persons, the headquarters of which are established within the national territory. |
| **II SECTOR-SPECIFIC COMMITMENTS** | | |
| Sector or subsector | Limitations on market access | Limitations on national treatment |
| Human health services (UN CPC 931) (…) 93122 Specialised medical services | (1) None (2) None (3) Subject to a maximum of thirty foreign hospitals (4) Unbound, except as indicated in the horizontal section | (1) Three years of professional practice in **A** required (2) None (3) **A**'s nationality required to establish an independent practice (4) Unbound |

In the *horizontal commitments*-section, **A** has established a national treatment limitation[158] for all sectors where commitments were made for services mode 3 (commercial presence of foreign service suppliers). Apart from that, **A** has established for all sectors that, apart from experts and

---

[157] Van Den Bossche/Prévost, 2021: 78, modified.
[158] National treatment can be limited to subsidies belonging to companies headquartered in **A**.

scarcity reasons, there is no facilitation of the market access of natural persons (mode 4).

In the *sector-specific commitments*-section, **A** has made a partial commitment regarding the subsector "Specialised medical services". As for cross-border supply of such services (mode 1) and the consumption of such services in other WTO members (mode 2), market access is fully granted. Foreign service suppliers providing cross-border services in **A** (mode 1) must prove three years of professional practice in **A** for being granted full National Treatment.

In contrast, the foreign commercial presence (mode 3) of such service providers in **A** is limited regarding the number of hospitals[159] and the nationality of suppliers establishing an independent practice. National treatment and market access of foreigners temporarily providing specialized medical services in **A** (mode 4) is even completely excluded (except for the exception stated in the *general commitments*).

---

[159] Since the number of *hospitals* was limited and not the number of e.g. services suppliers, this does not violate GATS Art. 16 (see above *Market Access*).

124

A (simplified) **assessment for determining if in trade in services NT is duly granted** can be done by asking these four questions:

1. *Commitment?* Has the affected member committed itself to NT in the concerned services sector and mode in its Services Schedule?
2. *Discrimination?* Are more favorable competitive opportunities[160] given to a domestic service / service supplier (than to the foreign service / service supplier) by internal measures?
3. *Like products?* Are the imported and domestic services / service suppliers "like" (see below)?
4. *No exception?* Is there no exception applicable that justifies the different treatment? (see below)

In trade in services, assessing *likeness* in NT is relatively similar to how it is done in MFN Treatment:

For determining if provided services and service providers (from different countries) are *like*, first an analysis in isolation has to be done: Determining if the services are *like* (in a competitive relationship) must be done *separately* from determining if the service suppliers are *like* (in a competitive relationship).
Only then an *overall* assessment determining a *competitive relationship* should be done.

Criteria used for determining likeness are e.g. the *characteristics* of the services and suppliers (kind/proceeding of service; size/assets/expertise of provider), substitutability for consumers and how they are classified (e.g. under the UN Central Product Classification).

Also in NT in trade in services **exceptions** may apply, such as services in the exercise of government authority or the permission to discriminate if

---

[160] No *actual* trade effects are necessary for that nor must be proven; the (theoretical) *opportunity* suffices.

125

the competitive disadvantages adopted are inherent to the foreign character of the service (language, physical distance, etc.).

However, National Treatment exceptions in trade in services are less important than e.g. in MFN or in trade in goods because members can anyway upfront decide how much they want to liberalize in this concern (by their services commitments). Therefore, they normally do not rely on exceptions.

# VI. Exceptions to the GATT

Even though the GATT establishes rules that all WTO members must abide by (like the MFN-Principle and the NT-Principle), it knows many exceptions to these rules.

 Although WTO members must e.g. not discriminate among themselves and, therefore, have to accord the best treatment given to one member also to all other members (MFN Treatment), they can exceptionally treat some members even *better*.

Of these many exceptions, the *Free Trade Agreement* and the *Developing countries exceptions* stand out. Both of them permit the non-compliance with the MFN-Principle, the former one for trade partners between which an FTA was concluded and the latter one for developing countries.

Apart from the FTA exception and the developing countries exception, there are other exceptions referring to the protection of important state matters, e.g. national security, health and morals, nature conservation and balance of payment.

The *GATS* exceptions are mostly similar to the GATT exceptions and are left out for reasons of conciseness.

# 1. Free Trade Agreements exception

In view of the non-discrimination rule (MFN-Principle and NT-Principle), all WTO members have to treat all WTO members equally in trade. If a trade advantage is granted to one member, it must be granted to all of them. However, that rule has one major derogation: **Free Trade Agreements** (FTAs).[161]

Free Trade Agreements (FTAs) permit a trade liberalization that goes deeper than the general liberalization established by the WTO for all of its 166 members. How this is done, is best demonstrated with an example:

If the general MFN-tariff on a certain good of WTO member **A** is 5% *ad valorem* and if **A** wants to reduce that tariff to 2% *ad valorem* for state **B**, with which it has an excellent relationship, it would have to lower this tariff not only in relation to **B**, but in relation to *all* WTO members (MFN Treatment). This might not be in **A**'s interest.
**If A concludes an FTA with B though, it can lower this tariff only in relation to B (!).** This means that the MFN-tariff on the mentioned good remains at 5% *ad valorem* while in relation (only) to **B** it can be reduced as desired to 2% ad valorem by **A**.


These FTAs lead to the first stage of economic integration between states, so called **Free Trade *Areas*** (see *Economic integration and Free Trade Agreements*).
If FTAs do not only liberalize trade between their members beyond general WTO levels[162] but also establish common trade rules (e.g. substantially the same tariffs and other restrictions) *towards third states*, they can also lead to the second economic integration stage – **Customs**

---

[161] Also called *Regional* Trade Agreements (RTAs) or *Preferential* Trade Agreements (PTAs).
[162] FTAs are, therefore, *discriminatory* against other WTO members that are not part of them (but exceptionally legal).

128

**Unions.** (GATT Art. 24, Understanding of the Interpretation of GATT Art. XXIV)

*Why did the founders of the GATT include arrangements that are in direct tension with its foundational MFN-Principle?*

In the years after the Second World War, also with the idea to create peace by economic entanglement[163], greater economic and political integration efforts emerged. Apart from plans to stronger interrelate the German and French economies (which led to the 1950 Schuman Plan and to the beginning of the European Integration), there were e.g. also secret trade liberalization negotiations between the USA and Canada. This interest in particularly deep and far-reaching trade partnerships between only *some* states was in contradiction with the goal to create a multilateral trade liberalization system with the same rules for everybody.

Finally, the compromise was to do both: On the one hand, common multilateral rules for everybody were established (MFN, NT), on the other hand exceptions were created to satisfy those who wanted to liberalize more. That is why the wide-ranging exceptions of Free Trade Areas and Customs Unions were integrated in the in principal *multilateral* GATT (and later also the GATS).

Some see in FTAs a "pathfinder for future multilateral disciplines"[164] because they often cover new issue areas (environment, digitalization, etc.) that might be put also on the *multilateral* liberalization agenda and become *multilateral* rules for all WTO members.

Others see the proliferation of FTAs as the reason for the slow multilateral WTO negotiations (*Why multilateralism, if we can liberalize bilaterally or plurilaterally?*). Again others say that the success of FTAs is not the reason for the paralysis of the WTO as a forum for multilateral trade negotiations but the *result* of it.

---

[163] Peace was also the main motivation for the establishment of the European Coal and Steel Community, first predecessor of the European Union.
[164] Trebilcock, 2020: 56.

129

## FTA conditions and Rules of Origin

There are two main conditions so WTO members can conclude an FTA in accordance with the GATT (which are usually not strictly enforced though):

An FTA must

**1. liberate** – i.e. eliminate restrictions on – "**substantially all trade**". This means that, in principle, trade restrictions between the FTA's members must not be maintained in any important trade area susceptive of liberalization.

**2. not lead to more restrictions for *third* countries**[165] than there were before the conclusion of the FTA.
However, even though no additional restrictions must be set for third countries, trade is regularly anyway diverted away from other possible trade partners to the members of an FTAs (due to the better conditions offered). This trade *diversion* is not prohibited. It is anyway not the *key* effect of most FTAs though (but additional trade *creation* among the FTA's members).

Apart from that, the WTO must be notified about the conclusion of the FTA (creating a Free Trade Area or a Customs Union), which is evaluated by the *Committee on Regional Trade Agreements*. This Committee issues recommendations to the General Council, which until now has never determined the inconsistency of an FTA with multilateral rules.[166]

The *periodic* review of the WTO members' trade policies and practices is done by the General Council meeting as *Trade Policy Review Body (TPRB)* based on reports by the members and the WTO Secretariat.

---

[165] Third countries referring here to *WTO members that are not parties to the FTA*.
[166] Although the matter was reviewed in one case by the *DSB*. (Trebilcock, 2020: 50)

130

If MFN Treatment does not apply due to the existence of an FTA, tariff rates vary *depending on the **origin of goods***. Therefore, WTO members need rules for determining the origin of a product – the so-called **Rules of Origin**.

Generally, each member has the liberty to determine its own Rules of Origin. In most cases, the origin of a product is where it was *predominantly obtained* or where its *last substantial transformation* took place. However, the origin of a good can e.g. also be the place where a particular *change in tariff classification* happened or where a certain percentage of *value was added* to it or where a particular *processing operation* took place.

The origin of a product does not only matter if there is a *preferential* treatment – of an FTA party or a developing country (see below) – but also for *non-preferential* anti-dumping duties (against dumping) and countervailing duties (against subsidies).[167]
For harmonizing the latter two (*non-preferential* Rules of Origin) the multilateral Agreement on Rules of Origin establishes some ground rules. Annex II of this Agreement focusses on the harmonization of *preferential* Rules of Origin (FTAs/developing countries), is less far-reaching though.

---

[167] For reasons of succinctness not included in this book. For a good summary, read e.g. the corresponding chapters of Van den Bossche/Prévost, 2021.

## 2. Developing countries exception

Some countries can be granted a better treatment than MFN (and NT) conditions even though they have not concluded an FTA. As with FTAs, discrimination takes place (against other WTO states not profiting from this better treatment) and, as with FTAs, it can be exceptionally legal.

The reason for this is that, with the huge number of members the WTO currently has (166), national economies of the members differ considerably. While some are very strong and competitive, others require protection and support for effectively and usefully participating in world trade. For instance, for a rapid transformation from traditional agricultural sectors to industrial or manufacturing sectors, often a temporary protection is necessary to cope with international competition.[168]

This is the reason why the WTO permits **economic development exceptions** or ***Special & Differential Treatment*** (*S&D Treatment*) for developing countries. (GATT Art. 18)

 The question if a WTO member is a *developed* country or a *developing country*, is decided mainly by **self-selection** of the respective member (!). If a member is considered a *Least Developed Country* (LDC) depends on the official UN classification though.

Developed country members must safeguard the developing country members' interests, which – thanks to the S&D Treatment provisions – can be done in accordance with WTO Law (legal/justified discrimination).

---

[168] On the downside, this could lead to inefficient manufacturing. Furthermore, often the most advanced developing countries profit *most* from such a protection (but need it *least*).

132

Special & Differential Treatment covers e.g.

- in trade in goods, the possibility of a **preferential tariff (and NTBs) treatment** (better than MFN Treatment) conceded by developed country members to developing country members. This is done under a developed country member's so-called *Generalized System of Preferences* *(GSP)* and, in principle, must be non-discriminatory *among developing countries*. Additional preferences are possible though if certain developing countries are situated similarly (and have similar trade, development, financial, etc. needs), and for LDCs.
  e.g. The EU *everything but arms*-arrangement eliminates *all* quotas and import duties for LDCs on all goods except for arms.
- in trade in services, the possibility of developed country members to offer a preferential treatment to services and service providers from (only) LDC ("**LDC Services Waiver**").
- the possibility of developing countries to temporarily impose higher customs duties (above MFN-terms) to establish a new industry ("**infant industry exception**").
- **longer time periods** in different matters, for example in WTO dispute settlement, and transitional periods for complying with some WTO obligations (e.g. the implementation of the TRIPS Agreement).
- **technical assistance and training** for developing country members by the WTO Secretariat.

This may sound "better" than it frequently is: MFN tariff levels have decreased with time, economic development exceptions are thus less valuable in comparison. Apart from that, developed countries often (reserve the right to) withdraw their preferential treatment of developing countries or exclude important goods from preferential treatment.

# 3. General Exceptions

Apart from exceptions thanks to an FTA or to the level of development of a WTO member, the GATT establishes exceptions for important state concerns like public health, morals and nature conservation. Most important public matters exceptions are included in the *General Exceptions* of the GATT (Art. 20). Some of them, like (inter)national security, balance of payments emergencies and safeguards against a serious injury of the domestic industry, are regulated apart though.

The General Exceptions represent exceptions to *any* GATT principle, be it MFN, NT or the prohibition of quantitative restrictions.

GATT Art. 20 is divided into two parts: a so-called *chapeau* (first part of Art. 20) relevant for *every* General Exception, and *different paragraphs* relevant *only* for the *respective* Exception the paragraph is dedicated to. For a measure falling under the General Exceptions, it has to meet **1.** the requirements of the respective paragraph it falls into and **2.** the ones of the *chapeau*.

For knowing if an otherwise illegal measure can exceptionally be justified under the General Exceptions,
**first conformity with the respective paragraph of Art. 20 has to be examined**[169]:

**(a) Public morals**: the trade-restrictive measure must be *necessary* so the goal of protecting public morals can be achieved.
Possible goals are e.g. preventing money laundering and fraud, promoting social inclusion and welfare of certain animals.

---

[169] Some of the paragraphs of GATT Art. 20 are left out here for reasons of conciseness: (c) gold and silver; (d) compliance with national laws; (e) prison labor products; (f) protection of national treasures; (h) commodity agreement obligations; (i) price stabilization schemes; (j) short supply.

**(b) Health** of humans, animals and plants: the trade-restrictive measure must be *necessary* so the goal of protecting the health of humans, animals or plants can be achieved.

This can e.g. be in relation to the smoking of cigarettes, air pollution and labelling of products (e.g. tuna products with a "dolphin safe" labelling requirement).

(…)

**(g) Nature conservation** of *exhaustible* natural resources including endangered species: the trade-restrictive measure must be *reasonably related* and *in proportion* to this goal (if we applied the at least by its wording narrower[170] *necessity*-requirement, it might be too late for endangered nature). Apart from that, the conservation of exhaustible nature goal must not only be reached by trade measures but together with domestic measures.

E.g. Fishing nets requirements guaranteeing that endangered sea turtles do not get entangled in them.

(…)


As for the assessment of the ***necessity** criterium of paragraphs (a) and (b),* three aspects must particularly be looked at:

- the importance of the protected value,
- the impact of the measure on trade (an import ban of course restricts trade more than a mere labelling obligation) and
- the contribution of the restrictive measure to protect the value.

Apart from the mentioned *necessity* and *relatedness/proportionality* requirements, the measures adopted due to morals, health and nature conservation must be "***designed for it***". This means, in principle, that the measures must *not* be *incapable* for reaching their goal – a criterium with a relatively low threshold and therefore mostly fulfilled.

---

[170] WTO, 1995: 584.

If the first part of the assessment can be affirmed (measure coincides with one of Art. 20's paragraphs (a) to (j)),

*second*, **compliance with the *chapeau* of Art. 20 has to be examined:**

The initial part of GATT Art. 20, the *chapeau*, refers to the *manner of application* of the trade restrictive measures. It mandates that there must be both

**1. no arbitrary or unjustifiable discrimination**

-when the *same* conditions prevail

*Country A prohibits imports of fox fur produced in local markets but not the fox fur produced in big factories because of animal health or public morals. In the local markets of B, hygiene measures and killing methods are the same as in big factories.*
In B's local markets and in big factories the same conditions of fox fur production may prevail. A's import prohibition may constitute an arbitrary or unjustifiable discrimination.

- **when *different* conditions prevail,** if the measure is not applied in a *flexible* manner.

*Imports of shrimps are only permitted by A if a **very specific** type of net that protects sea turtles from getting entangled is used for shrimp fishing (nature/environment conservation). In B not **exactly** the same turtle protecting net is available but (only) others that are as functional in regard to turtle protection.*

Although the nets available in **B** might not be exactly the same as those specified by **A, A** must remain flexible in the application of its restrictive measure and may have to permit also other fishing nets that are *as* good for turtle protection.

136

**2. no disguised trade restriction**, e.g. a measure that, at its core, is a *protectionist* measure with (mainly) protectionist motives of the imposing country.

# 4. Other Exceptions

Apart from the General Exceptions, the GATT provides exceptions e.g. for the following matters:

**1. National and International Security** (GATT Art. 21), which requires a trade restrictive measure to be **a)** *necessary* for the protection of domestic or international security for being permitted. The (inter)national security exception is available in case of **b)** *war* or other *emergency situation* and/or when *nuclear* or *military goods or services* are affected.

**2. Safeguards**[171] against increased imports (GATT[172] Art. 19, Agreement on Safeguards) that (might) lead to a serious injury of the domestic industry. Also here, a trade restrictive measure must be **a)** *designed for* preventing or remedying this injury and be applied to the extent (and as long as) **b)** *necessary*.

National products must be or threatened to be injured seriously by a **c)** *sharp and sudden increase of imports* of *like* or *directly competitive* products.

Apart from that, a **d)** *specific procedure* is required before the measure can be adopted:

An investigation has to be carried out and consultations with the WTO member(s) whose imports threaten the domestic industry must take place. These consultations focus on both **i.** the imports and measures taken to protect the domestic industry and **ii.** compensation for the by the safeguard measure affected state(s) (e.g. decreasing tariffs on other products). If no agreement on compensation can be found, the affected

---

[171] The terminology for measures against seriously injuring imports is *"safeguard measures"*. In contrast, a reaction to dumping is referred to as *"anti-dumping* measure" and to subsidies *"countervailing* measure".
[172] Not under the GATS.

138

member(s) is/are permitted to impose equivalent import duties to imports of the safeguarding member.
Moreover, the WTO Safeguards Committee has to be notified about the details of the safeguard measure.

Safeguard measures must be applied in a non-discriminatory way, i.e. to *all* imports of the injuring product, regardless of their origin.

**3. Balance of payments** emergencies.[173] For establishing a reasonable level of monetary reserves if they are **a)** very low or there was a serious decline, **quantitative restrictions** or **price-based measures** may be permitted. The latter refer e.g. to *import surcharges*, i.e. a tax added to all imports additionally to a tariff, and *import deposit requirements*, i.e. the importer must deposit upfront (without interest) a percentage of a good's value before receiving the good.

The measures taken in response to balance of payment emergencies must **b)** fulfill IMF-criteria and **c)** not exceed what is *necessary* to stop a current or imminent decline of monetary reserves.

---

[173] GATT Art. 12, 18; GATT Understanding on Balance of Payment Provisions.

# VII. WTO Dispute Settlement

The WTO dispute settlement system is[174] one of the most effective tools in International Law to effectively ensure compliance with international rules. As mentioned in the chapter on *International Law*, International Law in general has the "disadvantage" that there is no superordinated law enforcing entity guaranteeing its enforcement:

If **A** does not stick to an International Law provision, this may have negative consequences for **A**, but nobody *makes* **A**, with coercive power, comply with it.

This is similar in WTO Law. However, the negative consequences of not complying with it are often that severe that compliance is nearly always achieved in a short time period. That is what makes WTO Law so effective and valuable.

Since 1995, over 600 complaints have been subject to WTO dispute settlement, the USA and the EU being the leading complaining *and* responding parties. GATT provisions account for more than 400; anti-dumping duties and countervailing measures against illicit subsidies for more than 100 disputes respectively.[175]
A considerable percentage of all cases – approximately 70% – is appealed.[176]

---

[174] At least until recently, with the blockage of the Appellate Body by the US causing major problems.
[175] Van den Bossche/Prévost, 2021: 30; Trebilcock, 2020: 31.
[176] Trebilcock, 2020: 31.

140

## What happens when a WTO Member does not stick to WTO rules?

WTO members that consider a benefit they are entitled to under WTO Law is nullified or impaired (e.g. one other member violates the GATT, GATS, etc.) can have recourse to the WTO dispute settlement system. The proceedings (see below) finish with a Panel (or Appellate Body [AB]) **REPORT**.

In case the Panel (or AB) comes to the conclusion that a benefit was nullified or impaired,

- the violating member must ensure **COMPLIANCE** with the report within a reasonable period of time. This is done in about 80% of all cases at this point without any further actions being necessary.[177]

If the violating member does not comply with the Panel (or AB) report,

- **RETALIATION** by the complainant may follow after a successful (additional) *compliance dispute*. In this, the WTO Dispute Settlement Body authorizes the **suspension of an equivalent level of concessions** (e.g. tariff concessions) or obligations (e.g. obligations regarding intellectual property).

  Retaliation is, of course, trade destructive for both sides (but, as a last resort, anyway permitted).

The WTO dispute settlement system is *compulsory* and *exclusive* for settling disputes in the scope of *all* multilateral WTO agreements[178] (except for the Trade Policy Review Mechanism) plus the plurilateral Agreement on Government Procurement.

---

[177] Van den Bossche/Prévost, 2021: 48.
[178] See chapter *WTO agreements*.

It is **a)** only open for **members** (not companies or other states). Therefore, proceedings must be initiated by (WTO) *states* or the EU. In practice, the members initiate proceedings not "out of themselves" but at instigation of affected *companies* though.

Proceedings in the scope of the WTO dispute settlement system are furthermore only available when **b) WTO Law** (not any other area of International Law) is allegedly **violated.**

# WTO dispute settlement steps

WTO dispute settlement can be divided into the following steps:

**1. Consultations** (60 days or less/more if agreed) between the member(s) alleging a violation and the allegedly violating member(s). If the respondent agrees, other members with a substantial interest can join. Consultations are confidential and, if requested, with mediation. They delimit the scope of the dispute: the violated norm(s) and the violating measure(s) are identified. About ⅕ of all disputes are resolved at this stage.[179]

If consultations do not succeed, the complainant submits a

**2. Panel request** at the WTO Dispute Settlement Body (DSB), i.e. a request for the establishment of a "quasi-judicial" *ad hoc* Panel created only for the occasion of one dispute in concrete (and afterwards dissolved).

The DSB (a "political" organ composed by WTO members[180]) must grant the establishment of such a Panel at the latest at the second meeting at which the Panel request appears on its agenda.
The adoption of the establishment of a Panel is done by the non-existence of *negative consensus* against it, i.e. only if *all* WTO members agree unanimously (including the complainant (!)) that *no* such Panel should be established, it is not. If at least one member (even if it is only the complainant) disagrees, no negative consensus is given. Therefore, approving the request is, in practice, automatic.

---

[179] Van den Bossche/Prévost, 2021: 41.
[180] As mentioned above (see *WTO institutional structure*), the General Council in which the members are represented convenes (not only as formal General Council but) also as Trade Policy Review Body and Dispute Settlement Body.

Then, the *terms of reference* (scope of the dispute[181]) and the *Panel members* are determined. The panel members or *panelists* are three non-nationals of the parties, usually diplomats, trade officials, lawyers or scholars. They are chosen within 20 days by the parties (the Secretariat can make proposals). If they cannot agree, the Director General has 10 days to appoint (any) three panelists. Panel members must be impartial according to the WTO Rules of Conduct.

In addition, the *Working Procedures* (rules on timeframes and Panel meetings) are adopted by the Panel in consultation with the parties. The WTO offers basic Working Procedures in Appendix 3 of the Dispute Settlement Understanding (DSU) to the members in dispute (see Annex of this book). Usually more detailed or modified Working Procedures are adopted though by the Panels.

In principle, only the parties to a dispute participate in the Panel's sessions. If there exists substantial interest of other parties though, also *third parties*[182] may be admitted:

> In Panel proceedings third parties may participate in a *separate* session of the first panel meeting, receive (only) the first written submissions and can file one written submission.
> In Appellate Body (AB) proceedings third participants participate in the *same* session as the parties, receive *all* written submissions and can also file one written submission.

In addition, Panels *can* accept *amicus curiae briefs* (but in most cases do not do so; the AB *never* did), i.e. submissions of non-party experts assisting the Panel.

**3. Written submissions** of the complaining party and the responding party are filed.

---

[181] Claims or measures falling outside the *terms of reference* may not be dealt with by the Panel. This is necessary so the defendant can prepare a proper defense (due process).
[182] Called "third *participants*" in appellate proceedings.

144

The burden of proof is always with the party that asserts a claim or defense. As soon as a *prima facie case* has been made (there is sufficient evidence for presumption), the burden of proof shifts to the opposing party to refute it.

**4.** A confidential **oral meeting** with the parties in dispute (incl. an additional session for third parties) takes place, followed by a written rebuttal submission.

**5.** An **Interim Report** is issued by the Panel for the parties' comments.

**6.** The **Panel Report**[183] is issued by the Panel, translated into the WTO languages English, French and Spanish, and circulated to all members. The maximum time a Panel formally has for issuing its Report is **9 months** since its establishment. However, the actual average time Panels take is 1 ½ to twice this time.

**7.a.** The **Report** is finally **adopted by the DSB**, for which it has 60 days since the Report's circulation. With the adoption by the DSB, the Panel Report becomes legally binding (unless a Notice of Appeal is submitted, see below).

The adoption of Panel and AB Reports (as well as the authorization of retaliation; see below) by the DSB is done *automatically* thanks to the also here applicable *negative consensus*-rule (see **2.**).[184]

**7.b.i.** Between the issuance of the Panel Report by the Panel and its adoption by the DSB, the respondent (or complainant) can submit a

---

[183] WTO Law must be interpreted by Panels and the Appellate Body in accordance with the Vienna Convention on the Law of Treaties (see *Law of Treaties*), customary international law (see *Custom*) and the *effet utile*-principle (give meaning and effect to all the terms of a treaty).

[184] Before the foundation of the WTO (in the GATT *1947*) not the absence of negative consensus but the existence of (positive) consensus was necessary to adopt a Panel Report. Therefore, Panel Reports were only binding when they were adopted by the members by consensus; if one party (incl. the parties to the dispute) was against it, it could not be adopted.

**Notice of Appeal** (and the complainant [or respondent] a Notice of Other Appeal) to the DSB. This Notice of Appeal delimits the *terms of reference* of the appellate proceedings, whereas only issues of law (and not of fact) are appealable. The standard Working Procedures for Appellate Review usually apply (but the Appellate Body may modify them). The (often not met) maximum timeframe for appellate proceedings at the WTO Appellate Body (AB) is 90 days.

In contrast to the *ad hoc* dispute settlement Panels, the AB is a standing, i.e. *permanent*, tribunal. It is composed of in total 7 impartial experts (with "divisions" of 3 hearing appeals) appointed for four years (once renewable).

 In contrast to deciding by *negative consensus*, which is the general adoption modality of the DSB, the appointment of AB members requires (positive) *consensus*. This has led to a severe crisis of WTO dispute settlement (and the WTO itself and its rules in total) because the USA has been blocking AB members appointments since 2017.

In 2019, the required number of AB members to hear a dispute was not reached any more and, since then, the AB has been paralyzed. After the adoption of a Panel Report, most parties now appeal "into the void". This means that Panel Reports do not become binding (!)[185]. One of the "crown jewels" of the WTO – its highly effective dispute settlement system – is therefore (partly) incapacitated since then.

In theory, the next steps are:

**7.b.ii. Issuance** of the **AB Report by the AB**, translation and circulation.

---

[185] Unless the parties are members to the due to this situation created Multi-Party Interim Appeal Arbitration Arrangement (MPIA), which is obligatory for its members (EU member states + 25 others) and open also to other states.

146

**7.b.iii. Adoption** of the **AB Report by the DSB** in 30 days since its circulation as **upheld**, **modified** or **reversed**.

Panel and AB decisions are only legally binding *in the specific case* they resolve and only applied to it. The reasoning and clarifications however have precedent effects (the same issues must be resolved in the same way in a subsequent case):

> [Prior GATT Panel Reports] create legitimate expectations among WTO members, and, therefore, should be taken into account where they are relevant to any dispute.[186]

**8.a. Compliance** with the Panel / AB Report within a *reasonable* period of time. If no agreement can be found on the duration of this time period, an arbitrator appointed by the Director General decides. The granted reasonable time period usually does not exceed 15 months.
In about 80% of all cases compliance takes place at this point.[187]

In case of non-compliance:
**8.b.i. Compliance dispute**, whose procedure is mainly the same as the one mentioned in **1.–7.** but with shorter time frames (max. **90 days** in total).

After a compliance dispute confirming non-compliance of the respondent:
**8.b.ii. Remedies** taken by the complainant until compliance takes place:

- **Compensation**: At the request of the complainant, negotiations on a compensation for the time between the end of the reasonable time period and compliance (not for before[188]) take place.

---

[186] WTO Appellate Body DS8, 10, 11 (alcoholic beverages II, 1996).
[187] Van den Bossche/Prévost, 2021: 30, 47.
[188] WTO dispute settlement does not provide for retrospective compensation (or retaliation). However, it provides for comparably short timeframes.

*If no agreement on compensation can be reached within 20 days, the complainant can request authorization for retaliation at the DSB:*

- **Retaliation:** The complainant(s)[189] may suspend concessions (e.g. tariffs, IP protection) with regard to the respondent equivalent to the level of the respondent's illicit trade restrictive measures. If the respondent disagrees on the level of suspended concessions, an arbitral tribunal (usually the original Panel) decides.

As mentioned, retaliation is trade destructive for both sides. Developing countries sometimes cannot afford that and are, therefore, partly in disadvantage.

To at least in part mitigate the disadvantages of developing countries in dispute settlement, developing country *respondents* are offered longer time periods in the proceedings and discounted legal assistance and representation by the Advisory Centre on WTO Law (ACWL, Geneva).

Regarding general dispute settlement timeframes, it can easily be remembered:
It starts with **60 days (consultations)** and it ends with **60 days (DSB adoption). 9 months (Panel)** and **90 days (AB and compliance dispute)** is the total time.

---

[189] But not other members – there is no *collective* retaliation.

# VIII. Intellectual Property and TRIPS

## 1. International regulation of Intellectual Property

Intellectual Property (IP) can be understood as ownership of the result of creations of the human mind. Among other things, this includes patents (technical etc. inventions), copyright (works, i.e. books, pictures, music...) and trademarks (recognizable elements, i.e. signs, designs, expressions...).

Protection of this ownership/property is primarily a national concern (territorial sovereignty of states). Therefore, protection of intellectual property rights has to be granted by every state separately.[190]

**!** As a result, if one person or company wants its IP to be protected worldwide, in principle, it must request protection (and pay for it) in *every* state in which it wishes for protection.

However, there are several international treaties regulating IP and making its *international* protection easier. It is nevertheless recommended to consult local specialists or patent agents upfront when applying for IP protection in a country.

There are three major[191] *specific* treaties (regulating specific IP areas/categories) and one major *general* treaty (covering basically all IP areas):

the **Paris Convention for the Protection of Industrial Property** (*specifically* technical protective rights [notably patents],

---

[190] This means that the same IP might have different "owners" in different states.
[191] In addition, there is a large number of other treaties focusing on international IP protection or classification.

labelling/trademarks, competition)[192] administered by the World Intellectual Property Organization (WIPO).

the **International Convention for the Protection of New Varieties of Plants** (*specifically* phytosanitary/plant health) by the International Union for the Protection of New Varieties of Plants (UPOV).

the **Berne Convention for the Protection of Literary and Artistic Works** (*specifically* copyright) administered by the WIPO.

the **Agreement on Trade-Related Aspects of Intellectual Property Rights** (TRIPS, IP *in general*) by the WTO.


**Examples**

All these treaties e.g. establish, with variations of its scope, the obligation of their member states (*members*) to concede **National Treatment:** A foreigner from one of the treaties' members can **seek IP protection** in another member under the same conditions as this member's nationals.

The Berne Agreement goes deeper and completely eliminates the necessity of registering copyright between its member states. **National Treatment**, therefore, does not refer to the registration here but to the treatment of foreign copyright owners: their works must be **protected** equally to the works of nationals of the protecting member.

The European Patent Convention ("specifying" the Paris Convention) e.g. also makes it possible that **only one application** must be filed for a patent being protected in as many EU member states (and some other states) as the applicant wishes. Regarding trademarks, the Madrid

---

[192] There are various "sub-agreements" under the Paris Convention that are more specific: e.g. the European Patent Convention, the Patent Cooperation Treaty (patent filing and examination), Madrid Agreement Concerning the International Registration of Marks (incl. its Protocol), the Trademark Law Treaty and the Hague Agreement Concerning the International Deposit of Industrial Designs.

Agreement and its Protocol provide for a similar single registration for protection in several countries.

Apart from the **conditions for application** and the number of **countries one application may be effective in**, also the **level of protection** may differ from country to country. E.g. the TRIPS, among other things, establishes minimum protection standards for IP.

Despite the existence of important harmonizing and facilitating international treaties, the registration and protection of IP remains a primarily national concern, with the usual necessity of (sometimes tedious) individual applications at *every country* where the right(s) should be protected.

## 2. IP licensing

Once IP protection has been granted by a state, the owner/holder of the right can ***license*** this right (e.g. the use of a certain technology) to somebody in this state. This is, of course, normally not done for free but against the payment of a fee, called *royalty*. Franchises are often based on licenses of IP rights, with the franchisor licensing its "success formula" including trademarks etc. to the franchisees.[193]

> Licensing is a **middle ground alternative** to **exporting** from the owner's home country and **direct investment** in host markets. It can often produce, with relatively limited cost, immediate positive cash flows.[194]

---

[193] There might exist national law (or EU Law) restrictions though to international franchising and licensing.
[194] Folsom et al., 2016: 297, bold print added.

151

It creates a win-win situation for both the licensor (franchisor) and the licensee (franchisee): If the licensee succeeds, the paid royalties increase and the licensor also profits. Often licensing is combined with FDIs, e.g. in the form of a joint venture (that then has access to important IP).

Licensing is sometimes not offered though, e.g. due to the fear that competitors may be created (e.g. in countries where the production costs are much lower) or proprietary control e.g. over technology may be lost.

In regard to copyright, especially concerning music licensing, agency "clearinghouses" frequently take care of licensing, with sometimes thousands of rights being sold at once and then (part of) the fees being distributed to the copyright owners.

Apart from licensing, which is the legal form of using one other's protected IP, IP *piracy* (illegal use/production etc. of protected IP) is very common.

While for patents, trademarks and copyright normally a formal protection is (at least) available, there is no equivalent protection of *knowhow*: There are no exclusive legal rights to knowhow (e.g. the CocaCola recipe, business advice, trade secrets) that can be registered to be protected. This is why it is specifically hard to protect it internationally. Therefore, knowhow protection is often a question of confidentiality agreements with employees (and threatening high fines if broken) or even a question of penal law.[195]

---

[195] Folsom et al., 2016: 280, 281.

# 3. TRIPS

At first sight, the multilateral **Agreement on Trade-Related Aspects of Intellectual Property Rights** (TRIPS Agreement), appears to be the "foreign element" in WTO Law: While other agreements (like the GATT and the GATS) address (and promote) *trade*, the TRIPS Agreement protects *IP rights*. And protected IP (seemingly) limits trade because it requires permission from its owner to be used.

However, the lack of (or disparities in) IP protection can also be a barrier to trade. If IP is likely to be copied in another country (because it is not protected there), the holder is not likely to export its product to this country.
Apart from that, a lack of protection of IP might discourage innovation (potentially leading to exports and, finally, international trade).

The TRIPS Agreement establishes minimum standards, i.e. minimum rights for nationals of other WTO members for

- copyright (e.g. book authors: J.K. Rowling/Harry Potter),
- trademarks (e.g. three Adidas stripes, iPhone),
- geographical indications (Champagne, Tyrolean speck, Wachauer Marille [apricot]),
- industrial design, i.e. design of physical products manufactured by mass production (e.g. Eames chair, iPhone [designed by Jony Ive]) and
- patents (e.g. vaccines).

As mentioned, the standards set by the TRIPS Agreement are minimum standards. This means that the WTO member can exceed those standards and protect other members IP rights *more* (but not less). Furthermore, members are free in determining how to implement the TRIPS rules in their national legal systems.

In its core, the TRIPS Agreement establishes:

a) **MFN Treatment** and **NT** for the nationals of WTO members,
b) Minimum standards for **IP protection and transparency** of it and
c) Minimum standards and limits for **procedures** related to IP rights including dispute settlement.

## a. TRIPS – MFN and NT

As trade in goods and (partially) in trade in services, also the TRIPS Agreement knows the MFN-Principle and the NT-Principle. While in TiG and TiS these principles are applied to goods and services (providers), in the TRIPS Agreement MFN and NT do not refer to the protected intellectual property but to the **right holder**, i.e. the *person* whose IP rights are (to be) protected.

Therefore, there is no *likeness*-criterium (*like* products/services [providers]). Framed differently: **i.** all foreigners from all WTO members are always considered *like* and **ii.** all foreigners and all nationals from all members are always considered *like*. This makes the *likeness*-analysis obsolete.

Right holders (or applicants) from one WTO member must be treated the same (best) way as right holders from other members whose IP is protected by a member (MFN Treatment).
Right holders (or applicants) from WTO members must moreover be treated the same (best) way as nationals (right holders) from the member protecting the IP (NT).

154

Like in TiG and TiS, discrimination applies both to direct and indirect discrimination. An *indirect* discrimination in the scope of the TRIPS Agreement takes place when a distinction of (potential) right holders is not based directly on nationality but mainly *nationals of certain WTO members* are affected by it and profit from it, while the nationals of other members are/do not.

**Examples**

*Artists and authors from **A** must demonstrate a higher level of originality/creativity than **B**'s artists and authors for a copyright protection to be granted by **C**.*

**C** is *directly* discriminating the artists and authors from **A** (MFN-Principle).

*The EU / an EU member state establishes the rule that geographical indications (no matter where IP holders are from) have to fulfil special requirements when they relate to areas outside the EU.* [196]

Even though the special requirements rule is applied to all WTO members, potential IP holders from some countries (non-EU countries) have a disadvantage because they will be much more affected by the special requirements rule than potential IP holders. This has to do with the fact that non-EU IP holders are much more likely to apply for protection of geographical indications relating to areas outside the EU than EU IP holders.

The rule therefore represents an *indirect* discrimination discriminating non-EU nationals (NT-Principle).

---

[196] Similarly GATT Panel DS174/R, DS290/R (EC-Trademarks/Geographical Indications, 2005).

155

A (simplified) **assessment for determining if MFN and NT regarding IP protection is duly granted** can be done by asking these three questions:

1. *Discrimination?*
   **MFN:** Is a foreign country's national given a more favorable (protective) treatment than another foreign country's national by the protecting country?
   **NT:** Is a national from the protecting country given a more favorable (protective) treatment than a foreign country's national by the protecting country?
2. *Covered by TRIPS Agreement?* Some matters are not covered, e.g. IP exhaustion[197].
3. *No exception?* Is there no exception applicable that justifies the different (protective) treatment? (see below)


Exceptions to non-discrimination (MFN and NT) regarding the protection of IP are e.g.

- **security** reasons.
- exceptions to **exclusive copyright protection**. These may be permitted if they are limited, not against legitimate exploitation expectancies and not against legitimate interests (like the income of the IP owner).
- **compulsory licenses** for manufacturing patent-protected products (e.g. HIV drugs); with an adequate remuneration for the patent owner.
- **patentability** restrictions for the protection of the **public order, moral, health and environment**.

---

[197] Exhaustion of IP refers to the following question (not resolved by the TRIPS Agreement): *When an IP is released in a country's market with the consent of its owner, does his/her right to control the distribution of this IP end only in this country or worldwide?*

## b. IP protection and transparency standards

IP protection does **not** establish positive rights, i.e. the right to produce or market the protected product in a country. Instead, *negative* rights are conferred, i.e. the right to **exclude** others from the use of the protected products/IP.

For these negative rights, the TRIPS Agreement establishes minimum standards every WTO member must fulfil.

The nature and content of the different IP categories varies considerably and therefore requires a different level (and kind) of protection. This is why the TRIPS Agreement sets different minimum levels and rules for each IP category; for example:

**Copyright** in scientific, literary and artistic works must be protected by WTO members for the author's lifetime and at least 50 years after.

**Trademark** owners must be given the indefinitely renewable exclusive right to use a (trade)mark regarding identical/similar goods and services when a confusion might arise (for at least 7 years since registration/renewal).

**Geographical indications** protection must be offered so as to provide interested parties with the legal means to prevent a misleading designation (by others) regarding the origin of products.

**Industrial design** protection must be granted for at least 10 years in case of new/original independently created industrial designs.

**Patent** protection must be provided for at least 20 years from its filing for all new, actually inventive and industrially appliable inventions.

As for **transparency** of IP protection, the TRIPS Agreement establishes e.g. the obligation of all WTO members to publish regulation as well as judicial and administrative decisions relevant to IP protection.

## c. Procedural standards

According to the TRIPS Agreement, procedures and formalities can be a condition for the acquisition and maintenance of IP rights in the WTO members but are limited to what is **reasonable**.

If a state establishes rules and procedures for the granting of IP protection and this protection is officially granted, the state must guarantee an *actual protection* of these IP rights.

Therefore, the TRIPS Agreement requires members to have effective mechanisms in place so the IP rules/protection can be enforced, e.g.

- there must be **civil judicial procedures available** to enforce IP rights (prevent and deter IP infringements),
- **remedies** for IP protection must be **effective** and **expeditious**,
- **due process** (fairness, legal basis of decisions, etc.) must be guaranteed,
- **provisional and border measures** must be available (to prevent the introduction into commerce of IP infringing products).

The *TRIPS Council* monitors the members' compliance with the rules of the TRIPS agreement.
All disputes relating to TRIPS rules are subject to the **WTO dispute settlement system** (see *WTO Dispute Settlement*).

# D EU Competition Law

Effective competition is regularly considered as a basic element for the functioning of successful market economies.
Maintaining this competition is therefore key, which is the task of Competition Law.

First of all, Competition Law aims to act against competition restrictions caused by *private* actors (companies etc.) as participants in these markets. Private autonomy and contractual freedom companies generally enjoy are therefore limited to the extent in which they are counterproductive to the "general good", i.e., in this case, fair and free competition.
This part of Competition Law is usually referred to as **antitrust law** and includes the prohibition of cartels, merger control and the abuse of a dominant market position.

Second, Competition Law regulates state aid and public procurement as other potential market distorters, which is commonly designated **state aid law**. It is regularly directed at *states*.

Competition Law is an area of law dominated by the *national* law of individual states.[198] Its character and organization depends on the national economic interests and market orientation of the respective state – it has a *national* focus.

However, the anticompetitive actions of a company in one country may have effects that *exceed a country's borders*.

---

[198] Except for the EU, where Competition Law is partly internationally unified/harmonized (see below).

For such cases, International Law doctrine knows the so-called *effects principle*.[199]

According to this principle, a competition authority is competent to take up a competition issue if it has a (considerable) *effect on its own territory's competition*. It does not matter if the involved company is based in another country, or the distortive action is decided on or carried out in another country.

Let us remember what we said regarding the downside of International Law in the first chapter – it is often *not* enforceable. This is also valid for the mentioned doctrine:

International Law has not been able to clarify the issue how to effectively *enforce* (one affected country's) Competition Law *in another country* (!).

This is due to sovereignty concerns (a state is the *only* sovereign over its territory). These questions (and factual barriers) arise not only when one country's competition authority tries to enforce a national decision in foreign territory but already when the authority tries to investigate in another country (to be able to come to this decision).
Both investigation and enforcement in another state would require the approval by this state according to International Law.

There are also basically[200] no binding international rules governing international investigation and enforcement of Competition Law.

 In other words, there is no enforceable "World Competition Law".[201]

---

[199] Instead of the *effects* principle, in the EU another principle is primarily applied: the *implementation* principle. It refers to the place where the anti-competitive "agreement, decision or concerted practice is *implemented*". See e.g. CJEC *Ahlström Osakeyhtiö vs. European Commission* Judgment (joined cases C-89, 104, 114, 116, 117 and 125 to 129/85; 1988).
[200] With the important exception of EU Competition Law.
[201] In contrast e.g. to World *Trade* Law.

160

International Law and its sovereignty and territoriality principles[202] therefore regularly block more than facilitate the situation.

The only, but not entirely satisfactory solution International Law has found by now are **cooperation agreements** between states. These provide for formalized cooperation and (often *non-binding*) rules for application of competition regulations between the respective national competition authorities.[203]

Apart from these mostly bilateral agreements, multilateral attempts were made within the framework of International Organizations. E.g. the WTO, the OECD and the UNCTAD developed (non-binding) recommendations and principles for that matter with the – still far to reach – goal of guaranteeing international enforcement and harmonization of (parts of) Competition Law.

In addition, the International Competition Network (ICN), an informal network including representatives from over 100 competition authorities, aims to intensify *international cooperation* among these.

The huge exception from the mentioned regularly *national* character and international enforcement difficulties of Competition Law is the **European Union** (EU).

---

[202] A state has the *exclusive* power over its territory (and nationals), thus being subject only to International Law (and not any other law) and having the right to exclude anyone from interfering (sovereignty). As an element of a state's sovereignty, all (natural or legal) persons *within the territory of a state* are subject (only) to its laws and its own jurisdiction (territoriality).

[203] Such agreements exist e.g. between the EU and, among others, the USA, Canada and Japan. They are based on so-called "positive comity" where both parties can request (but not more) that the respective other party may take action against a violation of the requesting party's national Competition Law.

As established in the Treaty on the Functioning of the EU (TFEU), the EU has an **exclusive competence** in establishing "the competition rules necessary for the functioning of the internal market" of the EU. (Art. 3)

Thus, in the EU a type of International Law often referred to as *supranational* law for its often direct application in its member states (MS) regulates competition – *EU Competition Law*. It is focused on safeguarding the homogeneity of the EU's internal market[204] and keeping fair competition guaranteeing the free movement of goods, services, capital and persons within it.

EU Competition (Cartel) Law coexists with the national competition laws of its 27 MS and is primarily of importance where anti-competitive behavior has an **effect on trade *between* the MS**. In this case often both EU Cartel Law *and* the relevant national law can be applied to a competition violation by a competition authority or court, although there are several restrictions like prohibition of double punishment.[205]

Where a competition violation and its effect is limited to one MS only, usually (only) the *national* cartel provisions of the affected MS apply. However, *EU* Competition Law is triggered when a cartel involves businesses from different MS or impacts a significant part of the internal market, such as a whole country or a densely populated region. This means that even national cartels can have cross-border effects. Additionally, agreements between companies outside the EU may also be subject to EU rules if they are executed within the EU or significantly affect competition within its market.

Apart from the legislative function the EU has in Competition Law, it also has an important **enforcement competence** in this area, which is carried

---

[204] This internal market comprises all of the EU's 27 member states' territories.
[205] Regarding cartels (TFEU Art. 101), the application of national law is of no effect if it is stricter than EU Law though. In turn, the application of stricter national law is permitted regarding the abuse of a dominant market position (TFEU Art. 102). (Council Regulation (EC) No 1/2003 Art. 3)

out by the European Commission. This is a rather rare case due to the fact that normally EU Law, including the four fundamental freedoms, is (only) enforced by its *MS* (and not the EU institutions themselves).

In Competition Law, however – despite some national enforcement competences in particular areas and re-delegations of certain tasks to the $MS^{206}$ – the European Commission (COM) has substantial enforcement powers, i.e. to investigate a case or to impose sanctions against MS and individuals.


As mentioned before with a general character, also EU Competition Law can be divided into two parts: *antitrust law* focusing on private parties and *state aid law* focusing on states.

---

[206] Council Regulation (EC) No 1/2003 on the implementation of the rules on competition laid down in Articles 81 and 82 of the Treaty.

# I. Antitrust

EU antitrust law is addressed to *private* parties, called ***undertakings***, i.e. entities engaged in economic activity, regardless of their legal form. It is consistent with and safeguards the EU's fundamental freedoms (free movement of goods, services, persons and capital).

For being an undertaking covered by EU antitrust law regularly also a minimum degree of market power (abuse of power and mergers: 25-50%; cartels: 5 / 15%[207]) and a minimum of territorial relevance is required.[208]

The three main areas antitrust law covers are cartels, abuse of dominance and mergers.

 Antitrust law has a so-called vertical *and* horizontal *direct effect*. This means that all natural or legal persons can invoke antitrust law provisions *"directly" before MS courts* towards the state (*vertical*) and between each other (*horizontal*).

## 1. Cartels

### *What is a cartel?*

Cartels are arrangements between undertakings with cumulatively the following content and effects:

---

[207] 15% for vertical cartel agreements (different market level, e.g. manufacturer and distributor) and 5% for horizontal (same market level) ones.
[208] In contrast to antitrust law, for *state aid*, the market share is generally irrelevant, as the focus is on the distortion of competition rather than the size of the company.

**1. *market conduct is coordinated*,** i.e. there is an explicit or implicit agreement (*offer* and [also tacit] *acceptance*)[209] between the undertakings,

e.g. information is given by one undertaking on pricing or production quantity with the other modifying its conduct in reaction to it.

 Cartel law seeks a concurrence of wills between undertakings, *regardless of how it is expressed*. This includes written or oral agreements as well as collusion or coordinated behavior.

**2. *competition is restricted*,** i.e. the undertakings voluntarily restrict their commercial independence[210]. This can be done horizontally between competitors or vertically between non-competitors, e.g. between a producer, intermediary / distributor and retailer.

For knowing if this is the case, there are two alternatives of assessment:

*Did the coordination have the **clear purpose** to restrict competition?* (restriction by *object*)
Horizontal price or quota fixing and market sharing agreements are typical examples for this.
The COM does not need to demonstrate the actual effects of an agreement on the market when the by *object*-criterion is satisfied, however proof to the contrary remains possible.

*Did/does the coordination have an actual/potential restrictive **effect** on competition?* (restriction by *effect*)
Even though the coordination regarding market conduct might not be evidently *aimed at* restricting competition, it might have the same effect as such. For knowing if this is the case, an "assessment of the

---

[209] Merely factual (coincidental) parallel behavior is not prohibited, e.g. a price reduction after a price reduction of a competitor observed freely on the market.
[210] ...removing their ability to "determine their commercial strategy independently"(CJEU C-7/95 *John Deere vs. European Commission*).

165

counterfactual" (*as if* test) is done, i.e. it is analyzed how the price, quality and quantity of goods or services would be *without* the agreement.

**3.** there is a ***cross-border effect on trade***, i.e. undertakings of *several MS* are implicated *or* a *substantial part of the EU's internal market* (e.g. entire MS) is covered by the cartel *or* the undertakings are from third countries whose agreement or practice *impacts EU competition*.

Such cartels are prohibited by EU Law (Art. 101 TFUE), which means that the agreement on which they are based is **automatically void**. Therefore, it is not necessary that the COM declares them so.

If they have positive effects on competition though, by object as well as by effect restrictions may be **justified**. For that, there must be both

- **efficiency gains** resulting from the agreement, e.g. production or distribution improvements or economic or technical progress, that
    - o are passed on to consumers (consumer benefit) and
    - o cannot be attained otherwise (indispensable)

  and
- **no total elimination of competition**.

Due to the fact that the undertakings' agreement is void otherwise, they must assess beforehand if the requirements for justification are given and prove that.
For facilitating this self-assessment, the COM provides guidelines and *block exemption regulations* (BER), i.e. information on when these requirements are met in common business practices (e.g. joint research and tech transfer).

166

**Enforcement** of the EU cartel rules including investigation and sanctions is done by the COM, but partly[211] re-delegated to the MS's authorities.

Thanks to the direct applicability of the cartel provision contained in the TFUE, courts of the MS are competent to assess claims in relation to cartels. (Regulation 1/2003)

[211] Frequently regarding less serious competition infringements.

# 2. Abuse of a dominant market position

Undertakings that have a *dominant role* within the EU's internal market potentially affecting the trade in goods or services between the MS have additional responsibility.[212] They must not only comply with the mentioned cartel rules but also not impair competition in the EU's internal market in a certain way. This competition impairment may be result of this position of dominance or not (!) – see below.

Thus, a *1. dominant position within the EU internal market or a substantial part of it* is the first pre-condition for the application of the corresponding limitative TFUE provision (Art. 102).

Dominance is regularly given if one (or more) undertaking(s) **a)** holds a **high market share** (at least 25%) and/or other **additional barriers** to market entry for potential competitors are present. These can e.g. be technology lead (including important intellectual property rights) of the undertaking or *lock ins*, i.e. scenarios where the value (and user dependency) increases with the number of users (e.g. "everybody" having *iOS* or *Android* on their smartphone).
Thanks to this high market share and/or other barriers, this undertaking is **b) able to maintain prices higher** independently of its competitors, customers and consumers.

This dominance for itself is not forbidden. Neither is, for itself, the *2. adverse effect on trade between the MS* this dominance can have, which is the second pre-condition.
However, for *1.* dominant undertakings whose actions have *2.* adverse cross-MS trade effects, *3. abusive conduct* (third pre-condition, see below) *is* prohibited.

---

[212] This additional responsibility exists *irrespective of the causes* of that position.

168

This abusive conduct may be result of an undertaking's position of dominance or *not*.

In other words, a dominant undertaking has a special responsibility by virtue of its dominance and therefore must not take certain actions even though they are not taken (or *can* be taken) *because* of the undertaking's dominance. That means that, while abusive conduct by dominant undertakings is prohibited, the same conduct may not be so for other (non-dominant) undertakings.[213]

**Example**[214]

*i. For using specific Terms of Use regarding the collection of user data on various platforms and using this data to foreclose competitors, Facebook/Meta was charged with having **exploited** (see below) its users.*

*ii. Facebook claimed that other non-dominant platforms also applied such terms of use and, therefore, it cannot be due to its dominance that Facebook's user terms applied.*

Ad i. Facebook's conduct was found to be an *exploitative abuse* (see below) to the detriment of "the opposite side of the market, i.e. in this case the consumers who use Facebook"[215].

Ad ii. Facebook's argument of its terms of use design not being due to its dominant market position is in vain because abusive conduct by

---

[213] General Court (EU) *AstraZeneca AB and AstraZeneca plc vs. European Commission* judgment T-321/05, 1 July 2010.
Therefore, the terms "abuse of dominance" or "abuse of a dominant market position" are somewhat misleading.
[214] CJEU *Meta Platforms and Others vs. Bundeskartellamt* judgment C-252/21, 4 July 2023. See also Jaeger, 2021: 238.
[215] *Decision* of the Deutsches Bundeskartellamt B6-22/16, 6 February 2019.

dominant undertakings may *or may not* result from their position of dominance.

**Abuse** is given if one (or more) dominant undertaking's trade-restrictive conduct is

**a)** *exclusionary*, i.e. blocking the access of potential competitors to the market (*anti-competitive foreclosure*).

This can e.g. be the unjustified *refusal of dealing* with one competitor denying him/her access to essential goods/services/facilities etc.; *tying & bundling* (the purchase of another product being condition for the purchase of dominant product); and *predation* (incurring losses to foreclose a competitor).

*or*

**b)** *exploitative*, i.e. exploiting the undertaking's business partners and customers by making use of *lock ins* and the dependency they create (see Facebook/Meta example above).

This can e.g. be *disproportionate prices or business terms* that without the lock in dependency could not be attained by the undertaking; offering worse terms without justification to business partners competing with other partners to which better terms are conceded (*discrimination*); and artificially *limiting supply* (commonly resulting in higher prices) without any objective justification.

 It is of no importance if the dominant undertaking actually *intends* to abuse or not. If the mentioned conditions (dominance, adverse cross-MS trade effects, abusive conduct) are given, it must bear its consequences.

Abuse of market power is only **justified** if the dominant undertaking proves that there is/are

170

- an *objective economic reason* for its conduct (e.g. a quantity discount offered to everybody, where the cost per unit decreases if greater numbers of the product are purchased) *or*
- an *objective legal reason* (e.g. actions against the free-riding on the brand name) *or*
- *objective efficiency advantages* that also benefit consumers.[216]

As with cartels, acts against the abuse of power-prohibition are automatically void (and do not first have to be determined so by the COM).

They are enforced by the COM, enforcement competence which is partly re-delegated to the MS. Due to the direct applicability of the abuse of dominance provision contained in the TFUE, courts of the MS have jurisdiction to assess abusive conduct. (TFUE Art. 102; Regulation 1/2003)

---

[216] See CJEU judgments C-95/04 P; joined cases C-468/06 to C-678/06 and C-413/14; C-307/18; C-377/20 and e.g. Jaeger, 2024: 377.

# 3. Mergers

While cartels and abuse of market dominance are prohibited as such by EU Competition Law, mergers are, of course, not.

But, in order to prevent distortions of competition and maintaining a functioning market structure, market concentrations (to which mergers may lead) must be controlled.

While cartels and abuse of dominance[217] have their legal basis in the TFUE (primary EU Law), merger control is based on secondary[218] EU Law – the so-called *Merger Regulation* (2004).[219] Furthermore, in contrast to abuse of dominance and cartels, there are no parallel competences of national competition authorities *and* the COM in mergers. Merger control is *either* a national concern *or*, above certain thresholds, an EU concern ("one stop shop"). The MS' authorities and the COM can, however, refer cases to each other under certain circumstances. In addition, the MS' authorities must undertake inspections if requested by the COM. (Merger Regulation Art. 9, 12, 22)

According to the Merger Regulation, mergers between two (or more) undertakings are incompatible with the EU's internal market (and therefore an *EU* concern) if *all* the following elements apply[220]:

**1. *concentration*,** i.e. the lasting change of control of an undertaking resulting from a merger of previously independent (parts of or entire) undertakings. This can result both from a share deal (over 50% shareholding[221]) or an asset deal (purchasing most of another company's

---

[217] And also state aid (see below).

[218] Secondary EU Law refers to legislative acts adopted by the EU *based* on the EU Treaties while primary EU Law refers to the Treaties *themselves* (and some other legal documents).

[219] Council Regulation (EC) No 139/2004 of 20 January 2004 on the control of concentrations between undertakings (the EC Merger Regulation).

[220] Merger Regulation Art. 2.

[221] Holding 50% of the shares regularly constitutes a *dominant influence* over a company.

assets[222]) which brings permanent change of control or an elimination of independence of the acquired or merged company. It further can be horizontal (same market level competitors) or vertical (different market level, e.g. manufacturer and distributor).

**2. *EU dimension*,** i.e. a concentration of EU relevance, which is determined by a minimum of combined turnover of the undertakings EU-wide and worldwide. If the undertakings' commercial activity extends to *three or more MS*, the general EU-wide and worldwide turnover thresholds are set lower (and therefore easier to reach).

**3. *dominance / significant impediment to effective competition*** (SIEC), e.g. by a concentration specifically *creating or strengthening a dominant market position*. This may result in both a loss of competition between the merged undertakings and, if by the merger a competitor of other companies is removed, in less competition between other undertakings.[223]

There are two tests that may be used to determine if dominance is created or strengthened: a) the *dominance test*, which is largely based on the relevant market shares of the undertakings involved, and b) the (primarily used) *SIEC test* allowing a more comprehensive analysis of competition effects.

In contrast to cartels and abusive conduct, which – as mentioned – are generally prohibited, relevant[224] mergers (since they are generally allowed) must usually be *notified* to the COM. A standstill obligation will remain in effect for at least 25 working days from the date of notification,

---

[222] E.g. machines, real estate, intellectual property and contractual rights.
[223] See e.g. General Court (EU) *CK Telecoms UK Investments Ltd vs. European Commission* judgment T-399/16, 28 Mai 2020.
[224] Not every acquisition needs to be notified to the COM for review, but only when the involved companies reach a certain size. If mergers remain under this threshold and/or they affect mostly the market of only one MS, the must regularly be notified to the MS concerned (and not to the COM).

or longer if the Commission decides to initiate formal proceedings. If the COM finds that there are serious competition concerns in relation to the EU internal market, the undertakings have to wait at least three months until they can formalize the merger. If they do not notify or do not wait long enough, the merger transactions are void. (Merger Regulation Art. 7, 10)

If the COM issues a decision declaring the concentration compatible with the internal market or simply lets the three-month period[225] pass without deciding, a merger is considered approved.

If the COM comes to the conclusion that the planned merger has the just mentioned three elements (*concentration* with an *EU dimension* that is a *SIEC*), it prohibits the conclusion of the merger.

Enforcement, i.e. the reversal of transactions between the undertakings and the imposition of fines, is the (only) job of the COM:

Unlike the enforcement regarding cartels and dominance abuse, where national competition authorities share competence with the COM, the enforcement of merger control is centralized under the COM's authority, known as the "one-stop shop" approach. However, partly delegated enforcement to MS can occur under the referral mechanisms of the Merger Regulation (e.g. if the merger primarily impacts competition in a particular MS). (Art. 9)

---

[225] If no longer decision period is applicable. See Merger Regulation Art. 10.

# II. State aid

State aid law is, in contrast to antitrust law, not addressed to private persons or entities but to the *EU member states*.

Unlike antitrust law, the market share of the profiting undertakings is usually irrelevant and only the overall amount of aid matters.

Also unlike antitrust law, it generally[226] has **no** *direct effect* and its provisions can therefore not be invoked by individuals before courts.

The key task of state aid law is to **prevent public interference in competition** through economically valuable benefits.
Similarly to the EU Law provisions on cartels and abuse of dominance, also state aid is *generally prohibited* (but can exceptionally be justified) due to its potentially harmful effects on the EU's internal market.

In contrast to the EU, most states and customs unions with or without internal market tendencies do not or only very reluctantly prohibit state aid. This has to do with the high level of economic integration (four freedoms of the internal market) of the EU, which makes it necessary to limit state aid for ensuring fairness and non-discrimination between the EU MS's market participants.

> Apart from the EU, also the WTO has established a regime controlling state aid, the Agreement on Subsidies and Countervailing Measures (SCM Agreement, 1994). The SCM Agreement is generally applied relatively restrictively and to bigger cases[227] and – in contrast to EU Law, which *generally* prohibits subsidies – only prohibits *certain categories* of subsidies. Subsidies violations under the SCM Agreement are furthermore limited to sanctions of an inter-state nature (countermeasures).

---

[226] "Generally" meaning that there is one exception: The national courts of the MS are competent for determining if the standstill period (see below) was complied with and if compensation for resulting damages must be paid.
[227] Jaeger, 2017: 340.

175

(In principle prohibited) State aid, according to the TFEU (Art. 107) can be defined as follows:

An *1. economic advantage of state origin*

*2. granted selectively to* one or more *undertaking(s)*

that *3. distorts* (or threatens to distort) *competition*

and *4. affects trade between the MS.*

"Economic advantage" means the granting of better conditions than the normal market conditions. What matters is not the conceptualization nor the intention of their granting but its *effects*.
This can e.g. be a direct payment by the state to an undertaking but also loans and guarantees on non-market terms, tax or social security payment breaks or waivers or sales/investments in (failing) undertakings without an adequate return.

"*Selected* undertakings[228]" simply refers to not *all* (potentially profiting) undertakings but only *some* the state chooses to give the advantage to.[229]

"Competition distortion" and "effect on inter-MS trade", thanks to the mostly similar meaning of these terms in EU antitrust law (see above), does not require further explanation in this key essentials book.

If even one of these four constituent elements is absent, the measure does *not* qualify as prohibited aid. Benefits provided from state resources that do not meet all these criteria are unproblematic and permissible from an EU state aid law perspective.

---

[228] I.e. not consumers.
[229] Apart from the prohibition of offering special conditions to only *some* undertakings (without an objective justification and provided that the other three factors are also given), EU Law also provides for the general requirement to treat public and private undertakings equally. (TFEU Art. 106)

176

If all these four elements are cumulatively given though, state aid can only be conceded legally if an **exception/justification** is sought, for which the state has to request approval from the COM.

State aid is justified if it **a)** pursues *certain goals* (see below), is **b)** *proportionate* to them and, in the best case, **c)** also impossible to have been reached by the market itself (without state interference). Possible *goals* are especially those related to public interest / aid, e.g. improvements in disadvantaged regions, projects of common European interest, services of general economic interest (SGEI) and repairing damages caused by exceptional occurrences and natural disasters. (TFUE Art. 106, 107)

Furthermore, as with cartels, there are guidelines and *block exemption regulations* (BER) the COM provides for orientation.

The COM has broad discretion in determining if state aid[230] is justified and – unlike in EU antitrust law – there is no partial delegation of this task to the authorities of the MS (!). Therefore, it is an *exclusive* domain of the EU.[231]

If a state wants to seek a justification for state aid, this must be notified in advance and, generally, approved by the COM.[232] (TFUE Art. 107, 108)

After a state's request for conceding justified state aid (*notification*), there is a standstill period of two months[233]. During this period, the COM can decide that it is **a)** not a relevant measure or **b)** a subsidy compatible with the common market or **c)** initiate the second evaluation step (one

---

[230] The question if a measure *constitutes state aid* can be evaluated by national authorities and courts (*but not if it is justified or not*).
[231] The only area where the MS('s courts) are competent is in the appreciation if the standstill obligation was (not) fulfilled and to grant remedies for damages etc. (for a damaged undertaking against the infringing MS). (TFEU Art. 108)
[232] There are certain exceptions to the requirement for mandatory notification, such as aid covered by a *block exemption, de minimis* aid not exceeding 200 000 € per undertaking over any three fiscal years, or aid granted under an already authorised aid scheme by the COM.
[233] CJEU Gebrüder Lorenz Judgment 120/73 (1973).

additional month for finally allowing or prohibiting the subsidy). (Art. 108)[234]

If the COM **d)** does not react during the first two months, the MS can notify the COM about the putting in effect of the planned measure. After fifteen more days of additional standstill, the MS can finally do so.[235]

In contrast to antitrust, the COM holds the *exclusive* authority to assess the application of all grounds of justification under EU state aid law and is also *exclusively* competent for the public enforcement of EU state aid law. (TFEU Art. 108)[236]

All of the COM's decisions and procedural actions can be reviewed by the EU General Court and, in the final instance, by the European Court of Justice (CJEU).

Again unlike antitrust law, enforcement in this case does not cover fines for undertakings or MS but only *ordering the MS to recover unjustified state aid* (incl. interest) from the recipients.

 State aid law does not have a punitive nature.[237] The recovery of state aid serves (only) to neutralize the distortion of competition caused by the unlawful aid but not to "punish" the state (there are no fines etc.).

A violation of the implementation prohibition issued by the COM leads to the invalidity of the legal act implementing the aid, such as contracts or national decisions.

---

[234] CJEU *Sytraval/Brink's France* Judgment C-367/95 P (1998).

[235] CJEU Gebrüder Lorenz Judgment 120/73 (1973). If the measure has not been notified, it constitutes unlawful state aid and the two months-time limit does not apply.

[236] In certain specific areas, national courts have complementary competence alongside the COM to enforce prohibition measures. This includes the power to order the removal of illegal state aid (through recovery), issue injunctions to cease such aid, and grant compensation for damages caused by unlawful state aid measures. However, national courts are *not* competent to assess the compatibility of state aid with the internal market.

[237] Jaeger, 2024: 452.

178

In addition, illicit state aid may lead to claims from those who incur damages (especially competitors) against the unlawful state aid granted without permission.

# E Private International Law

The term "Private International Law" in its broader meaning covers any law, legal provisions or even legal practices relevant for private legal relationships with an international aspect.

More commonly though, when *Private International Law* is referred to specifically, it is meant and understood in its narrower word sense. This Private International Law *sticto sensu* (PIL) focusses on the following main questions in relation to a contract[238] (and also non-contractual obligations[239]) with international elements:

1. If parties disagree on contractual obligations, do not comply with the contract, or cause damages to each other, they will most likely try to find appropriate means of dispute resolution.
   But where (at which country's courts) do they litigate if they are based in different countries?
   **Determining where the dispute happens – *International Jurisdiction*** – is key task one of PIL, also referred to as *International Civil Procedure Law*.

2. After a court (or arbitral tribunal) is determined to resolve the case, which state's (or other) legal rules does it apply to the contract and related merits[240] in dispute?
   **Determining which rules are applied to merits with an international aspect – *International Conflict of Laws*** – is key task two (and according to some the *main* or *exclusive* task) of PIL.

3. Based on the now determined applicable rules, the court (or arbitral tribunal) will come to a decision determining what the parties must do (pay for damages, return goods/payments, etc.).

---

[238] Or, more generally, *legal transactions*.
[239] E.g. in family or inheritance law.
[240] I.e. actions, omissions, failures... actually taking place between the parties.

180

What happens if – despite a decision issued by a court of country **A** – a party based in country **B** does not comply with it? **Determining if decisions are recognized and enforced by another state – *International Recognition and Enforcement*** – is key task three of PIL.

The interesting thing about PIL is that, despite of its name, it is traditionally not *international* law (e.g. international conventions) that regulates PIL but *national* law.[241]

In some cases though, International Law has replaced national legal provisions. That is the matter e.g. in the European Union regarding all three areas (*Jurisdiction, Conflict of Laws, Recognition&Enforcement*) which are regulated by EU Regulations[242]. And it is also the case specifically with the international *Recognition and Enforcement* of foreign arbitral awards, which is regulated by the so-called *New York Convention* (see *Arbitration*).

---

[241] Despite of the fact that it is mostly *national* law by nature, it is anyway called "Private *International* Law". Since also International Law provisions partly regulating the mentioned areas are covered by the term, it can be stated that PIL is composed by both national *and* international law provisions. For more information, see chapter "Jurisdiction Requirements and Rules".

[242] See *Brussels Ia Regulation, International Conflict of Laws* and *International Recognition and Enforcement*.

# I. International Jurisdiction

Let us have a look at *International Jurisdiction* – i.e. the power of a court to decide a dispute.

## 1. Where to litigate?

This should be one of the first questions business partners concluding a contract with international elements have to ask themselves because it often determines the outcome of a dispute (!) that may later arise.

Parties can decide upfront[243] (e.g. in their contract) – within certain limits – where to litigate and choose a suitable court for disputes arising directly from their contractual relationship (breach of contract etc.) or in relation to it (damages/tort claims etc.).

It is highly recommended to make use of this possibility and establish which kind of body (litigation before a state court or arbitration before private arbitrators, see below) at which place (state/place of the court or of arbitration) is competent for deciding future disputes in connection to their contract. *Why is that so important?*

Depending on the court chosen,

- **procedural rules** (when to submit defense, timeframes …) apply, namely those from the state where it is located (!);

- **Conflict-of-Laws rules** (that tell us which country's etc. rules are applied to solve the case) apply, namely – again – those from the state where the court is located (!);

---

[243] They choose a competent court *upfront*, which is mostly done, but also *after* the dispute has arisen.

- **enforcement** of the court decision is guaranteed or not – since court decisions are generally only binding within a country whose court issued the decision.[244]

**Example**

*Contract party **A** is very convincing and manages to make the other party **B** agree to a court located in **X** seemingly very favorable for **A** to be competent for conflict resolution. In the end, the court actually decides in favor of **A**.*
***B**, based in **Y**, finally does not stick to the court decision's orders.*

**A**'s "success" could be in vain if the decision cannot be enforced because recognition and enforcement are possibly not granted to decisions issued by courts in **X** by the state (e.g. **Y**) where enforcement must take place (e.g. because **B**'s assets are there).[245]

Apart from that, there are many "soft" concerns parties should consider when opting for a court.

These include access of a court to evidence, a possible bias of the judge (e.g. in favor of its own national), convenience (e.g. connections to lawyers), travel, translation and court costs, lawyers (and co-counsel) costs and bar admittance requirements. Apart from that, certain state's courts (in the EU e.g. Italy and Greece) are known to work very slowly,

---

[244] In the EU enforcement of decisions by member states' courts is guaranteed though (exceptionally this is also the case in other countries). Generally, it is a state's own laws that determine under which conditions a foreign court decision is enforced in it, which regularly depends on where judgment is from.
In contrast, arbitral awards must be recognized and enforced nearly worldwide thanks to the New York Convention (see *Arbitration*).
[245] For this reason, it can (and does) happen that – in contrast to this example case – the court located in **X** does not take the case in the first place.

which can be made use of if parties want to delay the outcome of a process or avoided if parties want a quick result (as for the EU, very generally spoken, in the north, courts normally are comparably fast).[246]

Despite the relative freedom most legal systems grant parties to include such *forum selection clauses* (or *choice-of-court/forum clauses/agreements*), it is not absolute.

Several national legal orders (and public International Law) require at least some link[247] of the parties or their contract to the country whose courts will be competent for litigation.

This has to do both with sovereignty concerns and with the fact that litigation is somewhat considered by the implicated state as a service to its own citizens and businesses, which mostly costs more than it economically brings the state.[248] Apart from that, it can (and does) happen that both parties file a suit against each other on the same issue in different states (*parallel litigation* or *lis pendens*[249]), in which case e.g. US law tends to admit different locations of litigation whereas e.g. EU Law generally avoids them:

> When proceedings between the same parties involve the same cause of action and are brought in different EU member states' courts, all courts seised after the first one must stay their proceedings until the latter has

---

[246] See e.g. Council of Europe European Commission for the efficiency of justice (CEPEJ), 2022: *Study on the functioning of judicial systems in the EU Member States*, Council of Europe.

[247] Also a choice of court for itself creates some link to a country, which may or not be enough (but mostly is [!]). When there is no Choice-of-Court agreement and (only) the Private International Law rules of one country lead to the result that the courts of another country are competent, even this minimal link is missing (and therefore more cause for invoking *forum non conveniens* [see below] given).

[248] On the other hand, a state regularly has interest in guaranteeing rule of law and creating a secure environment where business want to settle.

[249] *Lis pendens* refers to the *pending legal dispute* in general, not implying necessarily that proceedings are running in parallel. Often proceedings are terminated from the beginning because of another *lis pendens*, i.e. there are no parallel proceedings in this case.

established (or not) jurisdiction. If it decides so, all other courts have to decline jurisdiction. (Brussels Ia Art. 29)

When parties included an exclusive choice of forum clause, all other courts have to stay their proceedings until the chosen court has decided about its jurisdiction. If it affirms its jurisdiction, all other EU member states' courts must decline jurisdiction. (Brussels Ia Art. 31)

If parallel litigation is not between EU courts but an EU court and a non-EU court, the EU court has two options. If it considers that the non-EU court's decision will be recognized and enforced and it is in line with "proper administration of justice", it can stay its proceedings. Otherwise (and if the non-EU court's decision is stayed or not expected within a reasonable time and/or if there is no risk of irreconcilable decisions), it can continue its proceedings.

As soon as there is a (in the EU court's country) recognizable and enforceable decision by the non-EU court, the EU court dismisses its proceedings. (Brussels Ia Art. 33, 34)

It must be mentioned that in countries with a *common law* tradition (US, UK, CAN, Australia, India…) courts can simply decide to not take a case even if they generally have jurisdiction (due to a legitimate forum selection clause[250] or a state's Private International Law rules leading to these countries' courts). This is called *forum non conveniens* and is usually only done if the plaintiff is no citizen of the state the court is located at and if another court is much better suited to deal with the case.[251]

A *practical* reason why *forum non conveniens* dismissal is used e.g. in the US – especially in tort cases – is because of the characteristics of US law.
US procedural law provides e.g. for extensive discovery, jury trials, lawyer's fees contingent upon the success of lawsuits etc.
US substantive law – although a state's court does not necessarily apply this state's substantive law – allows e.g. to sue for pain and suffering and, most prominently, punitive damages.

---

[250] When there is a legitimate forum selection clause, dismissal based on *forum non* is rare though.

[251] This can be for practical reasons, e.g. because all the evidence, witnesses and experts are located in another state, or because there are evidently closer links to another state with available and adequate courts.

Therefore, looking for adequate procedure and extensive compensation for damages, parties often practice "forum shopping" and choose the state's courts where they expect to have procedural benefits and get the biggest indemnity payment.
This practice is limited through by the inconvenient forum doctrine.

In contrast, in *civil law* countries (e.g. most European countries and Latin America) courts having jurisdiction[252] must take the case.

This may also have to do with the fact that civil law countries' rules generally "place an emphasis on the relationship between the court and the claim, as opposed to the U.S. emphasis on the relationship between the court and the defendant"[253] (*personal jurisdiction*).

That is also the reason why e.g. – in contrast to the US – contractual claims and non-contractual (e.g. tort) claims in the EU have to be assessed separately for finding out which court(s) has/have jurisdiction.

Consequently, if parties want to be completely sure their forum selection clause is successful, they should inform themselves about the relevant legal provisions and practice of the state whose courts they opt for (since in some cases a connection to this state is necessary). If e.g. an EU court is chosen, they are safe though.[254]

---

[252] There can be more than one country's courts having jurisdiction. If one of them is seised, in civil law countries, it must take the case over which it has jurisdiction.

[253] Folsom et al., 2016: 432.

[254] With some restrictions, e.g. **a)** insurance, consumer or employment contracts, where party autonomy to determine courts having jurisdiction is limited, and **b)** if the parties' Choice-of-Court agreement is null and void as to its substantive validity under the law of the state whose courts are chosen. (Brussels Ia Art. 24, 25; see *CoC agreements in Brussels Ia*)

# 2. Jurisdiction Requirements and Rules

For a court to establish jurisdiction the following elements are generally required:

First of all, there must be jurisdiction over a particular **person**, e.g. no immunity of the defendant, which may be the case e.g. for diplomats or for states before the courts of other states.

Second, jurisdiction must cover the **subject matter**, which must not have been removed from the decision power of the court, e.g. not a matter of purely administrative (non-judicial) competence or excluded from state court litigation due to an arbitration clause.

Third and most importantly, there must be **territorial competence**, i.e. a connection between the case (and/or the parties) and the territory of the state whose courts deal with it. As mentioned, even with forum selection clauses, to be sure, there generally[255] should exist a minimal link between the case and the court having jurisdiction over it. This is even more the case when parties (for whatever reasons) refrain from choosing a competent court and the court that will be competent has to be figured out.

*What tells a country('s courts) that this link is given, when it can exercise territorial jurisdiction?*

1. There are some **international treaties** that regulate (territorial) jurisdiction, which unfortunately do not count on very broad state acceptance.

Examples for these are the *Hague Convention on Choice of Court Agreements*[256], which is limited though to forum selection clauses, and

---

[255] E.g. in the EU such a link is not necessary if there is a forum selection clause.
[256] See *CoC agreements in international treaties*.

treaties in the area of international transport such as the *Convention on the Contract for the International Carriage of Goods by Road* (CMR). This Convention, apart from regulating judicial competence, also contains substantive law provisions though.

Moreover, the *Lugano Convention* for recognition and enforcement of judgments in civil and commercial matters must be mentioned, which is applicable in the EU including Denmark (which is excluded from *Brussels Ia*), Norway, Iceland and Switzerland.[257] Furthermore, there are some bilateral treaties regulating territorial jurisdiction.[258]

2. In the EU (except Denmark) there is a common framework for jurisdiction, regulated most importantly by the *Regulation (EU) No 1215/2012 on jurisdiction and the recognition and enforcement of judgments in civil and commercial matters* – **Brussels Ia or Brussels I***bis* **Regulation**[259] (explained below). Brussels Ia also regulates the important areas of recognition and enforcement of judicial decisions. It is supplemented by additional EU legislative acts focusing on order for payments procedure and small claims procedure. (Regulations 1896/2006, 861/2007 and 2015/2421)

3. Last but not least, as mentioned at the beginning of this chapter, Private International Law (PIL) is traditionally and *still* an area of law determined mostly[260] by **national law**. That is why in many cases it is still

---

[257] See *CoC agreements in international treaties* and *Brussels Ia Regulation*.

[258] There are also some international conventions regulating not jurisdiction but parts of the judicial process, such as the *Hague Service Convention* focusing on service of process, i.e. delivery to the defendant of the notice of the claim against him/her, and the *Hague Evidence Convention* focusing on discovery, i.e. the disclosure of evidence, access to witnesses, etc.

[259] The Brussels Ia Regulation is expected to be reformed in the next years under the new European Commission.
Apart from it, there are some narrower EU jurisdiction frameworks, like the Brussels IIa Regulation "on jurisdiction and the recognition and enforcement of judgments in matrimonial matters and the matters of parental responsibility" and the Succession Regulation, which regulates not only jurisdictional competence and enforcement but also the applicable law.

[260] As mentioned, in the European Union PIL is mainly determined by EU Law and not (any more) national law.

188

on the states themselves to decide (by internal lawmaking) if there are enough links of the case to their own courts or if other courts are more suited to deal with it. In the latter case, national law does not only determine that this country's courts are *not* competent but *which other country's* courts are. In Austria e.g. such a national law regulating jurisdiction is the *Jurisdiktionsnorm* (JN).[261]

As a very general rule it can be stated that a court regularly has competence if the parties agree on it and/or if it is the court (in charge of the state/area) of the defendant's domicile. As for businesses, national (and international) jurisdiction rules may have a tendency for the place of incorporation **or** the place of principal operations **or** another place of operations from where actions were performed (as for the EU, see *Brussels Ia Regulation*).

Another typical element of jurisdiction rules is that they include almost always special provisions for certain types of contract (e.g. sales, employment, insurance contract) and claims (e.g. contractual or non-contractual).

In many cases the claimant has various options where to litigate – e.g. a general court option *and* a special court option as a consequence of a specific type of claim – from which he/she can choose one.[262]

---

[261] The JN is in many cases excluded from application though due to Brussels Ia, which mostly is applied instead.
[262] As for the EU and the Lugano-area, see *Brussels Ia Regulation*.

## a. Choice-of-Court Agreements

Choice-of-Court (CoC) agreements by the parties to a contract/dispute are by far the most important ground for jurisdiction in international business.

Parties often can choose *any* court they want even though there is no connection at all between them or the contract (subject) and the place of the court.
Possible reasons for choosing a certain (country's) court with absolutely no link to the case can e.g. be that it is "neutral" ground (none of the countries the parties are based in) or that an other country's justice system is more reliable (to avoid e.g. despotic states' systems like some in Central Asia) or efficient (to avoid e.g. some southern European countries' courts that are known to be very slow; see also *Where to litigate?*).

It must be noted that, even though parties can *choose* any court, some courts can (and sometimes do) decline to decide / dismiss cases even if they have jurisdiction.[263] This is done especially if there is no link at all between the case and the court and another court seems more appropriate to decide a case (see e.g. *forum non conveniens* in the chapter *Where to litigate?*).

Regarding the **form** of CoC agreements, in the EU and most other legal systems they must be *in writing*[264] (often electronic messages providing a durable record of the agreement suffice, e.g. e-mails), though some legal orders also require the *signatures* of the parties.

---

[263] This possibility of declining to take cases despite a court having jurisdiction (due to a CoC agreement or a country's PIL rules leading to it) is not given in the EU thanks to Brussels Ia.
[264] In the EU, instead of written form, any form in line with (former) party practices is also valid. (Brussels Ia Art. 23)

190

CoC agreements are mostly integrated in the contract. Such contract clauses can be **permissive** or **mandatory**. *Permissive* means that parties agree to several possible courts of which one must be selected in case a dispute comes up. In contrast, *mandatory* means that only one area's court in concrete has jurisdiction and therefore is competent to resolve the dispute.

Nevertheless, even a mandatory clause[265] could be understood in some countries only as an *additional option* to the court that without this clause would have jurisdiction (e.g. the one at the defendant's domicile). Despite most legal orders interpreting a mandatory CoC agreement as **exclusive** anyway[266], this *exclusiveness* should be specified to provide for clarity in any case. If desired otherwise, it should be specified that the choice is **optional** to the court determined by regular jurisdiction rules.

Concluding an *exclusive* CoC agreement has particular relevance for the case that a party *enters an appearance* before a different court than the one indicated in the agreement (see below): This different court must generally decline jurisdiction in favor of the in the CoC agreement determined court.

Apart from that, such forum selection clauses can be focused strictly on the **contractual** relationship itself *or* englobe also matters **related** to the contract.

---

[265] Thanks to which the case is not opened up by the parties to several potential courts from the beginning.

[266] Such as, in the EU, *Brussels Ia*, concretized by CJEU jurisprudence (e.g. C-269/95).

If party agreement can be found, it is recommended to formulate the forum selection clause in a **mandatory** (only one court in particular is competent) way to later avoid discussions on finally choosing one out of various optional courts.

 It should also be specified expressly in the CoC agreement that this mandatory selection clause provides for **exclusive** jurisdiction of the chosen court.

 Moreover, unless intended otherwise, formulation should be done in a broad way, i.e. also covering disputes **related to** the contractual relationship (e.g. also tort claims and not only breach of contract claims).

**Example**

1. (…)

2. (…)

3. Jurisdiction and applicable law

All suits arising out of **or relating to** the subject matter of this contract shall be decided **solely** and **exclusively** by the state or federal courts located in New York City, New York.[267]

[applicable law clause]

4. (…)

5. (…)

[signature of both parties]

Usually, CoC agreements are incorporated up front in the contract and regularly together (in the same section of the contract) with a *Choice-of-*

---

[267] Folsom et al., 2016: 423, bold print added.

*Law* agreement (see *International Conflict of Laws*). Nevertheless, they can also be added later, e.g. when the dispute has already arisen. Then finding an agreement (that satisfies both parties) is usually more challenging though.

### Which law tells me if the CoC agreement is valid?

It is regularly the national legal provisions of the country whose courts were chosen in the agreement that determine the possibility and validity of a CoC agreement (as for the EU, see below).

## CoC agreements in Brussels Ia

As mentioned, in PIL and jurisdictional competence assessment there is a predominance of *national* law.

Nevertheless, EU member states mostly determine if one of their courts has jurisdiction – and in case not, which other EU member state's courts have – not by applying their internal laws but by all applying the same set of rules contained in an *international* legislative act – the already mentioned EU **Brussels Ia Regulation**.[268]

If **1.** the in a CoC agreement **chosen court is located in the EU** (except Denmark) and **2.** an **EU court is seised**, the court must apply the relevant provisions of Brussels Ia (Art. 25) instead of national law.[269]
Therefore, in the EU, only if the parties conclude a CoC agreement in favor of a non-EU (and non-Lugano Convention and non-Hague Convention state, see below) state, the *national* jurisdiction rules (on the

---

[268] This is nearly always the case with CoC agreements. If there is no CoC agreement, the defendant must also be *domiciled* in a Brussels Ia state (EU except Denmark) for Brussels Ia being applied.
[269] In international civil and commercial matters with some exceptions.

consequences of CoC agreements) of the EU country whose court is seised are applied.

Brussels Ia allows parties to choose *any* (EU) court they want even though there is no link at all between them (e.g. their domicile) or the contract/litigation subject and the place of the court. (Brussels Ia Art. 25)

**Example**

*Parties **A** and **B**, which are both based in Japan, conclude a contract with a clause indicating "all disputes arising out of the subject matter of this contract shall be decided by the courts of Sweden".*

If an EU court is seised, Brussels Ia Regulation is applied even though the parties are not based in the EU and, if Brussels Ia Art. 25's requirements are fulfilled, Swedish courts will have jurisdiction.

In relation to the mentioned *writing* requirement[270] for CoC agreements in the EU, it is also possible to include a CoC clause in the standard terms (such as GTC) of one of the parties. It is important though, for the validity of the CoC agreement, that the other party accepts these (and does not e.g. instead propose its own GTC with a contradicting CoC term).

### *What if the form requirements for a CoC agreement meet the Brussels Ia requirements but the contract itself is invalid?*

The CoC agreement is independent from the contract itself and must be dealt with separately. Therefore, a forum selection clause is not

---

[270] Or, instead, a form in line with party practices.

194

automatically invalid if the contract is void, e.g. because its (remaining) content is forbidden, factually impossible or contestable.

It is the court chosen by the parties in the formally valid CoC agreement that determines the applicable law to the contract including the CoC (according to the Conflict-of-Laws rules of the country[271] where it is located). This law does not determine questions of form (as Brussels Ia does) of the CoC agreement though but only if it is valid *materially*, e.g. if the offer or acceptance was timely, parties have the necessary legal capacity or consent was vitiated.[272] If the CoC agreement is considered invalid according to this law, it must be relied upon the general rules of Brussels Ia in order to determine which court has jurisdiction.[273]

This is, as mentioned, done regardless of the validity of the rest of the contract.

If e.g. the CoC is valid under Brussels Ia (formally) and the applicable law to the contract (materially), the chosen court has jurisdiction even if, according to the applicable law to the contract, the contract itself is invalid.

Apart from a violation of the mentioned formal requirements of Brussels Ia, a CoC agreement is of no effect in some cases where there is an imbalance of power (financially, information-wise, etc.) between the parties. An insurance company typically has more power than the person

---

[271] In the EU (except Denmark) it is often *EU* – and not national – law (e.g. the EU Rome I Regulation) that determines the applicable law.
[272] And, finally, it is also this law that determines if the rest of the contract (or parts of it) is contestable, void, etc.
[273] The so determined court then is bound by the decision of the first court regarding the validity of the CoC agreement. (see e.g. CJEU C-456/11)

insured, an enterprise more than its individual consumer[274] and an employer more than its employee. For protecting the respectively "weaker" party, party autonomy to determine courts having jurisdiction is limited regarding insurance, consumer and employment contracts (Brussels Ia Art. 10-23; see also *Brussels Ia Regulation*).

Nevertheless, CoC agreements concluded *after* the dispute has arisen or that offer the protected party an additional place of jurisdiction are permitted (and valid) though. (Brussels Ia Art. 25)

In addition, an EU member state's (MS) courts can also have *exclusive* jurisdiction, which means that, regardless of the parties' domicile or a CoC agreement, *only* these courts have jurisdiction.[275]

That is the case e.g. with claims concerning

**a)** rights *in rem* (e.g. property) of immovables as well as rent [courts of the MS where the property is],

**b)** proceedings on the validity of a company and its decisions [courts of the MS where the company has its seat[276]],

**c)** proceedings on registration and validity of intellectual property rights [courts of the MS where the registration has been applied for, has taken place or is deemed to have taken place] and

**d)** proceedings on the enforcement of judgments [courts of the MS where the judgment has been or is to be enforced]. (Brussels Ia Art. 24)

---

[274] A *consumer* being a natural person acting for a purpose outside his/her profession or trade and a *consumer contract* being a contract between a consumer and an entrepreneur (acting for an entrepreneurial purpose).

[275] When assessing which court has jurisdiction, it is recommended to *first* consult the list of exclusive jurisdiction matters contained in Art. 24 of Brussels Ia and then have a look at the general and special rules.

[276] The seat must be determined according to the PIL of the court dealing with it (Brussels Ia Art. 24), representing an exception to the autonomous EU law provision of Art. 63 Brussels Ia defining the domicile of a legal person. (Klauser/Kodek, 2018: Brussels Ia Art. 24)

## CoC agreements in international treaties

There are not many multilateral international treaties regulating CoC agreements. These establish common rules whose fulfilment generally guarantees effectiveness of the forum selection agreement, i.e. the court determined by it actually taking the case. In addition, they provide for binding enforcement of the judgment of the court chosen in the CoC agreement (this being of the utmost importance for parties!).

Examples of such treaties are the mentioned *Lugano Convention* "on jurisdiction and the recognition and enforcement of judgments in civil and commercial matters" (2007) and the *Hague Convention* "on Choice of Court Agreements" (2005).

The **Lugano Convention**[277] is applicable to a CoC agreement in civil and commercial matters[278] in two cases:

First, if **a)** parties confer in it jurisdiction to a court of a member country of the Convention to which Brussels Ia is not applied (Denmark, Norway, Iceland, Switzerland[279]) **and b)** at least one of the parties is based in one of the Convention's member states (the mentioned four and the EU MS).[280]

Second, if **a)** parties confer in it jurisdiction to a court of any member country of the Convention (EU MS including Denmark; Norway, Iceland, Switzerland) **and b)** the defendant is domiciled in a member country of

---

[277] Partly abbreviated here as *Lugano*.
[278] Except e.g. bankruptcy and related proceedings, questions of status and legal capacity of natural persons and arbitration. (Lugano Art. 1)
[279] Liechtenstein is, despite being part of the European Economic Area, is not covered by the Lugano Convention (nor Brussels Ia). Therefore, its national jurisdiction laws must generally be applied instead.
[280] In contrast to Brussels Ia, the Lugano Convention is therefore not applicable if parties agreed on a Lugano member state's court but none of them is based in a Lugano member state.

the Convention to which Brussels Ia is not applied (Denmark, Norway, Iceland, Switzerland).
(Lugano Art. 64, Brussels Ia Art. 73, 80)

CoC → DK/NO/IS/CH          +          party based in EU/DK/NO/IS/CH

                           *or*

CoC→ EU/DK/NO/IS/CH        +          defendant based in DK/NO/IS/CH


Otherwise, at EU MS' (except Denmark's) courts Brussels Ia is applied to the CoC agreement instead.

The Lugano Convention establishes mostly the same conditions for CoC agreements as Brussels Ia, i.e. regarding form (primarily written form), exclusive jurisdiction (in relation to insurance, consumer and employment contracts), CoC agreements being understood as exclusive (not optional) in doubt etc.
One important difference exists though: In case the same matter is brought before various courts, Brussels Ia provides for the court chosen in the CoC agreement to evaluate jurisdiction first, while the Lugano Convention provides for the court *first seised* to determine jurisdiction. (Brussels Ia Art. 31; Lugano Art. 27) This can lead to delays in the proceedings.


In 2015, the **Hague Convention** came into force. It covers CoC agreements in international civil and commercial areas excluding e.g. family and inheritance law matters as well as consumer, employment and carriage contracts. (Hague Convention Art. 2)

It is applied to CoC agreements if **a)** parties confer jurisdiction to one of its members' courts (EU MS including Denmark; Albania, Montenegro, Moldova, Ukraine, United Kingdom, Mexico, Singapore) and **b)** one of the parties is resident in a non-Brussels Ia (or Lugano) member of the

Convention[281] (Albania, Montenegro, Moldova, Ukraine, United Kingdom, Mexico, Singapore). (Hague Convention Art. 3, 26)

$$CoC \rightarrow EU/DK/AL/ME/MD/UA/UK/MX/SG$$

$$+$$

**party resident in AL/ME/MD/UA/UK/MX/SG**

Also the rules of the Hague Convention are mostly similar to those regarding CoC agreements contained in Brussels Ia: written form requirement (also electronically)[282], differentiation of the CoC agreement's and the (remaining) contract's validity, exclusivity in doubt of the CoC, etc. (Hague Convention Art. 3, 5)[283]

If a court according to the Hague Convention has jurisdiction, it must take the case, even if the same matter has been brought before another court of a non-member of the Convention before.
On the other hand, if a court of a *member* of the Convention is seised, it must suspend or dismiss proceedings in favor of the court that has jurisdiction in accordance with the Convention (due to a CoC agreement). (Hague Convention Art. 6)

Both the Lugano and the Hague Convention provide for rules generally guaranteeing recognition and enforcement by its members of the judgment of the court determined by a CoC agreement (see *International Recognition and Enforcement*).[284]

---

[281] If both parties are resident in states where Brussels Ia is applied, instead of the Hague Convention, Brussels Ia must be applied.

[282] With all *material* (not formal) validity questions resolved in accordance with the law applicable to the contract, which is determined by the Conflict-of-Laws rules of the country where the court is located.

[283] See also Kronke, Herbert et al., 2017: *Handbuch Internationales Wirtschaftsrecht*[2], Linde, Vienna.

[284] The *Hague Convention on Choice of Court Agreements* must not be confused with the *Hague Judgments Convention*, which regulates enforcement of judgments not only as a result of a court having jurisdiction *thanks to a CoC agreement*.

## No Choice-of-Court agreement and Court appearance

As mentioned, the most common ground for jurisdiction in international business are CoC agreements. The reason for most parties opting for CoC agreements is simple – they provide for foreseeability and security regarding contract breaches and related issues. Therefore, it is highly recommended for any parties engaging in international business activity to incorporate a forum selection clause in their contract.

This is not always the case though.

*What happens if the parties forgot, could not agree upfront on a court or the claim is not subject to a contract[285]?*

**a)** They generally can **agree** to a court being competent also **after** the dispute has arisen.

**b)** If they do not manage to do so, **entering an appearance** by the defendant before a court is usually possible. This means that the defendant appears in a (due to the jurisdiction rules leading to another court or a non-exclusive[286] CoC agreement in favor of another court) *non-competent* court the claimant e.g. has seised. This court then – due to this appearance – becomes competent. After that, the defendant generally cannot bring objections to this court's jurisdiction since he/she implicitly "agreed" to it by this act.

In the EU (and Lugano Convention states) *entering an appearance* means that the defendant is heard (lets him/herself be questioned) before court on the main issue (or other procedural issues) without objecting to the

---

[285] E.g. a tort claim not (sufficiently) related to the contract.
[286] If there is an *exclusive* CoC agreement in favor of an other country's court than the one seised, the seised court must stay its proceedings and, if the in the CoC agreement determined court establishes jurisdiction (which is likely), decline jurisdiction in favor of the in the CoC agreement chosen court. (Brussels Ia Art. 31) In other words, **entering an appearance can be avoided by concluding exclusive CoC agreements**.

jurisdiction of the court at the first chance.[287] In matters of insurance, employment and consumer contracts, if the defendant is the "weaker" party, the court must inform him/her that he/she can contest the jurisdiction according to Brussels Ia (Art. 26).[288]

c) If the parties cannot agree on a court (not before the dispute has arisen nor after) nor the defendant enters an appearance before a court, they have to rely on *legal provisions that determine which court has jurisdiction* in such a case. These are regularly the national jurisdiction rules of the country whose courts are seised but can also be of an international nature, like Brussels Ia[289] (which does not only regulate what happens if there is a CoC agreement [and if an appearance is entered] but also if there is not).[290]

---

[287] See e.g. CJEU C-112/13, 201/82, 25/81.
[288] The Lugano Convention, in contrast, does not provide for such an obligation of the court. (Lugano Convention Art. 24)
[289] And e.g. the Lugano Convention, which in this matter is identical to Brussels Ia.
[290] See *Brussels Ia Regulation*.

## b. Brussels Ia Regulation

If **1.** the **court seised** is located **in the EU** (except Denmark) and **2.** the **defendant** is **domiciled in the EU** (except Denmark)[291], in civil and commercial matters[292] with links to more than one EU MS[293] Brussels Ia must be applied to find out which court(s) is/are available for litigation.

As mentioned before (see *CoC agreements in Brussels Ia*), Brussels Ia establishes (relatively limited) formal criteria for CoC agreements, which generally permits the parties to **a)** *choose* the court competent for resolving their dispute. Brussels Ia also covers the case in which the defendant **b)** *appears* before a court, action which confers jurisdiction to it (no matter whether general and special jurisdiction rules are withstanding). (Brussels Ia Art. 25, 26)

If neither is the case, Brussels Ia provides for **c)** a *detailed rules pattern* that enables a seised court to find out which court(s) actually has/have jurisdiction.[294]

Brussels Ia distinguishes between so-called *general* rules and *special* rules. While the former provide for a venue where to litigate in *any* case, the latter usually determine alternative venues where parties can litigate instead if *certain types of claims* are presented. In other words, depending

---

[291] "A defendant not domiciled in a Member State should in general be subject to the national rules of jurisdiction applicable in the territory of the Member State of the court seised." (Brussels Ia Preamble (14))

[292] Excluding family and inheritance law matters, bankruptcy and related proceedings, questions of status and legal capacity of natural persons and arbitration. (Brussels Ia Art. 1)

[293] If both claimant and defendant are domiciled in the same country, the contract and claim have no link to another country and there is no forum selection clause in favor of another EU MS's court nor jurisdiction by appearance before another EU MS's court, Brussels Ia does not apply. The reason for this is that, in such a case, it is a matter of purely national concern (and *domestic* rules determine which court has jurisdiction).

[294] This replaces the national jurisdiction rules of the EU member states (except Denmark) in its area of application.

on the type of claim, parties often have two (or more) options where to conduct litigation, i.e. the claimant can choose between the "general rule's court(s)" and the "special rule's court(s)".

The *general* place of litigation is the **defendant's domicile**[295], i.e. the defendant can generally always be sued in the courts of the EU MS where he/she constantly lives.[296] As for companies, the general place of litigation is the seat of the defendant company (alternatively statutory or administrative seat or the "principal place of business"). (Brussels Ia Art. 4, 63; Lugano Art. 2, 60)

 Where litigation can take place depends on which of the parties is the claimant and which is the defendant.

The *special* rules, as mentioned, regularly provide for *alternative* (additional) venues of litigation.

> This alternative/additional character is sometimes not given though, namely where there is a protective intent, e.g. consumer claims (see below), claims between the employer and employee[297] or between the insurer and the insured.[298]

---

[295] Or, when there are *several defendants*, the claims are very closely connected (e.g. the producer and the distributor are sued) and irreconcilable judgments are at risk, "the place where any one of them is domiciled"(Brussels Ia Art. 8; Lugano Art. 6). The scope of this provision is heavily disputed though.

[296] To be precise, the question if a party (natural person) is *domiciled* in a country is determined by the law of the country where the court seised is located. If the court comes to the conclusion that a party does not have its domicile in the "court's" country, it must apply the law of the country where the party is (expected to be) domiciled. (Brussels Ia Art. 62)

[297] Brussels Ia Art. 20 et seq., Lugano Art. 18 et seq.

[298] Brussels Ia Art. 10 et seq., Lugano Art. 8 et seq.

In these cases, if the "weaker" party is sued, the by Brussels Ia's *special* jurisdiction rules determined venues are not optional to the *general* litigation place but normally *obligatory* and replace it.

In other words, there are special rules for certain types (or designs) of claims that normally make litigation possible also at other venues than the one determined by the general rules. In the following, the most important ones for international business are summarized.

As for **claims arising out of a company's branch's operations**, apart from the three optional *general* litigation places for companies (statutory or administrative seat or principal place of business), a business can also litigate at the courts of the country where its branch office (or other similar establishment) is located.[299] (Brussels Ia Art. 7, Lugano Art. 5)

Regarding the most important type of claims for businesses – **contractual claims** – this alternative venue is the *place of performance*. In sales of moveables this generally is the place of delivery and in services generally the place where the service is provided, in transport contracts generally the place of departure or, optionally, the place of the final destination. (Brussels Ia Art. 7, Lugano Art. 5)

The place of performance is not always easy to determine, e.g. when goods are delivered to several places (e.g. stores in France, Germany, Spain and Portugal). In such cases, one *principle place* must be determined.[300] For that, factors like quantity (to which country's stores most of the products go) or value (to which country's stores do the products go which have the highest total value) may be relied on.

---

[299] But, as indicated, only if the claim arises out of a company's branch's operations.
[300] See CJEU C-386/05.

204

Partly other special jurisdiction rules (though with partly not optional but compulsory litigation venues) apply e.g. for **consumer contracts**[301]. These rules primarily apply to contracts related to which an entrepreneur *pursues* his/her activity in the country where the consumer is domiciled (e.g. a company having branch offices in this country and selling products there) or *directs* his/her activity to this country (e.g. a company having no branch etc. at this country but advertising in this country or having an online shop directed [also] at this country).

Concerning such contracts, the consumer may sue the entrepreneur at the consumer's or the entrepreneur's domicile (but not at the [diverging] place of performance!). By contrast, the entrepreneur may sue the consumer *only* at the consumer's domicile (with limited options of CoC agreements: primarily to be concluded only *after* the dispute has arisen). (Brussels Ia Art. 17 et seq., Lugano Art. 15 et seq.)

Regarding (extra-contractual) **tort claims**, i.e. damage compensation claims[302], parties have two possible places to bring the claim – alternatively the place where the event giving rise to the damage happened or the place where the damage itself occurred.[303] (Brussels Ia Art. 7, Lugano Art. 5)

**Example**

*Company A releases toxic substances in a cross-border river in country X, which ruins the crops of company B watered with this river's (now toxic) water in country Y.*

---

[301] I.e., in short, contracts between a consumer and an entrepreneur/company.

[302] Except unjust enrichment, e.g. when money is accidently transferred to an account, the payback claim is not covered by Brussels Ia.

[303] I.e. not the place where the damage was discovered or where consequential damages occurred.

B can sue A in country X (place of event giving rise to the damage) or in Y (place of damage).[304]

As mentioned, an EU MS's courts can also have *exclusive* jurisdiction, which means that these courts are the only venue for litigation and, therefore, the mentioned general and special rules are not applied.

This is the case e.g. with claims concerning rights of immovables, the validity of a company and its decisions, registration and validity of intellectual property and the enforcement of judgments. (Brussels Ia Art. 24, Lugano Art. 22; see *CoC agreements in Brussels Ia*)

A (simplified) **assessment which court has jurisdiction under Brussels Ia** can be done in the following order (if the answer is *no*, the respectively next point applies):

1. **Is it a matter contained in the exclusive jurisdiction list of Art. 24?**
2. **Is there a CoC agreement and/or was an appearance entered before a court?** If there is/was, Art. 25 and 26 may be applicable.
3. **Is a special jurisdiction rule with a protective intent applicable (employee, consumer, insured – Art. 10-23)?** If there is, the special jurisdiction venue may not be optional.
4. **Which other special jurisdiction rules (Art. 7-9) and which general jurisdiction rules (Art. 4) apply?**

Last but not least, Brussels Ia also regulates recognition and enforcement of judicial decisions in the EU except Denmark (see *International Recognition and Enforcement*).

---

[304] Provided that Brussels Ia is applicable.

# II. Alternative dispute resolution

Alternative dispute resolution (ADR) refers to **any means of resolving a dispute other than by litigation at a state court**.

This can be *legally binding* or *not*.

## 1. Non-binding alternative dispute resolution

It is always recommended to contract parties to first try the non-legally binding means and only then, if they do not lead to a satisfactory outcome, opt for the legally binding ADR means (or litigation).
This has to do with the fact that parties, when they arbitrate or litigate *against* each other, they are not a *team* interested in the satisfaction of both parties[305] any more. They are usually *opponents* that want to get out as much as possible only for themselves because the contractual relationship is often anyway over afterwards.

Apart from the time and money invested in such confrontative legally binding conflict resolution means, parties might have to find new contract partners/clients, which again costs effort, time and money. Finally, there is also a risk of loosing in any court or arbitral proceedings, which can be mitigated by a compromise agreement instead. This might not be "perfect"[306] for any party, but avoids the risk of one party (and again, we do not know for sure which one it will be) being the loser. Apart from that, it often has to bear also the court and lawyers' costs of the other party.

---

[305] With the final goal of a successful and for both sides beneficial (long term) contractual relationship.
[306] But *acceptable*.

Examples for **not legally binding dispute resolution** are negotiation, mediation and conciliation.

Whereas **negotiation** is *only between the parties* and should always be the first step thanks to no additional costs, not conveying the impression that the issue is a "big deal", etc.

**Mediation** is negotiation between the involved parties with an additional third party that is not part of the contract and is objective[307]. This third party generally is not allowed to make "new" proposals, i.e. bring into discussion ideas that were not already brought up by the parties.

Also in **conciliation** a third, non-involved and impartial party is called in. Here his/her role is stronger than in mediation though since he/she is allowed not only to propose solutions based on the parties' suggestions but also based on his/her own expertise and experience with the subject matter. This entails, of course, a certain risk that points are brought up that one party does not want to address. At the same time, satisfactory, practical solutions might be brought up parties just have not thought about, e.g. due to intense prior negotiations on a certain detail that lead them to "not seeing the wood for the trees" anymore.

Mediation and conciliation require parties to *agree* on it, i.e. on a third party getting all (or most/some of) the background information on the issue in question and often the contractual relationship. It implicates also arranging additional meetings with the mediator or conciliator and/or letting him/her participate at the parties' regular meetings.
This, in some cases, can already be complicated, also since mediation and conciliation provoke additional expenses by the parties.[308]

---

[307] E.g. not a business partner or family member of any of the parties.
[308] And this in a possibly already complicated situation where the parties might have already lost money.

These additional costs are regularly minimal though compared both to the value of the transactions they try to find a solution for and the costs arbitral or court proceedings entail.

Mediation and conciliation can take place unregulated[309] or by using rules that must be followed regulating e.g. the mediation agreement, the proceedings, the costs and confidentiality. The International Chamber of Commerce (ICC[310]) e.g. provides for such *Mediation Rules* (2014) parties in dispute can use.

---

[309] A confidentiality agreement being highly recommended though.
[310] Not to be confused with the often identically abbreviated *International Criminal Court*.

# 2. Arbitration

As for **legally binding alternative dispute resolution**, first[311] and foremost *arbitration* must be mentioned as a very commonly used ADR method in international business.

 **Arbitration** means that not an official court (with judges) but a private tribunal (with private persons called *arbitrators*) is made competent to solve the dispute.

## a. Arbitration agreements and rules

For arbitration taking place, in contrast to litigation, *always* a party agreement is necessary, e.g. an *arbitration clause* incorporated in the contract[312], but also arbitration agreements concluded later are generally valid.

Such agreements (and arbitration itself) are allowed by most states *instead* of litigation (or sometimes *prior to* it). If there is an arbitral agreement, state courts confronted with the case will typically deny litigation.

As for **rules on arbitration**, apart from **national law**, there are some **model laws**. These are laws developed commonly by an international

---

[311] There are other even less formal possibilities of alternative conflict resolution trials than arbitration: the so-called *mini-trials*, which are only binding in exceptional cases though. By informally carrying out proceedings (nearly) *as if they were real*, mini-trials are generally intended to provide the parties with a clearer view of the case (and its arguments and possible outcome) before negotiating a settlement or bringing it before an actual judicial court or arbitral tribunal.

[312] Arbitration can also be included in a Free Trade Agreement (FTA) or a Bilateral Investment Treaty (BIT), specifically for giving investors the possibility to demand their rights against the states in which they invested (investor-state dispute settlement, ISDS).

institution that *cannot be ratified* by countries but have the specific goal of countries *incorporating* them (voluntarily) in their national legal systems. This way a certain level of international legal consonance can be reached. The *UNCITRAL Model Law on International Commercial Arbitration* (1985/2006) has e.g. been adopted in 93 states.[313]

**International law** (NYC, see below) is specifically important regarding the international *recognition and enforcement* of arbitral decisions, whereas **EU Law** only plays a secondary role.

In an **arbitration agreement**[314] the parties commonly

1. **agree on final and binding dispute resolution by arbitration** with respect to a defined legal relationship

2. **choose a country**[315] where arbitration should take place
   i.e. either of the countries where the parties are based or do business or *neutral ground*, i.e. a third country none of the parties has a connection to

 If – both at *ad hoc* and institutional arbitration (see below) – parties refrain from determining the seat of the arbitral tribunal (nor have left this decision to an arbitral institution), the arbitral tribunal itself decides.

3. **choose** the **rules for arbitral procedure** provided by an arbitral or other institution[316]

---

[313] https://uncitral.un.org/en/texts/arbitration/modellaw/commercial_arbitration/status.

[314] To make sure also claims only loosely connected with the contract are covered by the arbitration agreement, the used wording should, as with CoC agreements, include both disputes *arising out* of the contract and those *relating to* it.

[315] And possibly, a more precise location withing that country.

[316] It must be noted though that, if parties opt for an arbitral institution administering their case (see next point), they might not be able to choose *any* set of procedural rules but e.g. just the one issued by this institution.

e.g. the *Arbitration Rules* of the UNCITRAL (2021), of the ICC (2021) or of the ICSID (2022, for investment disputes)

4. **choose an arbitral institution**, which *administers* the case[317], offers its premises for the party hearings and provides a pool of arbitrators the parties can choose from
e.g. the ICC's[318] *International Court of Arbitration* based in Paris, the *London Court of International Arbitration* (LCIA), the *Vienna International Arbitral Center* (VIAC), the *Permanent Court of Arbitration* in The Hague or the *International Centre for Settlement of Investment Disputes* (ICSID) in Washington, D.C.

! These *arbitration institutions*, despite their (misleading) designation as "courts", do **not** issue judgments/awards. This is done only by the respective arbitral tribunals that (only) carry out their work (hearings etc.) there and are supported by the institution procedurewise.

While point **1.** is a must for a valid arbitration clause, points **2.**, **3.** and **4.** are optional but highly recommended.

Apart from that, parties can already **appoint arbitrators** in the arbitration agreement, which usually is not advisable though. This has to do with possible validity concerns of the agreement and questions of how to proceed if an arbitrator later, when the dispute arises, rejects his/her actual appointment.
In addition, parties usually prefer to choose an arbitrator well suited (with detailed expert knowledge) for the specific subject matter the dispute is about. This often is impossible to know at the (earlier) moment when a contract including an arbitral agreement is concluded.

---

[317] Keeps the parties up to date, sends relevant documents to the parties/arbitrators, supervises the proceedings and deadlines, etc.
[318] See *INCOTERMS and ICC*.

Therefore, arbitrators are frequently appointed when the dispute has already arisen. Arbitrators are often trade officials, entrepreneurs, engineers, lawyers or (other) experts or professors in the field and can be proposed by the parties[319] or by the arbitral institution.

Parties can (and often do) carry out so-called ***ad hoc*** – arbitral procedures, which refers to arbitration without having selected an arbitral institution to administer the case. Instead of the premises of arbitral institution, *ad hoc* arbitration takes place e.g. at (one of) the parties' premises or a conference center or hotel.[320]
This usually saves them money[321] but denies them the important procedural aids provided by an arbitral institution.

*Parties **A** and **B** opt for less expensive ad hoc arbitration establishing that both parties appoint one arbitrator. **B**, who has less interest in the procedure, does not appoint his/her arbitrator despite several "gentle reminders" of **A**.*

**B**'s behavior could block the procedure. If an arbitral institution had been chosen, (additional institutional fees would apply but) it would step in with specialist staff and expertise to assist **A**.

---

[319] Commonly *one* or *three* arbitrators (depending on the procedural rules, if applicable). E.g. each party chooses respectively one arbitrator and the third arbitrator is chosen by the two arbitrators (chosen before by the parties).
[320] Institutional arbitration (with an arbitration institution administering the case) can also take place at another place than the institution's premises, e.g. if cheaper and/or more convenient for the parties.
[321] Arbitration is usually only chosen in cases with a higher dispute value (hundreds of thousands or millions of euros) due to the fixed costs of arbitrators and the arbitral institution. By contrast, before state courts the state "funds" to some extent low value cases. Therefore, *the lower the amount in dispute, the more expensive is arbitration compared to state courts*.

213

In such *ad hoc* – procedures, parties are completely free to determine procedural rules, e.g. the commonly in this case used *UNCITRAL Arbitration Rules*.[322]

These Rules do not come "in a package" with an arbitral institution but are independent in this sense.

Apart from provisions on the appointment of arbitrators, the UNCITRAL Arbitration rules cover

> notice requirements, representation of the parties, challenges of arbitrators, evidence, hearings, the place of arbitration, language, statements of claims and defense, pleas to the arbitrator's jurisdiction, provisional remedies, experts, default, rule waivers, the form and effect of the award, applicable law, settlement, interpretation of the award and costs.[323]

Parties should also not forget to **include a Choice-of-Law (CoL) clause** in their contract (!), which the arbitral tribunal has to apply to the dispute for giving a decision. This can be a state's national law, or, by incorporation into the contract, uniform law (such as the UNIDROIT Principles) or even international commercial practice (see *Modern Lex Mercatoria*).[324]

As soon as the arbitral tribunal has issued its decision ("award"), it is legally binding and has *res iudicata* **effect**, which means that parties cannot go to courts (or other arbitral tribunals) afterwards for appeal. Review (and consequential annulment of awards) in front of state courts

---

[322] If they refrain from doing so, the arbitral tribunal decides which (procedural) rules to apply to the proceedings.

[323] Folsom et al., 2016: 459, 460.

[324] If they refrain from doing so, the arbitral tribunal decides which (substantive) rules to apply to the merits of the case.

is generally only possible when there were grave procedural shortcomings.

## b. Some Pros & Cons of arbitration

### Why do parties opt for arbitration?

This often asked question has clearly to do with the other option parties have – *litigation before a state court.*

Judges at state courts have proven legal knowledge and must be impartial, which is generally guaranteed by the fact they are not bound by political and administrative instructions, and cannot be removed from office or forcibly transferred.[325]

By contrast, arbitrators do not necessarily have a legal education and, in light of parties often choosing "their" arbitrator, are sometimes biased.[326]

The reason why many parties in international business anyway opt for arbitration simply has to do with its many advantages:

1. Arbitral proceedings are often **faster** than court proceedings. Delays in arbitral decisions are relatively frequent though.

2. Arbitral awards normally **cannot be appealed**, which leads to legal certainty after a shorter period of time and is often preferred to e.g. years of litigation through several legal instances. This lack of appealability can, of course, also be disadvantageous, e.g. when awards are heavily biased.

---

[325] Unless expressly provided for by law.
[326] Of course, also judges are sometimes biased.

3. If arbitrators are chosen by the parties, they can be sure the arbitrators have the necessary specialized **expert knowledge**[327], e.g. for a complex matter of dispute.

4. Unlike court judgments, awards are **recognized and enforced worldwide (!)**, which is certainly the biggest advantage of arbitration in international business.

This is thanks to the ***New York Convention*** *on the Recognition and Enforcement of Foreign Arbitral Awards* (NYC, 1958), which has 172 state parties guaranteeing mutual recognition and enforcement of awards.[328] It is one the most successful international treaties ever in private law.

 While, apart from the EU, international recognition and enforcement of foreign *court judgments* is often complex and depends on the national enforcement rules of each country respectively, recognition and enforcement of foreign *arbitral awards* is guaranteed nearly everywhere in a uniform convention, the NYC.

The huge advantage of that for international business transactions cannot be emphasized enough.

The NYC applies if recognition and enforcement should take place in a member state and the place of arbitration (whose award is to be recognized/enforced) was in any (!) other state. It establishes that arbitration agreements must be recognized by its members' courts if they are in written form (NYC Art. I, III, *electronic* written form will suffice in most countries).

---

[327] These likely have more specific expertise than a judge who has to deal with a broad range of different matters.

[328] The only *grounds for refusal* are e.g. certain procedural errors, invalidity of the arbitration agreement or award under the applicable law (or the law of the country where arbitration took place) and *ordre public*. (NYC Art. V)

216

Therefore, if parties want to make sure their arbitration award is recognized and enforced,[329] they must conclude their arbitration agreement *in writing* and plan (and apply) for recognition and/or enforcement in a *NYC member*.

A party applying for recognition and enforcement in a NYC state must only supply **a)** the authenticated award (or an authenticated copy of it), **b)** the authenticated arbitration agreement (or an authenticated copy of it) and **c)** a certified translation of both, to the competent authorities of the to be recognizing and enforcing state. (NYC Art. IV)

For guaranteed enforceability and the other mentioned reasons, it is understandable that arbitration is often preferred to litigation.

It is, arguably, *not optimal*.

Possible partiality of arbitrators[330] and, also due to non-appealability, unjust decisions are risked by parties opting for arbitration. In addition, there are no pre-trial provisional remedies[331] in arbitration. Plus, arbitrators often tend to split the differences between the parties instead of fully vindicating legal rights.[332]

It is finally on the importance parties give a potentially just[333] decision and enforceability conditions if litigation or arbitration is considered more appropriate by them.

---

[329] In accordance with the NYC.

[330] *De iure*, partiality is forbidden also in arbitration, see e.g. in Austria *Zivilprozessordnung* § 588, 589 & 611 (ZPO, Austrian Code of Civil Procedure).

[331] E.g. freezing funds, denying access to a company's establishment (e.g. to avoid destruction of evidence).

[332] *Splitting the baby* instead of the *winner takes it all*. This may, nevertheless, be beneficial for strong and longstanding business relationships. (Folsom et al., 2016: 457)

[333] This does not mean, of course, that arbitral awards are always unjust, which is not the case. The parties normally not being able to choose their judge(s) (but their arbitrator[s]) and non-appealability of arbitral awards are facts though.

# III. International Conflict of Laws

If one state's court has jurisdiction over an international business matter, this means that this court will apply the *procedural* law (timeframes of the proceedings, pleadings, motions, rules for evidence…) of the state where it is located.

*BUT* this does **not** mean that this state's *substantive* law ("lex fori") is applicable.[334]

If that was the case, it would cause a "race to the court", i.e. parties suing or requiring declaratory decisions at courts (declaratory relief[335]) without trying to solve issues amicably first just because they want a specific law to be applicable.

**Example**

*Contract parties **A** and **B** have been discussing for a while about a contractual question with no outcome. The application of French (substantive) law seems far more advantageous than Austrian law for **A** to get what she wants.*

*Variant a) According to the general and special jurisdiction rules of the applicable Brussels Ia Regulation, the courts of **both** countries (Austria **and** France) are possible places for litigation (both courts have jurisdiction).*

*Variant b) Since **A** is domiciled in Austria and **B** in France, the general place of litigation (defendant's domicile) is **either** France (if **A** sues **B**) **or**, if **B** sues*

---

[334] Whereas a *court* (a judicial authority) does not always apply its "own" state's substantive law, *administrative authorities* usually always do apply their "own" state's (public) law.

[335] A declaratory judgment of a court stating the rights and (existing or non-existing) obligations of the parties (e.g. party **A** does not owe anything to party **B**) without ordering specific actions or awarding damage compensation.

*A, Austria according to Brussels Ia. There are no alternative (special) places of litigation.*

A supposed possibility to influence the applicable law (*if the substantive law applied by a court was automatically the law of the state where it is located*), will in both **a)** and **b)** most likely lead to **A** suing **B** at the French courts without hesitation and further negotiations. Or, if **B** considers that Austrian substantive law is more beneficial for him than French law, he would try to be the first one in suing **A** at the Austrian courts.

If in **b)** **A** was domiciled in France (not Austria) and **B** in Austria (not France) and still the French law seems most beneficial for **A**, **A** might cause additional frictions to the contractual relationship to make **B** sue her at the (preferred) French courts.

Both omitting further negotiations and causing frictions on purpose is not optimal for party harmony and a solid contractual relationship.

Therefore, court competence does not necessarily mean that "its" national substantive law is applied.

If the substantive law of the state where the court is located is not automatically applied,

**how to find out which law to apply to the case?**

Basically every state (and the EU) has its own so-called **Conflict-of-Laws rules** ("statute"), which determine which state's substantive rules ("lex") are applicable.

This regulation of international conflict of laws is often seen as the core of Private International Law.

> **!** Conflict-of-Laws rules are only applied though if there is no *uniform law* regulating the matter.

If uniform law, such as the CISG[336] or CMR[337], is in place (e.g. thanks to a state having ratified it), in its area of application, the competent court does *not* apply its country's Conflict-of-Laws rules. Instead, it applies the relevant uniform law.

If uniform law does not cover all matters of a dispute (what is often the case), the competent court anyway has to apply its country's Conflict-of-Laws rules to find out which law it finally must apply to these remaining matters.

### But which Conflict-of-Laws rules to apply?

The Conflict-of-Laws rules of the *state whose courts are competent* are applicable. That means that the court dealing with the case does not only apply the procedural rules of the state where it is located but also its Conflict-of-Laws rules. In the EU, these rules are mostly harmonized by Regulations common to all EU MS except Denmark.[338]

That is why, if certain conditions are met (see *EU Regulations and Rome I*), an EU court commonly does not apply the Conflict-of-Laws rules of its "own" country but an EU Regulation instead.

This has the advantage that, no matter to which court in the EU we go, we (theoretically) get the same substantive result, e.g. *not* one and the same contract being considered valid or not because different law is applied to it.

---

[336] *United Nations Convention on Contracts for the International Sale of Goods*, which all EU MS except Malta have ratified.

[337] *Convention on the Contract for the International Carriage of Goods by Road*, which all EU MS have ratified.

[338] The so-called Rome I Regulation (contractual obligations), Rome II Regulation (non-contractual obligations), Rome III Regulation (divorce and legal separation; but with several MS not participating), Succession Regulation, etc.

*If foreign law is applicable as a result of the application of the Conflict-of-Laws rules, what does the court do?*

Once an applicable state's (or other) law has been determined by means of the Conflict-of-Laws rules by the court having jurisdiction, it must apply this law to the merits of the dispute.[339]

This is, of course, often challenging because the competent judge most likely does not have broad knowledge and insight of every foreign legal order including foreign judgments/case law, scholarly opinions, etc.

That is why the court applying foreign law typically has wide latitude in determining it, with the parties commonly providing experts to explain the most substantial characteristics of the foreign legal system and the specific legal rules in relation to the case subject. Often affidavits (official declarations by the parties/experts under oath etc.) including translations of the applicable legal provisions are submitted.

If the support of the parties to the conflict is not given or insufficient, the court will typically inquire at the Ministry of Justice[340] of the country where it is located. If necessary, it will request experts' opinions on the subject (e.g. from a university professor from its "own" country or the foreign country whose law is applied). If none of that leads to a sufficient outcome in reasonable time, i.e. the court still is unsure which specific legal provisions are applicable and how to interpret/apply them, the court commonly can apply its "own" country's law instead.[341]

Another occasion when the national substantive law of the place of the court (*lex fori*) is applied is when compulsory provisions apply. These are **a)** so-called *overriding mandatory provisions*, referring primarily to laws

---

[339] E.g. if the contract was breached, there is warranty or damages to be compensated for.
[340] See e.g. Austrian Federal Law on Private International Law (IPRG) §4.
[341] So – although Conflict-of-Laws rules and the law they refer to prevail – there is still a chance that the court applies its own national law instead. This nevertheless is not the regular case.

with a protective intent (of weaker parties or public interests[342]), and **b)** those concerned with *public order (ordre public)*, referring to general public values and order (expressed by certain laws).[343]
If there are *overriding mandatory* or *ordre public* provisions, the national legal order does not replace entirely the foreign legal order applicable according to Conflict-of-Laws rules. They only override individual provisions of foreign law in their (limited) scope, i.e. just in the matters they regulate (see also *EU Regulations and Rome I*). All other provisions of the foreign legal order must still be applied.

For assessing if an *overriding mandatory provision* of the *lex fori* should be given effect to, Rome I establishes some criteria: nature & purpose of the provision and consequences of its [non-] application. (Rome I Art. 9)

Incompatibility with *ordre public* must be "manifest"(Rome I Art. 21) and is regarded at the very end of the analysis determining which law to apply. They are the subject of somewhat of a *negative control of the results* of one's *Which law is applied*-analysis.

---

[342] E.g. in Austria in consumer law (e.g. in GTC with consumers: grossly disadvantaging incidental provisions as well as objectively unusual, surprising provisions [ABGB §864a & 879]), employee protection and immovable property transfer rules.
[343] E.g. in Austria and several other European states expropriation without compensation, succession only for male heirs, legal impossibility of compensation for pain and suffering, legal impossibility of dissolution of marriage...

## a. Choice-of-Law Agreements

Similarly[344] to CoC agreements (see chapter above), parties are mostly free to decide which law to apply to their contract and related matters in international business.[345]

A basic requirement that regularly must be given though is that the contract etc. has a **foreign (international) element**, i.e. that parties are domiciled/based in different countries and/or their contract is concluded and/or executed in another country.

If parties agree on foreign law being applied to their purely national contract (with all of its elements in one country), usually the national law of the country where all these elements are located is applied – this entirely or only regarding peremptory law (whereas non-peremptory national law is replaced by the chosen foreign law[346]).

As with forum selection, some legal orders also require a minimum link between the parties/case and the chosen legal order for Choice-of-Law agreements being valid/effective.[347] In the EU, i.e. when a European court has jurisdiction, party freedom in this regard is specifically pronounced. (see e.g. Rome I Art. 3, Rome II Art. 14)

Such Choice-of-Law (CoL) agreements are regularly included in the contract *upfront*, usually in the same section of the contract as Choice-of-

---

[344] But maybe a bit more limited.

[345] But often not e.g. in family law, property law, consumer private law, etc.

[346] This is e.g. the case in the EU. (Rome I Art. 3)

[347] E.g. generally US commercial transactions, where the Uniform Commercial Code (UCC) requires "a reasonable relation" between the transaction and the state chosen by the parties whose law should be applied. (UCC §1-301)

223

Court (CoC) agreements. But they can also be made later, e.g. after the dispute has already arisen.

For predictability and certainty reasons (and to avoid later discussions on it), it is highly recommended for parties to incorporate both a CoC and a CoL already in their contract.

 As with CoC clauses, a CoL clause should be drafted in an *obligatory* manner (mandatory[348] and exclusive) to avoid later discussions with the other contract party.

 It is also recommended to formulate it in a *broad* way, in order to cover not only disputes connected directly to (arising from) the contract but also issues *related* (indirectly) to it.

Formally, a *choice of law* can only be made regarding national law of a country and not concerning *uniform law*[349], such as the UN Sales Convention (CISG) and the UNIDROIT Principles (PICC, see corresponding chapters below).

Nevertheless, uniform law can be included in the contract – as part of the parties' private autonomy – not by a formal *choice of law* but (only) by *incorporating* it in the contract (as parties can do with GTC). This way, the CISG or PICC are applied to the contractual relationship.

Since uniform law does not cover all possible matters of a dispute though, in addition the national law of a country always applies for the

---

[348] *Mandatory* means that the parties do *not* include in their CoL clause that the law of two (or more or any) countries can be applied to the contract from which (one of) the parties then should choose one but only *one* country's law. It happens very rarely though that parties formulate a CoL in a permissive (not mandatory) way.
*Exclusive* means that *only* the law chosen (and not optionally also the law the Conflict-of-Laws rules lead to) is applicable.
[349] I.e. sets of (in our case) substantive law with several states applying them, typically of an international non-state nature.

case that the incorporated uniform law does not cover a relevant matter.[350]

Thus, parties can choose both e.g. the PICC **and**, *subsidiarily*, a national law (with the national law only actually being applied if a relevant matter is not covered by the PICC etc.).

Irrespective of uniform law being incorporated *and* a national law chosen **or** *only* a national law chosen, special attention must be given to the choice of law of *states that are parties of the CISG*:

> If contract parties e.g. decide in their sales contract that Austrian law should be applied, this *includes* the CISG (of which Austria is a member), resulting in not the Austrian internal law being applied to the contract but (mainly) the CISG.
> If they do not want that, apart from choosing Austrian law, they must *expressly exclude the CISG from being applied*.

As mentioned, wherever *overriding mandatory* or *public policy* provisions apply, the applicable law may be interfered with by individual national rules of the state where the competent court is located.

The question if the CoL agreement is valid materially is answered commonly by the national law chosen in the agreement.[351]

---

[350] Apart from the national law being a "gap filler", its peremptory provisions override incorporated law.
[351] E.g. in the area of application of Rome I (contractual obligations).

## b. EU Regulations and Rome I

As mentioned, for a court deciding which law to apply to the merits of a dispute, it relies on the Conflict-of-Laws rules[352] of the country where it is located.

In the EU member states (MS) except Denmark common EU Regulations are applied though in their respective area of application instead of national Conflict-of-Laws rules.

These cover

1. Contractual obligations (Rome I Regulation[353]),
2. Non-contractual obligations (Rome II Regulation[354]),
3. Divorce and separation (Rome III Regulation[355], limited to 17 of the 27 EU MS),
4. Matrimonial property and of registered partnerships[356] (including also jurisdiction and enforcement, limited to 18 of the 27 EU MS)
5. Maintenance of families[357] (including also jurisdiction and enforcement) and

---

[352] If and in the areas where no *uniform law* is applicable.

[353] Regulation (EC) No 593/2008 of the European Parliament and of the Council of 17 June 2008 on the law applicable to contractual obligations.

[354] Regulation (EC) No 864/2007 of the European Parliament and of the Council of 11 July 2007 on the law applicable to non-contractual obligations.

[355] Council Regulation (EU) No 1259/2010 of 20 December 2010 implementing enhanced cooperation in the area of the law applicable to divorce and legal separation.

[356] Council Regulation (EU) 2016/1103 of 24 June 2016 implementing enhanced cooperation in the area of jurisdiction, applicable law and the recognition and enforcement of decisions in matters of matrimonial property regimes.
Council Regulation (EU) 2016/1104 of 24 June 2016 implementing enhanced cooperation in the area of jurisdiction, applicable law and the recognition and enforcement of decisions in matters of the property consequences of registered partnerships.

[357] Council Regulation (EC) No 4/2009 of 18 December 2008 on jurisdiction, applicable law, recognition and enforcement of decisions and cooperation in matters relating to maintenance obligations.

6. Succession[358] (including also jurisdiction and enforcement).

In the remaining areas (e.g. company law, creation of marriages, parentage, property law and capacity) the internal (national) Conflict-of-Laws[359] rules of the state whose court has jurisdiction and deals with the case are applied.

Contractual relationships being most relevant for international business transactions, let us have an illustrative view at the Rome I Regulation (*Rome I*).

Rome I regulates Conflict-of-Laws in the EU MS except Denmark[360] in contractual relationships in **1. civil and commercial matters** excluding the areas covered by other EU Regulations (see above) as well as e.g. company law (including the validity of a company and its decisions) and securities law, questions of status and legal capacity of natural persons and CoC and arbitration agreements. (Rome I Art. 1)

Apart from this material scope of application, the main requirements for Rome I being applied are that **2.** the merits of the case have a **foreign element** (no matter to which EU or non-EU country (!); Rome I Art. 1) and

---

[358] Regulation (EU) No 650/2012 of the European Parliament and of the Council of 4 July 2012 on jurisdiction, applicable law, recognition and enforcement of decisions and acceptance and enforcement of authentic instruments in matters of succession and on the creation of a European Certificate of Succession.

[359] E.g. in Austria the (federal) *Bundesgesetz über das internationale Privatrecht* (IPRG). By contrast, in the United States there is no unified regulation for determining conflicts of law. There the Conflict-of-Laws rules are the case law of the US state where the competent federal court is located, which varies considerably from state to state. (Folsom et al., 2016: 445)

[360] The preceding *Rome Convention* (1980) is still applicable in Denmark and some of the MS's overseas territories. The UK has adopted a materially with the Rome regime mostly coincident Conflict-of-Laws regime (on a domestic level) and is not bound any more by the CJEU's decisions.

**3.** an **EU court** (except Denmark) has jurisdiction (and deals with the case).[361]

## Validity of the contract (including CoL agreements) in Rome I

Rome I regulates which country's law is applied if the parties have *not* concluded a CoL agreement[362]. At the same time though it acknowledges the freedom of choice and, establishes as a first rule that "a contract shall be governed by the law chosen by the parties"(Rome I Art. 3).

It establishes some lax general criteria for CoL agreements (explicit or implicit but clearly demonstrated conclusion[363]), the remaining **material validity** (vitiated consent, legal capacity of parties, legality of content, etc.) of the agreement being determined by the law chosen by the parties. This rule *also* applies to the *rest of the contract.* (Rome I Art. 3)

By contrast, the **formal validity** of the CoL agreement and *also of the remaining contract*, is given if it is in accordance with *optionally*:

a) the law of the country where either of the parties is at contract conclusion (if they are in the same country, only this country) or
b) the law of the country where either of the parties has his/her habitual residence at contract conclusion or
c) the law chosen in the CoL agreement by the parties. (Rome I Art. 11)

---

[361] Rome I is *universal* in the sense that – in contrast to Brussels Ia – it is not necessary that the defendant is based in the EU; it can also be based in a third (non-EU) state and Rome I may anyway be applicable. *Universality* of Rome I is also given due to the fact that its rules might lead to the law of a *non-EU* state, which then has to be applied by an *EU* court to a case. (see below)

[362] And no *uniform law* is applicable (see initial part of the chapter "International Conflict of Laws").

[363] A CoC agreement in favor of one state's courts is e.g. a strong indication for the parties having agreed implicitly also on this state's law being applied.

In face of this variety of options, it is regularly the case that at least one of the mentioned laws provides for no formal requirements for CoL agreements. Therefore, parties are relatively free how and also *when*[364] and regarding *which law*[365] to conclude the CoL agreement.

Peremptory & overriding mandatory provisions and *ordre public*

As for the law applicable to the contract, Rome I establishes that in **cases with no foreign elements**, the national ***peremptory*** law provisions (*ius cogens*) of the state where the competent court is located must be applied. This means that, in such cases, the chosen[366] foreign law is applied *only* where the court's national law (*lex fori*) provides for the parties' possibility of altering or waiving provisions[367]. (Rome I Art. 3)

In cases with **foreign elements**, but which **do not exceed the EU's** internal market (all EU MS), EU peremptory law must be applied. This is only relevant if parties choose non-EU Law to be applied (otherwise EU Law would anyway be applied). (Rome I Art. 3)

Not to be confused with the just mentioned *peremptory* provisions of the *lex fori* which generally *are* replaced by the foreign law chosen (or otherwise applicable) by the parties (just not in contracts with no foreign elements (!)), so-called ***mandatory*** and ***ordre public*** (public policy) provisions *always* override the otherwise applicable foreign law.

---

[364] Before or at contract conclusion (e.g. as a contractual clause) but also after, even during proceedings (!). (Rome I Art. 3)

[365] Uniform law like the CISG or basically the law of any of the world's states.

[366] In this case it can only be the law *chosen by the parties* (and not also the law determined by the general Conflict-of-Laws rules) because the general Conflict-of-Laws rules do not lead to a foreign law *if there are no foreign elements*.

[367] "provisions of the law of that other country which cannot be derogated from by agreement" (Rome I Art. 3).

In other words, mandatory and public policy provisions are those provisions of the legal order where the competent court is located[368] that *always and in any case* are applied. They are narrower and to be construed more restrictively than *peremptory* provisions. (Rome I, Preamble (37))

Rome I provides for such cases

1. if the respect for *overriding mandatory* provisions "is regarded as crucial by a country for safeguarding its **public interests**, such as its political, social or economic organization" (Rome I Art. 9) and
2. if (otherwise) applicable foreign law "is manifestly incompatible with the **public policy** (*ordre public*) of the forum" (Rome I Art.21).[369]
   Manifest incompatibilities with *ordre public* are looked for at the very end of one's *Which law is applied*-analysis.

## Applicable law without CoL agreement in Rome I

As mentioned, it is highly recommended for parties to incorporate a CoL agreement in their contract and Rome I also provides for it as the standard case. But it can (and does) happen that parties forget about it, do not want to bring this issue up at contract conclusion or cannot agree on one legal order to be applicable.

---

[368] As for *overriding mandatory* provisions, also those of the law of the country where the contractual obligations are *performed* may be taken into account in limited cases. (Rome I Art. 9)

[369] Bold print added. As for the difference between public *interests* and *policy* see the examples mentioned in the initial part of the chapter *International Conflict of Laws*.

*Which law is applied to the contract if parties refrain from choosing it?*

Uniform law, if applicable and in the material scope it covers.[370] If uniform law is not applicable or, if it is, for matters not covered by it, the following applies:

Whereas parties usually have several options by law which *court* is competent (although they did not choose any court; see *Brussels Ia Regulation*), Rome I provides for only one option of *applicable law*.

This means that in Brussels Ia both the general *and* special rules can apply and they are optional/cumulative, and in Rome I *only one* rule applies which is obligatory/exclusionary.[371]

Rome I provides for special rules in those cases where Brussels Ia establishes special rules *due to the necessity of protection* of the typically "weaker" party, i.e. consumer, insurance and employment contracts. Additionally, there is a special rule for carriage contracts in Rome I.

Apart from these cases, i.e. if it is *any other contract type*, (only) the **"standard" rules of Rome I** apply.

These clarify, depending on the contract type, that the law of the following country is applied:

a) **Sales contract** – country of habitual residence of the seller
b) **Services contract** – country of habitual residence of the service provider
c) **Contract** relating to **rights in rem** or **long-term tenancies**[372] of **immovables** – country of location of the immovable

---

[370] See initial part of the chapter *International Conflict of Laws*.

[371] Rome I (only contractual obligations) is also narrower in scope than Brussels Ia, which covers also non-contractual claims.

[372] If tenancies have a duration of maximum six months, the country of habitual residence of the landlord and the tenant (if it is the same country and the tenant is a natural person). (Rome I Art. 4)

d) **Franchise contract** – country of habitual residence of the franchisee
e) **Distribution contract** – country of habitual residence of the distributor
f) **Auction sales contract** – country where auction takes place
g) **Contract on financial instruments** in the context of stock exchanges – generally country that supervises the trading system[373]
(Rome I Art. 4)

*All other*[374] contracts than carriage, consumer, insurance and employment contracts and those just mentioned in points **a)** to **g)**, are subject to the law where the party effecting the "**characteristic performance**" has his/her habitual residence. [375]

 The *characteristic* performance is generally the act (or omission) that is **not monetary**.[376] This means that the party that does not pay for something but has to do (or *not* do) something (and usually gets paid for it) typically effects the characteristic performance in a contract.

The ***habitual residence*** of legal persons (e.g. companies) is their *place of central administration* and of entrepreneurs (natural persons acting in the course of their business activity) their *principal place of business*[377]. If the

---

[373] Verschraegen in Rummel/Lukas/Geroldinger, 2023, Art. 4 Rom I-VO.

[374] E.g. bank contracts (with clients generally the bank effects the characteristic performance), hedges (e.g. sureties where the guarantor effects the characteristic performance), licensing contracts of intellectual property rights (the holder of the right effecting the characteristic performance).

[375] In this point, many national Conflict-of-Laws rules coincide with Rome I. E.g. the Austrian IPRG also refers to the law of the state, where the party that provides the characteristic performance has/her its habitual residence (in the absence of a CoL agreement). (IPRG §35)

[376] In some cases, e.g. credit contracts, also a monetary performance can be characteristic (e.g. the payment of the credit amount by the bank to its client).

[377] Note that, in contrast, Brussels Ia offers various options for where a company can be considered to be *domiciled*: the *principal place of business* (as in Rome I), but alternatively also the *statutory seat* or the *administrative seat* of the company. (Brussels Ia Art. 63)

contract was concluded by a branch (or other similar establishment) or the branch must perform the contractual obligations, *habitual residence* refers to the *place where the branch is located*.

The relevant moment of when to determine the habitual residence is *contract conclusion*. (Rome I Art. 19)

Where "all the circumstances of the case" point at another country due to **manifestly closer links**[378] to this country, this country's law must be applied instead of the mentioned rules for different contract types (points **a)** to **g)**) and the *characteristic performance* rule.

This is also the case for contracts not included in the mentioned list that by nature do not have a characteristic performance (e.g. barter contracts).

Let us have an illustrative view at two of the four contract types Rome I has **special rules** for (carriage, consumer, insurance and employment contracts) – *carriage contracts* and *consumer contracts*.

As for **carriage contracts**[379], Rome I distinguishes between carriage of goods and of passengers.

For *carriage of goods* the law of the country where the carrier has his/her habitual residence applies if the (initial) receipt, (final) delivery, or habitual residence of the consignor are also situated in this country. If not, the law of the place of delivery is applicable.

However, parties can freely conclude CoL agreements that diverge from these applicable laws. (Rome I Art. 5)

---

[378] Even though one could suppose that there is a similar *manifestly closer links*-rule for jurisdiction (court competence), in civil and commercial matters there is **no** such rule. So even though there are *manifestly closer links* to a country('s courts) *other* than the one determined in accordance with the regular jurisdiction rules, this other country's courts do not become competent.

[379] Including consumer contracts.

233

To *carriage of passengers* contracts the law of the country where the passenger has his/her habitual residence applies, if the departure or destination is in this country. If not, the law of the country where the carrier has his/her habitual residence applies.

Party freedom regarding CoL agreements is limited in carriage of passenger contracts. Only the law of the country of the

- passenger's habitual residence,
- carrier's habitual residence or his/her central administration,
- place of departure or
- place of destination

can be chosen. That means that a state's law to which the parties or the contract have no connection at all cannot be chosen. (Art. 5 Rome I)

It is important to mention though that in international transport law there are some **international agreements,** such as the *Convention on the Contract for the International Carriage of Goods by Road* (CMR). All EU member states are parties to the convention, along with 31 other states (58 parties in total). CMR's and the other pertinent conventions[380] replace Rome I in their area of application. Rome I and the applicable law it leads to then only serve as a gap filler for matters not covered by the CMR.

**Consumer contracts**[381] are contracts between a consumer[382] and an entrepreneur that *pursues* his/her activity in the country where the consumer has his/her habitual residence (e.g. a company having branch offices in this country and selling products there) or *directs* his/her activity to this country (e.g. a company having no branch etc. at this

---

[380] E.g. the *Convention concerning International Carriage by Rail* (COTIF) including the appendix *Uniform Rules concerning the Contract for International Carriage of Passengers and Luggage by Rail* (CIV), and the *Convention for the Unification of Certain Rules for International Carriage by Air* ("Montreal Convention").

[381] Excluding e.g. carriage contracts, rights in rem and tenancy of immovables.

[382] A natural person concluding the contract not for business reasons.

country but advertising in this country or having an online shop directed [also] at this country).[383]

These contracts are subject to the law of the country where the consumer has his/her habitual residence. (Rome I Art. 6)

Apart from that, CoL agreements are limited in consumer contracts so that the *peremptory* provisions[384] of the law of the state of habitual residence of the consumer must *in any case* be applied. Therefore, if another country's law is chosen, its provisions are only applied in the areas where the habitual residence state's law can be derogated from.[385]

Rome I has a **universal** character: It is possible that Rome I's (standard or special) Conflict-of-Laws rules lead (not only to an EU MS's law but also) to a **non-EU** state's law. This law must be applied by the court dealing with the case.

 It can (and does) happen that an **EU court** must apply **non-EU law**, i.e. the law of a country that is not an EU MS (!).

---

[383] This consumer contract concept coincides with its equivalent in Brussels Ia (see above).

[384] Peremptory provisions are usually only applied if the contract has no foreign elements (in this case the peremptory provisions of the *lex fori*), see *Peremptory & overriding mandatory provisions and ordre public*.

[385] This means that, depending on the configuration of the national (consumer) law of the consumer's habitual residence (peremptory or not), this law is often applied in all cases where it is more advantageous for the consumer (e.g. in Austria, KSchG §13a). This means that, in the end, the otherwise applicable law and the law of the consumer's habitual residence must be compared, so that the more advantageous one of both is applied.

A (simplified) **assessment which law is applicable** can be done in the following order (if the answer is *yes*, the respectively next point applies):

1. **Is it a case involving foreign elements?** If not, the *lex fori* is applicable.
2. **Is *no* uniform law applicable?** If it is, the uniform law, e.g. the CISG, is applicable (and in areas not covered by it, the law determined with the applicable Conflict-of-Laws rules or chosen in a CoL agreement).
3. **Is an EU Regulation on applicable law applicable?** If not, the internal *Conflict-of-Laws rules of the* state where the court is located are applicable.
4. **Are there no overriding mandatory provisions applicable?** If there are, these provisions override the otherwise applicable provisions (with the rest of the otherwise applicable law still being applied). (Rome I Art. 9)
5. **Is there *no* valid CoL agreement?** If there is, the law chosen in the CoL agreement is generally applicable. (Rome I Art. 3, 10, 11, 13)
6. **Is it *no* carriage, consumer, insurance and employment contract?** If it is, Rome I Art. 5-8 are applicable.
7. **Then the "standard" rules of Rome I Art. 4 apply.**
8. **Are there no *ordre public* provisions applicable?** If there are, these provisions replace the otherwise applicable provisions (with the rest of the otherwise applicable law still being applied). (Rome I Art. 21)

# IV. International Recognition and Enforcement

In the preceding chapters we saw *which court* deals with our case and *which law* it must apply to "solve" our case. If this court now issues a judgment, parties must *follow the measures and orders* contained in it.

This is regularly not a problem if these orders must be fulfilled in the same country where the court is located because the national authorities are bound by a national judicial organ's decisions and will "make" the parties comply with it.

If this judgment's content must be fulfilled in another state, party compliance with it regularly is not guaranteed because the authorities of one state are not necessarily bound by the decisions made in another state.

Since parties do not litigate as an aim in itself but due to the (binding and enforceable) effects of its results, guaranteed recognition and enforcement of judgments is of the utmost importance in international business.

Recognition and enforcement of judicial decisions is mainly a **A) matter of national concern**. If the conditions established by the national law of a country[386] are met, also foreign judgments can be enforced. This fact, unfortunately, implies a broad variety of different rules and, in the end, often huge difficulties to *enforce* a judgment in an other country than the one where the deciding court is located.

Apart from enforcement, where judgments are only (or also) of a declaratory nature, i.e. stating the rights and (existing or non-existing)

---

[386] In Austria e.g. such a national law dealing with recognition and enforcement is the *Exekutionsordnung* (EO). Austria being a member of the EU, the EO is in many cases excluded from application though due to Brussels Ia, which mostly is applied instead (see *Recognition and Enforcement in Brussels Ia and Lugano*).

obligations of the parties[387] without ordering specific actions or awarding damage compensation, *recognition* of judgments is of importance.

Therefore, some **B) international conventions** emerged, such as the mentioned *Hague Convention on Choice of Court Agreements* (*Hague Convention*, 2005)[388] and the *Hague Judgments Convention* (HJC, 2019). These are, unfortunately, (still) relatively limited in state participation, the former currently having 34[389] and the latter 29[390] state parties.

These guarantee, with some exceptions[391], the recognition and enforcement of judgments between their respective member states.[392] The *Hague Convention on CoC Agreements*, however, regulates enforcement of judgments *only* as a result of a court having jurisdiction *thanks to a CoC agreement* (!)[393] (Hague Convention Art. 3).

Between the EU MS (except Denmark) and the *non-Brussels Ia states* Denmark, Norway, Iceland, Switzerland, the *Lugano Convention* (*Lugano*, 2007), which covers both jurisdiction and recognition&enforcement, is applicable (see *CoC agreements in international treaties* and below).

Apart from these (and other) multilateral agreements, there are several *bilateral* international agreements, which provide for reciprocal

---

[387] E.g. party **A** does not owe anything to party **B**.
[388] See also "CoC agreements in international treaties".
[389] All 27 EU MS as well as Albania, Montenegro, Moldova, Ukraine, United Kingdom, Mexico and Singapore.
[390] All EU MS except Denmark as well as Ukraine, United Kingdom and Uruguay.
[391] E.g. *punitive damages*, i.e. awarding a compensation for damages that exceeds the damage sum (the actual loss or harm suffered). (Hague Convention Art. 11, HJC Art. 10) Apart from that, several matters are excluded from the Conventions, e.g. family and inheritance law, status and legal capacity of natural persons, carriage, insolvency, validity of companies and their decisions, etc.
[392] If these are effective and enforceable in their "home" member states. (Hague Convention Art. 8, HJC Art. 4)
[393] Between EU MS Brussels Ia is applied instead though.

recognition and enforcement of the judgments of the courts of both state parties.

In the **C) European Union** (EU) recognition and enforcement of judgments of an other EU member state is generally granted and sort of automatic.

This is thanks to the mentioned Brussels Ia Regulation (*Brussels Ia*), which is supplemented by additional EU legislative acts focusing on (automatically recognized and enforced) order for payments and small claims procedure.[394]

*Recognition and Enforcement in Brussels Ia and Lugano*

**Brussels Ia**, as mentioned[395] covers two big areas: *1. Jurisdiction* and *2. Recognition and Enforcement*.

*As for the former*, Brussels Ia establishes formal criteria for **CoC agreements**, which generally permits the parties to *choose* the court competent for resolving their dispute. It also covers the case in which the defendant **appears before a** (possibly not competent) **court**, this act conferring jurisdiction to it. And, finally, if neither is the case, Brussels Ia provides for a detailed **rules pattern** that enables a seised court to find out which court actually has **jurisdiction** (see *Brussels Ia Regulation*)

*As for the latter (Recognition and Enforcement),* Brussels Ia provides for the recognition and enforcement in one EU MS (except Denmark) of *any*

---

[394] EU Regulations 1896/2006, 861/2007 and 2015/2421.
[395] See *CoC agreements in Brussels Ia* and *Brussels Ia Regulation*.

239

decision[396] issued by the courts of an other EU MS (except Denmark). It is of no importance according to which law the deciding court had jurisdiction nor where the parties are based. It is necessary though that the decision to be enforced elsewhere is enforceable in the country where it was issued. (Brussels Ia Art. 39)

These decisions are recognized automatically without the necessity of a procedure.[397] Also enforcement in the scope of Brussels Ia does *not* require a declaration of enforceability ("exequatur"). (Brussels Ia Art. 39)

The only requirements are that the person seeking recognition and enforcement[398] provides the competent recognizing foreign court or authority[399] with

> 1. an **authentic[400] copy of the judgment**,

> 2. a **certificate with the main information** of the decision issued by the original court[401] and

> 3., if required by the recognizing court or authority, a **translation** of the judgment or the certificate. (Brussels Ia Art. 37, 53)

A judgment must be enforced by the state in which its enforcement is sought according to its national enforcement law.[402] If the foreign judgment already includes concrete enforcement measures/orders that are *not known* in the enforcing state's law, a measure with "equivalent

---

[396] Including authentic instruments (official documents) and court settlements. (Brussels Ia Art. 58, 59)

[397] If recognition of the judgment is refused, any interested party can apply for a "decision that there are no grounds for refusal" (Brussels Ia Art. 36)

[398] Which is the judgment *creditor*, e.g. the party entitled to payment or a certain action by the other party (*debtor*).

[399] Information on the competent court and related matters can be found e.g. in the *European Judicial Atlas in civil matters*, available on https://e-justice.europa.eu/.

[400] Authenticated (certified) according to the legal requirements of the state where recognition and enforcement should take place.

[401] For which a form is provided in Annex I of Brussels Ia.

[402] Under the *same conditions as national judgments* of the enforcing state. (Brussels Ia Art. 41)

effects" and "similar aims and interests" must be applied by the enforcing court/authority. (Brussels Ia Art. 39, 54)

The person against who the enforcement is sought[403] can **apply for refusal** of enforcement (Brussels Ia Art. 46, 47) Possible grounds for this refusal are all grounds existing under the law of the enforcing state *and* those listed in Brussel Ia (e.g. *ordre public*; irreconcilability with other judgments between the parties; conflict with Brussel Ia's protective provisions for consumers, employees and insureds; etc.). (Brussels Ia Art. 45)

Let us have a quick look at the points where the recognition and enforcement provisions of the **Lugano Convention** – applicable in the EU (including Denmark), Norway, Iceland and Switzerland – and of Brussels Ia differ.

Judgments of the EU MS' (except Denmark's) courts are recognized and enforced in the *only-Lugano* states Denmark, Norway, Iceland, Switzerland) and *vice-versa* according to the Lugano Convention.

*Recognition* is similarly automatic as in Brussels Ia and does not require a special procedure. (Lugano Art. 33).

There is an important difference though regarding *enforcement*:

> **!** While enforcement in Brussels Ia does *not* require a declaration of enforceability ("exequatur"), in Lugano such a procedure *is* necessary. (Brussels Ia Art. 39, Lugano Art. 38 et seq., 53 et seq.)

Another difference is that Lugano requires the person seeking enforcement to have an address in the enforcing state or appoint a representative there, which is not necessary according to Brussels Ia. (Brussels Ia Art. 41, Lugano Art. 40)

---

[403] This is the judgment *debtor,* e.g. the person who shall be made (not) do something according to the judgment.

The grounds for refusal (non-recognition) of the enforcement of a judgment coincide with those in Brussels Ia. (Brussels Ia Art. 46, 47; Lugano Art. 34, 35)

Last but not least, it must be mentioned that both Brussels Ia and Lugano are *not* applicable to *arbitral awards*, whose application is nevertheless ensured by the New York Convention. (see *Arbitration*; Brussels Ia Art. 1, Lugano Art. 1).

# V. Uniform Law

**Uniform law** refers to sets of legal rules, typically of an international non-state origin, that *several* states apply and which are also intended for this. This can be substantive law (like the CISG) or procedural law (like the *UNCITRAL Model Law on International Commercial Arbitration* and the *ALI/UNIDROIT Principles of Transnational Civil Procedure*). The goal of uniform law is legal unification across states.

On the one hand, uniform law can be contained in an *international convention* states can ratify and are thus bound by it and must apply. In this case uniform law is **International Law** applicable in the member states of such a convention.
Prominent examples for this kind of uniform law are the CISG, CMR and NYC.[404] Such uniform law included in international conventions generally must be applied *instead of* national (or even European) law.

 The European Union (EU), as a supranational organization, has the competence to adopt uniform legal acts for all of its 27 member states[405] without a ratification. Due to its validity in several – 27 – states all EU Law[406] is, strictly speaking, uniform law.

On the other hand, uniform law can be a simple legal "text" (not available for ratification) provided with the objective that states incorporate it in their national legal system. In this case, the proposed uniform law is for itself not binding law[407] (not international nor national law) but *can* become binding **national law** if a state decides to adopt it as part of its

---

[404] See chapters *UN Sales Convention (CISG)* and *Arbitration*.
[405] In its areas of (exclusive and shared) competence.
[406] Except for legal acts directed only to one state/entity (e.g. some EU "decisions").
[407] Or, put differently, it does not have the force of law.

243

national legal order. It is not applied *instead* of national law but *as an element* of national law (finally, it **is** national law as soon as adopted). This kind of uniform law is often also denominated **model law** since it serves as a model for states' national legislative activity. Of course, in this case, states have all freedom to modify the proposed legal text, which is why some say it is not *uniform* law but only *harmonizing/harmonized* law.[408]

A successful model law example is e.g. the *UNCITRAL Model Law on International Commercial Arbitration*.

Apart from these two types of uniform law, there are also (*model* or) **standard**[409] **contractual terms**/clauses provided for their individual integration in contracts by the parties.

Also these are just (shorter) legal texts with no binding value until they are incorporated in a contract of two (or more) private parties. This makes them binding between these parties. Strictly speaking, they then do not become *law* (as adopted by a state) but *legally binding* in a concrete contractual relationship. Just like model law, they can be modified according to the needs of the parties.

Instead of standard terms, parties – as part of their contractual freedom – often can also opt for uniform (or model) law[410] to be applied to their contract.

The most prominent example for standard contract terms are the INCOTERMS[411], while the UNIDROIT Principles[412] are designed to be both model law (for *states* integrating them in their national legal orders) and a set of contractual terms *private parties* can opt for.

---

[408] See e.g. Ferrari et al., 2023: 6.
[409] Or *model* contractual clauses.
[410] Or parts/articles of it.
[411] See *INCOTERMS*.
[412] See *UNIDROIT Principles of International Commercial Contracts (PICC)*.

# 1. UN Sales Convention (CISG)

The *United Nations Convention on Contracts for the International Sale of Goods* (CISG) was concluded in 1980[413] at a conference in Vienna in the framework of the United Nations Commission on International Trade Law (UNCITRAL) and can be seen as the most successful example of uniform sales law. Currently, 97 states are parties to the CISG, including most European states[414], North America, most parts of Latin America, Australia, Russia and China. Ratification of the CISG is still lacking in many parts of Africa and Asia but has been increasing in the last years.

CISG members
No CISG members

*Image: Alinor, wikimedia commons, modified by Karoline Schreiber.*

---

[413] And, from an International Law standpoint, entered into force in 1988. In Austria in 1989.

[414] All EU MS except Malta. In Denmark, Finland, Iceland, Sweden and (non-EU) Norway though the CISG does not apply to contracts of sale (or to their formation) where the parties' places of business are in Denmark, Finland, Iceland, Sweden or Norway.

The substantive law applied to a sales contract is determined according to the Conflict-of-Laws rules of the state whose courts are competent to hear a case. As we have already heard, parties can agree on a certain court being competent and on which state's law is applicable to their contract. While the CISG (since it is not a *state's* law) cannot be chosen as a formal *choice of law*, parties can *incorporate* the CISG in their contract (similarly to GTC).

By this incorporation, the CISG replaces (only) the dispositive (non-peremptory) provisions of the state law applicable to the contract. This applicable state law (which can be chosen by the parties as their formal choice of law) also serves as a *gap filler* for issues not covered by the CISG.

Although parties might not have explicitly **chosen** the CISG to be incorporated to their contract (**option 1**[415]), it can still happen that the CISG is applied – before even looking at the Conflict-of-Laws rules of a country. That is the case when the parties to a contract are **based** in different contracting states of the CISG (and a contracting state's court is competent for resolving the dispute) (**option 2**). If these conditions are not met, it can anyway happen that the CISG is applied to a sales contract; namely when the **Conflict-of-Laws rules** or a **CoL agreement lead to the application** of the law of a country that is part of the CISG (**option 3**).[416]

In other words, when country **X**'s rules (or the parties' CoL agreement) lead to country **Y**'s law to be applied to a contract, that does not

---

[415] Parties can incorporate the CISG in their contract even though the contractual relationship is *merely domestic*: If both parties are based in Austria and decide the CISG should be applied, it replaces Austrian non-peremptory law in the areas it regulates. Since the CISG is dispositive (suppletive), parties can also decide that one/some article(s) of the CISG should not be applied to their contract or modify articles of the CISG according to their needs and wishes.

[416] In case a contracting state did not opt out of this rule, such as China and the USA.

necessarily mean that **Y**'s internal legal order is actually applicable. It is generally not (but the CISG instead) if **Y** is a CISG member.

!
• Even if the parties to a contract decide explicitly that **Y**'s legal order should be applied to their contractual relationship, this only means that **Y**'s domestic contract law is applied to the contract *if **Y** has not ratified the CISG*. If it has done so though, the CISG is applied. If parties want to prevent that (and want **Y**'s *internal* laws to be applicable), they do not only have to put that into their contract but also that they *exclude the CISG from being applied*.[417]

**Example**

*A car manufacturer based in Japan (**A**) sells 30 cars to an Austria-based car dealer (**B**) who is a UK citizen.*

The CISG is applied to this contract because both of the parties' places of business are in different CISG contracting states (if a contracting state's court is competent), even though the applicable Conflict-of-Laws rules would lead to another state's substantive law. The citizenship of the parties does not matter, only where their businesses are headquartered.

***B** sells 10 of the imported cars to a car dealer in Morrocco (**C**) (which is not a contracting state of the CISG).*

If litigation takes place in Morrocco and Moroccan Private International Law (Conflict-of-Laws) rules refer to the substantive law of a CISG contracting state (e.g. of Austria) to be applied to the case, the CISG is primarily applied and **not** Austrian substantive law. Even if **B** and **C** agree

---

[417] E.g. with contractual clauses like "Austrian law applies, *excluding the UN Sales Convention / CISG*" or "subject to the ABGB and UGB".

that Austrian law should be applied to their contract, it does so only in case they also expressly exclude the CISG from being applied.

It is important to note that the CISG only covers goods, i.e. movable property, and that the purchase of goods for the personal use (of the buyer him/herself, his/her family or home)[418] is excluded from the application of the Convention.[419] (CISG Art. 2) For, therefore, concerning primarily the entrepreneurial sale of goods, the CISG is especially relevant in international business and company law.

**Example**

*The mentioned car dealer **B** (based in Austria) buys a car exclusively for family use from the car manufacturer **A** (based in Japan).*

The CISG is not (automatically) applied although both **B** and **A** have their places of business in the CISG members Japan and Austria. Supposing that Austrian courts are competent for resolving a dispute arising from the mentioned contract, Austrian (European) Private International Law[420] has to be looked into and checked to which country's legal system the Conflict-of-Laws rules lead.

*Some months later, **B** buys a plot of land for parking the cars that are up for sale from the German real estate investment company **D**.*

---

[418] Other excluded goods are e.g. securities, airplanes and ships. (CISG Art. 2)
[419] If the seller "knew nor ought to have known that the goods were bought for any such use"(CISG Art. 2 (a)). Moreover, if goods are bought for the mixed use (personal *and* business use), the CISG is generally applicable.
[420] In this case the Rome I – Regulation is applied (even though Japan is no EU member); which would refer to the law of the state, where the party that provides the *characteristic performance* has its habitual residence (Japan). (Rome I Art. 4 (2))

248

The CISG is not (automatically) applied either, in this case because a plot of land is not a good but immovable property. Therefore, also here the relevant Conflict-of-Laws rules determine the applicable substantive law.

Contentwise, it must also be mentioned that – in comparison to national civil law – the CISG is more limited:

It regulates only the conclusion of a contract and the rights and obligations of its parties. It does not regulate other important questions such as the validity itself of the contract, i.e. if the parties have the necessary legal capacity (age, soundness of mind, etc.) for the contract, or if the subject of the contract is legal, e.g. if certain drugs can even legally be sold. The result of error (e.g. if something is sold for "100 000" and A thinks the currency is British *pounds* and B thinks it is *euros*) is not regulated either in the CISG, nor is the effect of the contract on property (if and when the sales contract actually leads to the buyer becoming the legal owner of the good). For these issues it must be relied on the substantive law the Conflict-of-Laws rules refer to. (CISG Art. 4)

That being said, let us have a quick look at the substantive rules the CISG provides.

## Substantive rules of the CISG

As mentioned, the CISG plays an essential role in the international sale of goods between businesses. Therefore, it is worth displaying *grosso modo* some of its most vital rules.

The CISG in many cases resembles the correspondent contents of many European civil codes. One of the oldest ones in force and also a model for some more recent civil codes in Europe is the Austrian *Allgemeines Bürgerliches Gesetzbuch* (ABGB, 1811), which in the following will be compared with the CISG in some occasions.

### a. Contract conclusion

Let us have a look first at the conclusion of a contract. Generally, a sales contract is based on the agreement of two (or more) parties: The seller makes an *offer*, whose terms are approved by the buyer through his/her *acceptance*. This is common to both the CISG and most national civil law regulations in the world. When it comes to the details, some questions may arise though:

i. *Until when can the seller revoke his/her offer at the latest?*

ii. *Do the acceptance terms have to be exactly the same as the offer terms or may there be a slight difference between them?*

iii. *Does the buyer's acceptance of an offer lead to a binding sales contract if it is expressed after the deadline provided by the seller?*

It is exactly in those (important) details where Austrian law and the CISG differ.

**Ad i.**

Whereas Austrian law provides that an offer can be revoked only until the buyer has received it, the CISG gives the seller more flexibility. It allows him/her to revoke the offer even after the buyer has taken note of it, namely until the latter actually expressed his/her acceptance. (ABGB §861 et seq., concretized by judicature and doctrine; CISG Art. 16) This, of course, may lead to buyers accepting offers faster (and faster business transactions in general) but, on the other hand, gives them less security (because a seller could at any point just revoke his/her previously made offer).

**Ad ii.**

According to Austrian law, there has to be a complete consensus between the parties on the contract terms. If the acceptance does not wholly match the offer, it is generally seen as a new offer (made now by the *buyer*), which the seller must accept for him/her being bound by it. In contrast, the CISG provides that also an acceptance that does not completely match an offer can lead to a binding contract. This is the case when the seller does not immediately object to it and additions or deviations from the offer constitute merely insignificant changes to the offer, e.g. minor alterations of delivery times (but not considerable changes regarding the price, the product, delivery time and place, etc.).[421] (ABGB §869 et seq., concretized by judicature and doctrine; CISG Art. 19)

**Ad iii.**

If the seller gives the buyer a deadline for his/her response to an offer, Austrian civil law considers it as *final*. That means, that a late acceptance does not directly lead to a binding contract (but only a new offer, this time from the *buyer*). On the contrary, the CISG stipulates that a "late

---

[421] CISG Art. 19 generally qualifies also the "price, payment, quality and quantity of the goods, place and time of delivery..." as *material alterations* of the contract terms. Nevertheless, in cases when party customs/habits or pre-negotiations, general commercial practices or the special circumstances of the case point in the other direction, this assumption may be refuted. This is especially valid in cases where the modified acceptance is beneficial for the seller. See e.g. Kronke, 2017: 68.

acceptance is nevertheless effective as an acceptance" if the seller is informed about it "without delay"(CISG Art. 21). In other words, although the deadline is already past – if it is not past by far and the buyer communicates his/her late acceptance – the seller is still bound by his/her offer.

**Example**

*Company **A** sends an E-mail to company **B** containing an offer about the sale of*
*"200 X-900-microwaves for 30 000 €, delivered on December 15 before 5:00 PM. Answer expected by October 26."*
*The applicable Conflict-of-Laws rules refer to the CISG to be applied to their contract.*

*Since in the country where **B** is based, October 26 is a holiday, **B** sends his reply to **A** on October 27 stating that he is sorry for the delay but that he agrees to **A**'s offer to be "delivered on December 15, as always before 4:00 PM".*

Despite the delayed acceptance, the contract is concluded successfully with the slightly earlier delivery time limit being a party custom if A does not directly insist on the later delivery time.

If Austrian civil law had been applied, there would not have been a binding contract (unless A had answered B in a further step that he agreed to B's changed terms).

As we can see, when compared to the ABGB, the CISG slightly lowers the threshold for contract conclusion, at least in the two mentioned aspects i. and ii.. This may lead to more fluid commercial transactions but also possible misunderstandings between the contracting parties.

## b. Obligations of the parties and passage of risks

The **seller** must **deliver** the good (incl. documentation) to the buyer and **transfer property**[422] to him/her. (CISG Art. 30)

When and where to deliver?

If the parties did not agree on any **delivery date**, it has to be delivered "within a reasonable time after the conclusion of the contract"(CISG Art. 33).

If no **place of delivery** was agreed on, it is

1. if carriage is involved – the first carrier the good is handed over to for transmission to the buyer,
2. if no carriage is involved – the place where certain goods to be manufactured or produced are manufactured or produced,
- in other cases – the place of business of the *seller* during the conclusion of the contract. (CISG Art. 31)

If a location where to deliver was agreed on contractually by the parties, *this* place is the "place of delivery". The place of delivery may also be affected if parties use standard clauses, such as the INCOTERMS (see below). As for multimodal INCOTERMS DAP, DPU and DDP, the place of delivery and passage of risks is e.g. their destination, i.e. in case of doubt the place of business of the *buyer*.

---

[422] As mentioned, the question if property/ownership was actually transferred is resolved by the applicable national civil law and not the CISG.

What exactly has to be delivered?

The **good to be delivered** has to be in accordance with the contractual terms in quantity, quality and description. If the contract does not concretize the good, it must be in conformity with both (former) practices between the parties and international commercial usage and practices (CISG Art. 9; see also *Lex Mercatoria*)[423]. If such do not exist, it must fulfil the conditions mentioned in Art. 35 CISG in line with the standard of the country from which it is exported:

> (2) Except where the parties have agreed otherwise, the goods do not conform with the contract unless they:
> (a) are fit for the purposes for which goods of the same description would ordinarily be used;
> (b) are fit for any particular purpose expressly or impliedly made known to the seller at the time of the conclusion of the contract, except where the circumstances show that the buyer did not rely, or that it was unreasonable for him to rely, on the seller's skill and judgement;
> (c) possess the qualities of goods which the seller has held out to the buyer as a sample or model;
> (d) are contained or packaged in the manner usual for such goods or, where there is no such manner, in a manner adequate to preserve and protect the goods. (CISG Art. 35 (2))

It must be noted though that the seller is not liable for products not corresponding with these conditions if the seller knew about it or must have known about it. (CISG Art. 35 (3))

The moment relevant for determining if the product is in line with the contract or the mentioned parameters is not the conclusion of the contract but the "**passage of risk**":

When products are sold they are subject to several risks from the time they are initially produced or stored by the seller to the time they are

---

[423] See e.g. Welser et al., 2015: 214, 215.

finally placed at the buyer's disposal. These risks include the damage or destruction and loss of a product, which may happen deliberately, negligently or accidentally.

The *passage* or *transfer of risk* can therefore be understood as the moment when the risk of (especially *accidental*) deterioration or loss of the product passes from the seller to the buyer, i.e. when the seller stops being liable for it and the buyer starts being liable. Being liable in this case generally means having to bear the costs of the deterioration or loss (having to offer another product for free or having to pay the full price despite not having received a [functioning] product).

This is also one of the main issues the so-called *INCOTERMS* focus on, which replace the corresponding parts of the (dispositive) CISG if the parties decide so (see *INCOTERMS*).

Regarding risk transfer, the CISG in general coincides with Austrian law[424], which in case of accidental (i.e. no fault or contract breach by either of the parties) deterioration or loss of the good in question generally determines the moment of the (**planned) take over** of the good by the buyer. Therefore, the moment of the take over by the buyer is of the utmost importance.

In case the good is handed over first to a carrier (to be brought to another carrier or to the buyer), the risk passage takes place when the seller hands over the good to the first carrier.[425]

The situation is different though if a place for handing over the good to a *carrier* was agreed on: Even though the seller hands over the good to a prior carrier (to bring it to the place where hand over to a carrier should

---

[424] See ABGB §§1447, 492, 905, concretized by judicature and doctrine.

[425] Keep in mind that in Austrian law, in consumer contracts the risk passes from the seller (enterprise) to the buyer (consumer) at a later moment, namely when the last carrier hands the product over to the consumer. (KSchG §7b) If, in Austria, you buy a book on Amazon and it gets wet and unreadable because of the rain during the transport, the risk (and costs) has to be borne by Amazon.

take place contractually), here it is not the first carrier but the *carrier at the agreed place* where the risk passes. (CISG Art. 66-69)

If the loss or deterioration was not accidental (e.g. force majeure) but goes back to the fault of the buyer or of the seller, generally the party that has acted in a negligent/faulty manner[426] and/or in breach of contract is liable.

Whereas the seller must deliver and transfer property, the **buyer** is obliged to 1. pay the price for the sold good at the moment when it is placed at his/her disposal (unless the parties agreed otherwise or he/she has not had the opportunity to examine the good) and 2. to take delivery of it. (CISG Art. 53, 58)

## c. Breach of contract

That leads us to another vital issue – the **breach of contract** by one of the parties.

Many national legislations distinguish different types of contract breaches, such as impossibility of performance (e.g. if a Picasso painting is destroyed, it cannot be delivered any more), delay (of the seller and also of the buyer – if he/she does not pick up the good at the agreed time) or warranty if the delivered product has a defect (e.g. a smartphone's screen brightness cannot be adjusted).

The CISG, in contrast, does not distinguish primarily by the type of breach but by its significance for the other party. Therefore, some claims are only

---

[426] As we can see below though, regarding damage claims due to contract breaches, the CISG does **not** demand that the damaging party acted with fault/negligence (although there are some exceptions to this rule).

256

available to the other party if they are *fundamental* – no matter whether it's a case of impossibility of performance, delay or warranty.

A breach is **fundamental** when the execution of the contract is of no interest (or to be expected) any more for (by) the aggrieved party and the other party could foresee that[427]. (CISG Art. 25)

**Example**[428]

*B orders 400 roll-ups displaying the program of a conference taking place on October 21. A delivers them on October 27, when the conference is already over.*

A must have foreseen that **B** has no interest any more in the roll-ups that were customized specifically for that conference. It therefore is a fundamental breach of contract.

If the roll-ups had not been customized for this occasion and were reusable (and **A** was not informed about the conference), contact breach would most likely not have been fundamental, with different legal remedy options for the affected party **B**.

---

[427] The analysis if that is the case must be based on an overall assessment of objective criteria such as the nature and extent of the breach, consequences for the other party (such as additional expenses and efforts) and the timely possibility of repair or replacement. Nevertheless, the mere possibility of repair or replacement itself does not necessarily lead to the qualification of a breach as *non-fundamental*. See e.g. Krejci, 2013: 415.
[428] Let us suppose the CISG is applied to this example case.

If there is a (fundamental or not) breach of contract because no delivery takes place, what can the parties do?

The CISG distinguishes between legal remedies available to the seller, on the one hand, and legal remedies available to the buyer, on the other.

If the **seller breaches the contract** by _not delivering at all_, the buyer always has the following options:

i. He/she can simply insist on the seller fulfilling the contract (and wait as long as he/she feels appropriate).

ii. He/she can fix an additional reasonable period of time by when the seller has to deliver and, after this period has passed (without delivery), declare the contract avoided. (CISG Art. 46, 49)

If the breach (by not delivering at all)[429] is _fundamental_, the buyer can also

iii. directly declare the contract avoided (without having to offer an additional time period for performance).[430] (CISG Art. 49)

The buyer (**B**) from the afore mentioned _customized roll-ups_ example can therefore directly declare the contract avoided without giving the seller (**A**) another option to deliver them and, therefore, is entitled to not pay for them (or get the paid money back if he has already paid). [option **iii**]

In case of _non-customized and reusable roll-ups_ ordered without any conference in connection (a non-fundamental contract breach), **B** would have to fix an additional reasonable time period, e.g. November 10, and

---

[429] In case the fundamental breach has not yet happened but is certain to happen, the (to be) affected party can even beforehand declare the contract avoided.

[430] Austrian law differs here from the CISG and does not provide for this instant option for terminating the contract. (see ABGB §918)

258

can only terminate the contract if **B** does not deliver the roll-ups by then. [option ii]

**B** can, of course, also decide to wait indefinitely for the delivery [option i] and, at a later moment, take the mentioned step of offering an additional time period for performance and afterwards ending the contract.

If the **buyer breaches the contract** by _not "delivering" at all_, i.e. he/she does not pay as agreed, the options of the seller are similar:

i.      He/she can simply insist on the buyer fulfilling the contract (and wait as long as he/she feels appropriate for payment).

ii.      He/she can fix an additional reasonable period of time by when the buyer has to pay and, after this period has passed (without payment), declare the contract avoided.

iii.      If the breach is <u>fundamental</u> (e.g. because the buyer is in dire financial straits), the seller can right away declare the contract avoided.
(CISG Art. 62-64)

In addition to that, the seller can also terminate the contract if payment is not the problem but reception of the good by the buyer. In case the buyer does not take delivery, the seller can

iv.      insist on the buyer taking delivery (and legally enforce it) or

v.      offer an additional reasonable period of time taking delivery and, in its absence, declare the contract avoided. (CISG Art. 64)

What if the good is delivered to the buyer but there is still a (fundamental or not) breach of contract because the product is defective?

As mentioned, the CISG does not distinguish primarily between impossibility of performance, delay or warranty (but instead focusses on the (non) fundamentality of the contract breach). Nevertheless, it does provide different legal remedies for the cases when delivery did not take place at all (see above) and for when it did take place, but the delivered good is deficient[431].

That is the case when the product does not conform with the contract because of deviations in quality or quantity (or rights) from it.

If that is the case, the CISG provides for different remedies:

i.      **repair** (or provision of missing components) of the good, which is available in any case

ii.     delivery of a **substitute** (non-deficient) **good** instead of the delivered deficient one, which can be required by the buyer only if the contact breach is fundamental

iii.    **price reduction** by the buyer in proportion to the reduced value of the delivered, regardless of the fundamentality of the breach[432]

iv.     alternatively to i., ii. and iii., **termination of the contract**, only if the contract breach is fundamental
        (CISG Art. 46-50)

---

[431] That is also when, in many legal orders, *warranty* comes into play.

[432] Even though the buyer directly declares *price reduction*, the seller must still be given the chance to provide *repair* (i.) or a *substitute good* (ii.). If the seller does so, the buyer must accept that. The seller requiring price reduction can **set an appropriate additional time period** for repair or substitute delivery though (which is *recommended*). If the buyer does not comply with it, nothing stands in the way of a price reduction.
In practice, price reduction is of limited importance due to the anyway given possibility of no-fault compensation for damages (see below).

All these remedies are subject to two conditions:

**1.** The duty of the buyer to *give notice* to the seller of the defect within a reasonable time after he/she (should have) discovered it.[433]
**2.** The assertion of the claim during a maximum period of two years since the good was handed over.
(CISG Art. 39)

If the buyer forgets to give notice on time, even though the maximum time limit of two years has not passed yet, the mentioned four remedies remain unavailable to him/her.

**Example**[434]

*Beverage supplying company **B** buys ten new trucks from the truck manufacturer **A** for its soft drinks deliveries to supermarkets. Already after the first week eight of **B**'s ten drivers complain about backache due to the non-functioning seat suspension of the trucks' seats. Apart from that, the trucks work perfectly fine.*

Since the contract breach of **A** is not fundamental, **B** can require the trucks to be repaired by **A** [option **i**] but he is not entitled to demand new trucks instead [option **ii**] nor declare the contract avoided [option **iv**]. If **A** does not repair the trucks (or just does not reply to **B**'s request), **B** can reduce the price of the trucks in relation to their now lower value (in this case, only a low percentage of the overall trucks' costs) [option **iii**][435].

---

[433] The duty of the buyer to give notice ceases if the seller must have known about the defect. (CISG Art. 40)
[434] Let us suppose the CISG is applied to this example case.
[435] In case **A** does not repair the trucks and nor delivers substitute trucks, some authors affirm that he/she can not only require price reduction but also declare the contract avoided. See e.g. Krejci, 2013: 416.

Nevertheless, **B** may only require repair and a price reduction if he gives notice of the defect within a reasonable time (not much longer than a few weeks) after he was informed of it by the drivers.

### What if the breach of contract has lead to financial damage of the contracting party?

In addition to the mentioned remedies, **both the seller and the buyer** can claim **compensation for damages** resulting from the contract breach.

In other words, while the aforementioned options are directed to save (or cancel) the contractual relationship itself, the below mentioned options are for compensating the aggrieved party for the damages that may have arisen *as a consequence of* the breach. The use of one of the aforementioned remedies does not exclude the use of the below mentioned ones (i.e. *both* can be claimed).

Unlike in many national civil regulations, the CISG's compensation for damages rules are based on a *no-fault / strict liability*. That means that a party generally is liable for damages caused by his/her breach of contract even though his/her has not acted with negligence or fault. (CISG Art. 74 et seq.)

Nevertheless, there are several exemptions to this rule. A party is e.g. not liable if

> the failure was due to an impediment beyond his control and that he could not reasonably be expected to have taken the impediment into account at the time of the conclusion of the contract or to have avoided or overcome it, or its consequences. (CISG Art. 79)

That means, that, for example in situations of natural disasters or strikes (which are outside the parties' sphere of influence), the party violating the contract cannot be made liable. The party suffering the damage

262

cannot rely on failures for compensation either if he/she him/herself was the reason for the failure in the first place. (CISG Art. 80)

An important limit – in this case not to the occasions when damages can be sought but to the *amount* of that has to be compensated – is furthermore constituted by the following requirement:

! The injuring party must only compensate for damages he/she could have foreseen at contract conclusion as a consequence of contract breach.

If this requirement is given though, he/she must compensate not only for the direct loss a party actually had but also for (indirect) loss of profit[436]. This also includes interest in case the buyer does not pay (on time). (CISG Art. 74, 78)

**Example**[437]

*A has been looking for the relatively compact "Freezequick 900"-ice cream machines for her tiny ice cream shop. Unfortunately, these machines are sold out everywhere and not produced any more. Finally, she finds out that B is still offering the desired machines for 10 000 € each. She orders five machines and starts renovating one of her rooms for the machines and orders platforms fitting exactly the size of the "Freezequick 900" to put them on (total price for the platforms: 2000 €).*

*Unfortunately, the agreed delivery date (June 15) is not met by B, who informs A that the machines are out of stock and that he cannot deliver them because "there's no place on earth where you can still get the*

---

[436] Austrian law again differs here from the CISG since, **a)** there is no foreseeability-criterion and **b)** not always loss of profit (but often *only direct loss*) is compensated for. (see ABGB §1293 et seq. &1323 et seq.) On the other hand, both Austrian law and the CISG provide for an obligation of the aggrieved party to mitigate (minimize) damages. (CISG Art. 77, ABGB §1304)

[437] Let us suppose the CISG is applied to this example case.

*compact and effective machines you need". It takes **A** three months to again get delivered similar, but slightly bigger, ice cream machines somewhere else. These need new platforms since the old ones are too small. In addition, due to the contract breach by **B**, **A** could not sell ice cream during the entire summer (June 15 to September 15). Lost profit amounts to at least 15 000 €.*

Since the execution of the (main obligation of the) contract cannot be expected any more, there is a fundamental contract breach and **A** can declare the contract avoided instantly. If she has already paid the 50 000 € for the machines, **B** has to reimburse the sum.

Apart from the contractual relationship which **A** can terminate as mentioned, she can also claim compensation for damages. If **B** was informed upfront that **A** will order platforms for the ice cream machines, **A** is entitled to the direct loss of 2000 € for the now useless old platforms. Since **B** knew that **A** needed specifically these (or very similar) compact and effective machines, he must also compensate **A** for the secured profits **A** would have made if the contract had not been breached – i.e. the loss of profit of 15 000 €.

Finally, it must be noted that the CISG only includes rules for material damage but not for personal damage. (CISG Art. 5) For determining compensation for personal damage, the relevant national civil law has to be consulted.

In summary, the legal remedies provided by the CISG can be categorized as follows:

| breach | no delivery (by seller / buyer) | incorrect delivery (by seller) |
|---|---|---|
| fundamental | - contract fulfilment<br>- immediate termination of contract<br>- compensation for damages | - repair<br>- substitution<br>- price reduction<br>- immediate termination of contract<br>- compensation for damages |
| not fundamental | - contract fulfilment<br>- termination of contract after additional time period<br>- compensation for damages | - repair<br>- price reduction<br>- compensation for damages |

# 2. UNIDROIT Principles of International Commercial Contracts (PICC)

The *UNIDROIT Principles of International Commercial Contracts* (PICC or [UNIDROIT] Principles) are a set of substantive rules for all types of international commercial contracts[438] adopted by UNIDROIT in 1994. UNIDROIT is an independent International Organization with currently 65 member states. It is based in Rome and pursues the goal of internationally harmonizing private law through uniform rules, conventions and model laws[439]. With the aim of compiling (and restating) actual trade practices, after a drafting period of 20 years, the PICC were adopted in 1994. UNIDROIT regularly updates the Principles, with the 2016 version being the most recent one.

While the CISG is an international agreement created by official government delegations and ratified by states and with state parties, the PICC are quite the opposite. They were drafted by (non-state) independent experts, cannot be ratified by anybody and do not have state parties.

Nevertheless, also the PICC represent uniform law, i.e. sets of (in our case) substantive law applied by several states parties can agree on to be incorporated in their contracts.

The functioning is (partly) different though. Whereas the CISG is susceptible to be applied to a contract without its parties actively deciding so (because parties are based in CISG members or the Conflict-of-Laws rules lead to it), the PICC are only applied to a contract if the parties decide so.[440]

---

[438] Especially for sales contracts.
[439] Laws made with the objective that as many countries as possible incorporate them in their legal systems (and by that reach international legal unification).
[440] Except, of course, if the case is subjected to arbitration and the arbitrator decides to apply the PICC as expression of the *lex mercatoria* (see below).

As with the CISG, the parties are free to choose only one or some of the PICC articles to be incorporated in their contract or opt for the Principles in their entirety except for one or some articles. It must be noted though that the PICC are chosen in much rarer cases by parties than the CISG.

Apart from this use of the PICC by **a)** *parties* actively integrating them in their contract, the PICC are also addressed at **b)** *states* as an orientation for their national private laws (and therefore legislative harmonization).[441] The PICC can also serve for supplementing national legal regimes and even the CISG when it has gaps or is ambiguous.

Apart from contracting parties and states, the PICC are often used **c)** by arbitrators that apply the *lex mercatoria* (see *Lex Mercatoria*). That has to do with the fact that the PICC were created with the clear objective to "reflect current trade practices" by independent subject-matter experts (and not governments that had to find consensus, as is the case with conventions like the CISG). This advantage of not depending on state consensus – as optional *soft law*[442] – also allowed them to cover a broader area of regulation than e.g. the CISG.[443]

### *Substantive rules examples*

Let us have a quick look at some of the substantive rules the PICC provide. Far from being exhaustive, in the following some additional aspects to what we have seen in our description of the CISG are briefly referenced in relation to the UNIDROIT Principles.

---

[441] For this reason, the PICC are – to some extent – *both* model law and standard contractual terms.
[442] This optional soft law, of course, becomes binding "hard" law as soon as the parties agree on the PICC to be applied to their contract.
[443] Folsom et al., 2016: 127-129.

## a. Standard terms

As we have seen before, under the CISG (unlike under Austrian law) a contract can also be concluded if the acceptance by one party does not completely match the offer. Condition for that is that the acceptance does not "materially alter" the terms of the offer. (CISG Art. 19) The UNIDROIT Principles include a very similar rule (PICC Art. 2.1.11) but, in addition, regulate the important and common case when two parties both use their own standard terms (GTC etc.). This "battle of forms" is not expressly regulated by the CISG.[444]

If both parties use diverging standard terms, the PICC provide that a contract is anyway concluded based on the "agreed terms" of the parties. This means that – if parties raise certain terms individually and negotiate– a contract is concluded with these terms in its center.[445] These "agreed terms" are complemented by the default rules of the Principles and, in the very rare case that the parties' standard terms are "common in substance", the matching standard terms. (PICC Art. 2.1.22)

In Austrian law, if parties refer to their GTC, there usually is dissent (and therefore no contract). Only in the rare case the GTC only diverge in secondary terms, a successful contract conclusion can be assumed (but only regarding the non-diverging terms). If parties have already started performance of the contract (and none of the parties did not conclusively accept the other's GTC either), the *hypothetical will of the parties* has to

---

[444] If the buyer answers to the seller's GTC with his/her own GTC, this will generally be seen as a "material alteration" of the seller's contract terms, which hinders contract conclusion according to the CISG. Regarding individual clauses that are not completely coincident, the CISG provides for a remaining validity of the parts of the clause that *are* coincident. If parties use different INCOTERMS, in most cases their non-inclusion in the contract must be supposed. See e.g. Bernstorff, 2020: 35.

[445] If parties explicitly – and not only automatically e.g. by using order forms with the respective GTC on
the reverse side – insist on their (diverging) standard terms though, no contract is concluded.

268

be looked for. This hypothetical party will usually depends on the complexity and costs of contract rescission (reverse transactions etc.).

Whereas the PICC seem to be relatively "generous" regarding contract conclusion under standard terms used by both parties, when only *one* party uses such terms, it tends to protect the other party (at least in some cases).

If, for example, the standard terms used by one party include "surprising" clauses, these become ineffective (if they have not expressly been accepted). In other words, if the adhering party "could not reasonably have expected" such a clause, the contract is concluded without it. This "surprising" nature can be due to the terms' presentation, language or content. (PICC Art. 2.1.20)

**Example**

*A, a travel agency, offers package tours for business trips. The terms of the advertisement give the impression that A is acting as a tour operator who undertakes full responsibility for the various services comprising the package. B books a tour on the basis of A's standard terms.*

Notwithstanding **B**'s acceptance of the terms as a whole, **A** may not rely on a term stating that, with respect to the hotel accommodation, it is acting merely as an agent for the hotelkeeper, and therefore declines any liability.[446]

Other examples are the use of a term requiring local arbitration in a foreign language or a choice of foreign law clause in insurance contracts.[447] Although in business contracts it generally must be expected

---

[446] UNIDROIT, 2016: 70, italics and bold print added.
[447] Folsom et al., 2016: 132.

that standard clauses such as the INCOTERMS are to be found also in GTC, it is anyway recommended to explicitly include such terms in the contract *on an individual basis*.

Austrian law similarly regulates that individual clauses with a) unusual content included in GTC that are b) not expressly referenced nor c) to be expected are excluded from a contract if they are d) disadvantageous for the contractual partner. In consumer contracts concluded in connection with an entrepreneurial activity in Austria this provision even applies when foreign law is applied to the contract.[448] (ABGB §864a; KSchG §13a)

## b. Force majeure and hardship

The CISG's compensation rules, as mentioned before, are based on *strict liability*, which leads to a party being liable for damages caused by his/her breach of contract even though his/her has acted diligently. There is an important exemption to this rule though:

Liability is excluded if there is an unexpected and uncontrollable impediment that could not reasonably be avoided or overcome. Apart from that, the party confronted with this impediment must inform the other party of the impediment. (CISG Art. 74-79)

The PICC provide for the same kind of exception by the name **force majeure**. Consequence of invoking it is the non-liability of the affected party.[449] Nevertheless, both parties can – if the conditions for it are given (CISG's "[fundamental] contract breach", PICC's "[fundamental] non-

---

[448] This is due to EU Rome I Regulation, which establishes that in consumer contracts a choice of foreign law by the parties must not deprive the consumer of protection by peremptory provisions of the law where he/she has his/her habitual residence. (Rome I Art. 6)

[449] As mentioned, the CISG and the PICC are based on a liability concept that generally does *not* require fault but counts with some exceptions like force majeure. Austrian law, in contrast, works the other way round: *Fault* is necessary as a *condition* for liability. (ABGB §1295) Since in case of force majeure fault is not given, there is (automatically) no liability. Therefore, there is no need for an exception for force majeure.

performance") – terminate the contract or withhold performance etc. (PICC Art. 7.1.7; CISG Art. 79)

Apart from *force majeure*, the PICC knows another related concept, which – as to its remedy – is completely different from the CISG: **hardship**.

Hardship refers to the situation when the "equilibrium" of the contract is not given any more due to significantly increased costs or a return performance that has lost (most of) its value.[450] (PICC Art. 6.2.2)

Additional criteria for hardship to be invoked are that

(a) the events occur or become known to the disadvantaged party after the conclusion of the contract;

(b) the events could not reasonably have been taken into account by the disadvantaged party at the time of the conclusion of the contract;

(c) the events are beyond the control of the disadvantaged party; and

(d) the risk of the events was not assumed by the disadvantaged party. (PICC Art. 6.2.2)

**Example**

*Since most experts state that "demand for respiratory masks will remain high at least for one more year", **A** buys one million masks (7 € per mask) to sell in his market for a price of 10 € each within the next year. After two months, demand surprisingly falls with the market price dropping first to 4 € and then to 1 €. Since demand is very low now, half of the masks will not be sold at all and have to be thrown away due to their expiry date. Export options are very limited too.*

---

[450] Also the complete disappearance of a market can be mentioned in this regard as a potential "breaker" of a contract's equilibrium.

Although in this case there are certainly some indications of an "alternated contractual equilibrium", the competent court will have to decide if *hardship* is given and which consequence there is (see below its special role according to the PICC).

As indicated, what is most special of hardship under the PICC is not the concept itself but its **remedy**.

Even if hardship is proven, this does not lead to an excuse of performance. For that, several additional steps must follow:

1. The disadvantaged party must try to renegotiate "without undue delay".
2. If renegotiation fails in a reasonable time period, parties "may resort to the court".
3. If they do so, the court analyses if hardship is given.
4. If the court finds hardship, it decides (based on what it finds appropriate and not based on a clear regulation in the PICC of when it has to do what!) if it is reasonable to either
   a. terminate the contract or
   b. adapt the contract. (PICC Art. 6.2.3)

This special role of the judge being competent to freely decide if the contract should be terminated or adapted (and how to adapt the contract!) may be considered inappropriate or risky by the parties, in which case they may waive or adapt this article (since the PICC are optional soft law).

**Example**

*A, an exporter, undertakes to supply B, an importer in country X, with beer for three years. Two years after the conclusion of the contract new legislation is introduced in country X prohibiting the sale and consumption* *of alcoholic drinks. **B** immediately invokes hardship and requests **A** to renegotiate the contract. **A** recognizes that hardship has occurred, but refuses to accept the modifications of the contract proposed by **B**. After one month of fruitless discussions **B** resorts to the court.*

If **B** has the possibility to sell the beer in a neighboring country, although at a substantially lower price, the court may decide to uphold the contract but to reduce the agreed price.

If on the contrary **B** has no such possibility, it may be reasonable for the court to terminate the contract, at the same time however requiring **B** to pay A for the last consignment still en route.[451]

If the conditions for both force majeure *and* hardship are given, the affected party may decide what to invoke. If he/she wants to exclude his/her liability, it makes sense to pursue force majeure. If the goal is to renegotiate or to keep the contract alive on revised terms, hardship will be the more appropriate remedy.

In general, it must be said that the hardship provisions of the PICC are relatively open. That is why it is recommended to parties to include in their contract more precise provisions adjusted e.g. to the special features of the transaction in question. For example, the ICC offers a standard hardship – and also force majeure – clause parties can opt for instead (and further adjust to their needs) – see Annex.[452] Another way to

---

UNIDROIT, 2016: 226, italics and bold print added.
[452] The ICC hardship clause provides for a similar solution as the PICC with a) the judge deciding whether to terminate or to adapt the contract. However, it also offers the parties two alternative options: They can instead opt for b) the judge having the right (only) to terminate the contract or c) the party invoking the clause having this right.

deal with the risks of force majeure or hardship (and generally liability) is, of course, to include an insurance obligation in the contract.[453]

Also International Law knows hardship, namely in the sense of the so-called *clausula rebus sic stantibus* ("as things stand"-rule). According to this general principle of law and international customary law, contracts may be terminated if a a) fundamental circumstance for consent changed, this was b) unforeseen and c) there was a radical transformation of the extent of obligations of the affected party. While e.g. the German Civil Code (BGB §313) explicitly covers hardship, the Austrian ABGB is silent in this regard. Nevertheless, civil law doctrine and judicature have established a concept similar to the international (and German) hardship provisions.

---

[453] Parties can e.g. establish in their contract that one of the parties must take care of taking out insurance in line with the so-called "Institute Cargo Clauses". Most of the world's transport insurances are based or influenced by these clauses published by the International Underwriting Association of London. They are differentiated by their coverage in A (all risks covered), B (named peril covered) and C (limited named peril covered) clauses. Also the INCOTERMS 2020 CIP and CIF clauses establish insurance coverage, which must be provided by the seller "complying with the cover provided by the Clauses (A) of the Institute Cargo Clauses" or similar clauses.

# F Lex Mercatoria

Private autonomy, i.e. the possibility private entities (or persons) to freely organize their contractual relationships among themselves, has – quite logically – led to several customs and practices between private individuals. Questions of how a contract is structured, what it covers, and how/where/by when parties have to fulfil it generally remain optional and at the discretion of the parties.

Nevertheless, parties tend to reduce their options to what is *common* in international business. If out of 100 contract options, 60% of the enterprises in a certain business sector choose only 10, the remaining 40% are very likely to also choose the same 10 options. That is how international business customs and practices emerge. Due to their wide dissemination and often proven functionality, contractual partners tend to only accept (or at least prefer) these (and not other) contract forms or contractual contents. And if they act in line with what is common and usual in business and are anyway sued, naturally, they want the deciding authority (judge, arbitrator, etc.) to take that into account.

That is, of course, nothing new – already in the Middle Ages the so-called "lex mercatoria" or *merchant law* regulated the way merchants dealt with each other economically within an empire's borders and between empires. What is special about this *lex* is that it did not have its origin in an institutionalized sovereign (emperors, kings…) or a state as we would refer to it now but was established by the "ordinary" people and the actual way they traded among themselves. Not rules were *set* but practices *evolved* into rules. In a further step, these first only factual rules were recognized by significant institutions such as trade guilds, which consolidated them and applied them in disputes. This made binding rules with a (quasi)legal character out of them.

It can even be said that all European trade / company law, at its beginnings (starting in the 12$^{th}$ century) was customary law, which complemented and modified general civil law.

# Modern commercial practice

In modern times, the state and its legal regulation activity has also accessed what was originally dominion of the merchants themselves. Nevertheless, custom and practices and the imposition of what is most common remain of significance.

## 1. Custom in (public) International Law

Also International Law takes account of *what is most common*, namely in one of its official sources: the *general principles of law*. (ICJ Statute Art. 38) These can be understood as the most important common principles of the major (national) legal systems in the world.

Some scholars say that there is a new (modern) lex mercatoria (juridified commercial practices and usages; see below) and that this new *lex mercatoria* nurtures[454] itself of the mentioned general principles. This does not surprise, because in international commercial arbitration and international investment law, amongst others, these principles are of vital importance.

Among these general principles of law of relevance for international business law are

- the principle of *good faith* in the performance of contracts (*pacta sunt servanda* – agreements must be kept) and their interpretation,
- the obligation of paying default interest in case of late payments,
- the duty or obligation to mitigate damages and

---

[454] See e.g. Fernández Rozas et al., 2013: 41.

- the possibility to adjust (or terminate) contracts if fundamental circumstances changed (*clausula rebus sic stantibus*).

Some of these principles took the next step and became (also) another source of International Law – *international customary law* (or, shorter *international custom*). In this case *custom* does not refer to the behavior of private individuals but to the actions of *states* primarily. Therefore, in modern International Law, factual state practice is considered law if it is **a)** general [*consuetudo*] and **b)** regarded as legally binding [*opinio iuris*]. (ICJ Statute Art. 38; see *Sources of International Law*)

Not surprisingly, states (and International Organizations) in many cases acted in line with the mentioned general principles of law and considered them as legally binding, which is why they became (also) international customary law. This is e.g. the case for the mentioned general principles *pacta sunt servanda* and *clausula rebus sic stantibus*. But also the principle of *good faith* finds its equivalent in the international custom of *estoppel*, which can be defined as the prohibition of contravening one's own former actions if the other party counted on these and would be harmed by the change in behavior.

As for other international custom examples, please go back to the chapter *Sources of International Law*.

# 2. Custom in (private) Business Law

Despite the mentioned fact that some scholars consider the International Law sources *general principles of law* and *international customary law* of importance for international business law (which undoubtedly is correct to some extent), they remain (public) International Law. They are, therefore, focused on the regulation of the actions of states and International Organizations and *not* of the behavior of private parties (entrepreneurs and consumers).

Nevertheless, also private law knows some (remainders of) customary legal rules. In Austria the rule that the principal heir of a farm must be able to "wohl bestehen" (well exist) after the legator(s) decease(s), is e.g. considered customary law. This usually implies a reduction of the takeover price of the farm.
Customary rules in Austrian company law are e.g. the structure of account books or the rules on commercial confirmation letters.[455]

In contrast to commercial customary *law*, which if only of importance in some niche areas of business law, the so-called commercial *practice* plays a more significant role. Despite this not being law strictly speaking (but a matter of fact), it is of legal significance on various levels.

First of all, commercial practices serve for interpreting law. Austrian company law, for instance, provides as follows:

> Regarding the meaning and effect of actions and omissions, entrepreneurs must take into account the customs and practices

---

[455] Commercial confirmation letters ("Unternehmerische Bestätigungsschreiben") are written notifications about the content of contracts that were concluded verbally before. According to traditional doctrine, customary law says that if the contracting party does not react to a commercial confirmation letter that does not coincide with the verbal contract, this amounts to *acceptance* of the changed terms. This is partly refuted though by more modern Austrian law doctrine.

applicable in business transactions among themselves. (UGB §346, translated)

Second, commercial practices can (especially when laws or contractual clauses provide for it) become of <u>substantive legal importance</u>, even though they still remain facts.[456]

An example for such a commercial practice is the applicability of (any) General Terms and Conditions (GTC) in contractual relationships among merchants. Despite the importance of some *concrete* model contracts/GTC or INCOTERMS in international trade, it generally cannot be assumed that parties tacitly agree on them in specific to be applied to their contract though.

Also when the CISG is applied, parties to a contract are not only bound by what they explicitly agreed on. According to Article 9, they are also bound by
**a)** the (former) usages and practices between themselves and
**b)** by generally known and regularly observed usages in international trade. (CISG Art. 9)

It must be noted though that the question if a commercial practice (to be taken into account in line with the CISG) is *existent* (or not), is determined not by the CISG itself but by the applicable national law. (CISG Art. 4) It is therefore advisable for the parties to inform themselves about the existence of commercial practices beforehand.[457] An example for a widely accepted international commercial practice are the *Uniform Customs and Practice for Documentary Credits* (see *Uniform Customs and Practice (UCP)*) published by the ICC.

---

[456] That is demonstrated also by the fact that if peremptory law appears that is in opposition to commercial practices, these practices lose their legal recognition.
[457] A list of commercial practices in Austria can e.g. be found on the website of the Austrian Federal Economic Chamber: <u>https://www.wko.at/oe/news/handelsbrauch-liste</u>.

Nonetheless, both in Austrian law and the CISG, parties can exclude the application of commercial practices if they explicitly agree so in their contract.

In summary, it can be said that customary *law* plays an only subordinate role in national and international business law whereas factual commercial *practices* are of major importance thanks to statutory law actively providing for their aid in interpretation, concretization and supplementation.

## 3. Modern Lex Mercatoria

As stated, the key importance of commercial usages and practices does not lie in their *direct* legal effect as *legal provisions* (which they are not in most cases) but in their role of *indirectly* becoming of legal importance as *matters of fact*.

Nonetheless, some scholars consider that these commercial usages and practices in their totality cease to be matters of fact and become actual law: the modern *lex mercatoria*.

> (…) there is an important "juridifying optimism" that clearly believes that the new *lex mercatoria* will achieve its objective by transforming itself from its own system and under the weight of the needs of international commerce into a perfect and finished legal order.[458]

These scholars see the origin and precepts of this new "law" in the above mentioned *general principles of (economic) law* and/or institutions like the ICC and UNIDROIT and their (model) rules, principles and conventions. Apart from that, its legal rules also stem from the actual regular behavior of (dominant) business partners, if this is not anyway

---

[458] Fernández Rozas et al., 43, translated.

coincident with the general principles of law or international model contracts or clauses. But this new "legal order" is, according to its proponents, not only equipped with binding legal provisions but also with "judicial" authority and sanctions in case the *lex mercatoria* is not observed.[459]

An example for these sanctions is the boycott, i.e. the abstention from commercial relations with the non-abiding party as a means of protest or punishment. This can be referred to a certain product (because e.g. its characteristics do not match business custom), to an unfamiliar or prejudicial practice realized by a company (e.g. usage of unconventional "surprising" clauses in GTC) or to a particular market actor in total (e.g. because of its discriminatory employment policy). This way enforcement of *lex mercatoria* works, or should work, automatically.

As for the settlement of disputes, the new *lex mercatoria* works with arbitration. This is, in fact, what can be considered the key and most vital element of this new merchant "law" since, in some cases, arbitrators actually apply it in their awards (arbitral decisions).

 In other words, (private) arbitrators sometimes do not apply law in its traditional sense (e.g. Austrian national law or the CISG) to the case they decide but commercial practices instead.[460]

Especially the *UNIDROIT Principles of International Commercial Contracts* (see *UNIDROIT Principles of International Commercial Contracts (PICC)*), drafted by independent experts based on best practices in international commercial contracts, are often resorted to by arbitrators as a "general statement of international contract principles" and "international custom".[461]

---

[459] See e.g. Fernández Rozas et al., 2013: 41-43.
[460] This is of course not possible if parties explicitly include a choice of law agreement in their contract. If they do not do so though and there is also no close and evident link of the contract to a certain state, arbitrators have considerable discretionary powers.
[461] Folsom et al., 2016: 128.

282

This is why, occasionally, "multinational companies enter into contracts with each other that are no longer subject to any national jurisdiction or to any national substantive law".[462]

Despite the strong argument for the *lex mercatoria* of being (partly) applied by arbitrators, the corresponding arbitral awards are still dependent on national law and authorities regarding enforcement. One of the major advantages of arbitral awards in comparison to state court decisions is, though, that they can be enforced nearly everywhere in the world. This goes back to the worldwide (172 parties) ratification of the New York Convention (NYC, which requires its contracting states to recognize and enforce the awards of foreign arbitral tribunals. (NYC Art. III; see also *Arbitration*)

In conclusion, irrespective of the merely theoretical discussion if consolidated commercial practices can be designated as a new *lex* between businesses or not, especially in international arbitration these practices often exceed their before mentioned role as mere interpretation and supplementation aid. This is because they are, in fact, partly applied *as if* they were law by arbitrators (and in the end also enforced as would law be).

---

[462] Fernández Rozas et al., 2013: 43.
It must be noted though that **a)** the explicit election of the *lex mercatoria* by the parties is quite rare (but not necessary for it to be applied by the arbitrator) and that **b)** the *lex mercatoria* usually cohabits with a national legal order in its application.

# G Contractual Terms

As we have seen in the preceding chapters, as part of their private autonomy, parties have several options regarding the law that is applied to their contract: the law of a state (e.g. German law), uniform law emerging from an International Organization (e.g. CISG, UNIDROIT Principles), the *lex mercatoria* ("juridified" commercial practices) …

On the other hand, private autonomy as the "freedom of contract" does not only comprise the flexibility of the parties to choose which law should be applied. It also allows parties to "create" law, i.e. legally binding provisions for each other as part of the contract. For that, within the limits the applicable law sets, they can freely formulate their own terms as they please and use their own preferred wording. A common result of that are, however, imprecisions and ensuing misunderstandings and possible "gaps" that have to be filled by potentially unwanted provisions of the applicable law.

In order to avoid that, parties do not only regulate as much as possible and reasonable explicitly in their contract, but also regularly a) use broadly accepted and understood terminology in their contracts and c) rely on model contracts and model contract clauses that have proven themselves.

As for the common terminology used in commercial contracts, e.g. regarding shipping and payment one often finds vocabulary such as

- *carriage forward* (*C/F*, German: "unfrei"), generally meaning that the buyer assumes the costs of delivery.
- *carriage paid/free* or *free domicile* (German: "frei Haus"), generally meaning that the seller assumes all costs and risks for transportation to the buyer's premises.

284

- *cash on delivery* (German: "Nachnahme"), generally meaning that the buyer has to pay upfront, i.e. before he/she has the possibility to inspect the good.
- *documents against payment* (German: "Kasse gegen Dokumente", see *Payment against documents*), generally requiring the buyer to pay before receiving the good (and being able to inspect it), but only after the seller has provided the relevant documents.[463]

Such terminology is regularly used and generally interpreted correctly by both parties. Some (other) of that terminology is ambiguous or has various meanings though.[464] This is why it is not recommended to use special terms without clarifying their concrete meaning in the contract.

The easiest way to avoid that is to use model clauses with a clearly defined meaning.

Apart from the INCOTERMS and the UCP600 we have a closer look at below, commonly used clauses are e.g. the *FIDIC Conditions of Contract*, which are published by the International Federation of Consulting Engineers (FIDIC) and usually used in construction and plant building. Also the UN Economic Commission for Europe (UNECE) offers contract conditions popular in the area of plant and machinery business. In some cases, also national standards parties can contractually opt for reach an overreaching significance, such as the *ÖNORM B 2110* in Austrian construction contracts.

Of course, parties can also agree to integrate[465] individual articles of the CISG, the PICC or other international substantive law frameworks in their contract (instead of deciding that the entire Convention/Principles should be applied to their contract).

---

[463] See e.g. Bernstorff, 2020: 15, 16.

[464] E.g. the term *price subject to change/confirmation* (German: "Preis freibleibend"), meaning **either** that the buyer is contractually bound but can increase the price if the market price increases **or** that the buyer is not bound contractually and can offer a new price the seller can accept or not.

[465] By reference or copy-paste.

# I. INCOTERMS[466]

## 1. ICC and INCOTERMS

The ICC is no International Organization (such as the UNO or UNIDROIT) but a private business organization founded in 1919, which is based in Paris and represented in all over the world. Its members are national and subnational chambers of commerce, big enterprises, banks and business associations. It has three main tasks:

1. It sets **optional rules for business transactions**, such as the INCOTERMS or the *Uniform Customs and Practice for Documentary Credits* (UCP 600, see *Documentary Credits and securing performance*).

2. It provides **dispute resolution services**, specifically in the areas of arbitration and mediation. For that purpose, it offers procedural arbitration (2021) and mediation rules (2014) and has established the *International Court of Arbitration* in Paris[467], which has achieved great global significance. In its framework, the ICC offers its premises as well as supervision and support for arbitral proceedings taking place there.

   ! The International Court of Arbitration does **not** issue judgments or awards. This is done only by the respective arbitral tribunals that carry out their work (hearings etc.) there.

---

[466] The Incoterms® Rules are protected by copyright owned by ICC. Further information on the Incoterm® rules may be obtained from the ICC website (https://iccwbo.org/business-solutions/incoterms-rules/). Incoterms® and the Incoterms® 2020 logo are trademarks of ICC. Use of these trademarks does not imply association with, approval of or sponsorship by ICC.

[467] Not to be confused with the intergovernmental organization *Permanent Court of Arbitration* in The Hague.

286

3. It represents its members by communicating the standpoint of world economy and **advocating for its policy objectives** at International Organizations and meetings, such as the WTO, the G20 and the UNO, where it has observer status.

The most important set of clauses used in international sales contracts are undoubtedly the so-called *INCOTERMS*. They are used in 90% (!) of all international sales contracts in over 120 countries around the world and primarily regulate transport and related costs and risk obligations. Based since their beginning on the globally most common actual commercial transport practices, the INCOTERMS are published and regularly revised since 1936 by the International Chamber of Commerce (ICC).

"INCOTERMS" stands for ***In**ternational **Co**mmercial **Terms*** and refers to optional standard contractual terms for international *and national* sale (of goods) contracts.[468] They do not cover all parts of a sales contract but focus on the **a)** tasks – including packaging, notices, documents, (un)loading, insurance and customs clearance, **b)** risks and **c)** costs associated with the *transportation* of goods.

**Example**

*The furniture chain **A** based in **X** buys 500 plain walnut tables (1x2m) from the woodwork company **B** based in **Y** for 200 000 €.*

The parties do not only have to agree (as done here) on the costs, size, quality and quantity of the product but must also arrange transportation and agree on its terms, e.g. where must the tables be delivered to, who

---

[468] In this point there is a clear parallel with the CISG, which also refers to sales contracts on (movable) goods. It must be noted though that, while the INCOTERMS are indeed commonly used in *sales* contracts, the only requirement for their usage is *transportation*. Therefore, they are in principle also eligible to be used in other contract types.

picks them up, where and when to pick the tables up, who pays for transportation and organizes it, how (and who) to package the tables so they arrive undamaged, who is liable if they are damaged anyway, who pays export and (import) customs duties and makes sure all export and import formalities are dealt with?

All these issues can be easily clarified by integrating one of the INCOTERMS clauses in the contract.

## 2. Incorporation and interpretation

While the INCOTERMS regulate important questions in relation to the transportation of goods, they do not cover other important contract contents, such as the specification of the sold good, payment terms, warranty and general (exclusion of) liability, the court (or arbitral tribunal) competent for the settlement of disputes, law applicable to the contract and the passage of propriety.
These questions must be regulated separately in the contract. If parties refrain from doing so (or leave some areas unregulated) or if they regulate something that contradicts peremptory law[469], the applicable state or non-state law has to be relied upon (e.g. Spanish civil law, the CISG or PICC).

*After* having clarified these essential contract contents, parties often decide to include INCOTERMS in their (inter)national sales contract if goods must be transported.

### a. How to include INCOTERMS in a contract?

Despite INCOTERMS being extremely common in international sales contracts, an automatic tacit inclusion of an INCOTERMS clause because of it being "commercial practice" cannot regularly be assumed.

This is why they must be incorporated actively in a contract: An INCOTERMS clause may be included in a contract by reference (e.g. "INCOTERMS 2020 Free Carrier / FCA") or by inserting the entire text of the clause in the contract.

An INCOTERMS clause can also be formulated in a way it is applicable to numerous business transactions. In order to avoid misunderstandings

---

[469] **See** *Peremptory & overriding mandatory provisions and ordre public*.

and legal complexities regarding its incorporation in the contract, it is recommended though to not (only) include it in a company's standard terms (GTC etc.) but to explicitly do so on an *individual* basis.

This inclusion of an INCOTERMS clause should generally be done **a) explicitly** (e.g. a clause merely printed on the back of a contract is usually not enough) and **b) when the contract is concluded**, e.g. mentioned in connection with the purchase price (the mere mentioning in e.g. an order confirmation generally does not suffice). INCOTERMS can also be added later but this should be expressly confirmed (in writing) by both parties.

It is further recommended to precise **which version of the INCOTERMS** is integrated in the contract, the newest one being the INCOTERMS *2020*. If such a reference is missing, in case of doubt the newest (English) version applies.

Emphasis must be placed on the importance of the *place of delivery* to be specified by the parties when using an INCOTERMS clause. To avoid misunderstandings, it is further useful to not only include a (general) place of delivery (e.g. a big port) but to also precise the exact point within this place. As a result of not determining the *exact* point of delivery/destination, according to the INCOTERMS, "the seller may select the point that best suits its purpose".

If parties forget to name a place of delivery (e.g. because the GTC of both parties contradict each other in this regard, which makes them inapplicable), the place of delivery and passage of risks depends on the respective clause used. In case of doubt, when clauses EXW and FCA/option A are used, the assumed place of delivery is generally the *seller's premises*. When DAP, DPU and DDP are used, the place of *destination* is also place of delivery, in doubt the *buyer's premises*. As for CPT and CIP, the place of delivery is the handing over to a carrier, so in case of doubt delivery most likely will take place at the *carrier's premises*. Finally, FCA/option B itself *requires* the parties to name "another place" for delivery; otherwise option A must be assumed (see above).

The INCOTERMS clauses can of course be modified or supplemented by the parties as expression of their contractual freedom. This is associated though with the risk of losing the provided interpretation aids (see now).

## b. How to interpret INCOTERMS?

The INCOTERMS are phrased in a clear, easy to understand manner and, also thanks to the constant revision work of the ICC, are less susceptible to interpretation complications than freely formulated clauses. Nevertheless, where interpretation based on the text of the clause (and additional party clarifications in the contract) remains insufficient, the INCOTERMS themselves provide for two interpretation aids:

a) the *introduction* preceding all clauses, which explains what the INCOTERMS are, how they are structured and how they should be used

b) an *explanatory note* for INCOTERMS users preceding each clause, where the general nature and specifics of the corresponding clause are mentioned

Apart from that, former practices and usages between the parties of the contract (and commercial practices in general e.g. expressed by the PICC) as well as, especially regarding terminology, the CISG may help to determine the meaning of the INCOTERMS.

# 3. INCOTERMS for all modes of transport

The INCOTERMS 2020 include 11 clauses covering each the same issues (tasks, risks and costs). They differ in two things though: **1.** the mode of transport they are available for and **2.** the level of tasks, risk and cost taking.

Whereas seven clauses are open for all modes of transport, four of them should only be used for sea and inland waterway transport. In this chapter focus will be on the mentioned seven clauses available for all modes of transport, i.e. air, rail, road and water.

As for the level of risk and cost taking, these seven clauses range from *very beneficial for the seller* (and very disadvantageous for the buyer) to *very disadvantageous for the seller* (and very beneficial for the buyer). On the one end of this range we find the *Ex Works* (EXW) clause, which imposes the least set of obligations on the seller, whereas on the other end of this range we find the *Delivered Duty Paid* (DDP) clause, which imposes the maximum level of obligations on the seller. In between these extremes we find the remaining five clauses that represent compromises *between* the mentioned minimum and maximum clauses.

All these seven clauses (and also the remaining four clauses for water transport) are structured the same way, "A" standing for the seller's obligations and "B" standing for the corresponding buyer's obligations:

| | |
|---|---|
| 0 | Explanatory notes for users |
| A1/B1 | General obligations |
| A2/B2 | Delivery/Taking delivery |
| A3/B3 | Transfer of risks |
| A4/B4 | Carriage |
| A5/B5 | Insurance |
| A6/B6 | Delivery/transport document |
| A7/B7 | Export/import clearance |

| A8/B8 | Checking/packaging/marking |
| A9/B9 | Allocation of costs |
| A10/B10 | Notices |

Let us have a look at the mentioned EXW clause to get a better understanding of how this structure common to all INCOTERMS 2020 clauses is e.g. "filled" with material content:

## EXW | Ex Works[470]

**A1 General obligations**
The seller must provide the goods and the commercial invoice in conformity with the contract of sale and any other evidence of conformity that may be required by the contract. Any document to be provided by the seller may be in paper or electronic form as agreed or, where there is no agreement, as is customary.

**B1 General obligations**
The buyer must pay the price of the goods as provided in the contract of sale. Any document to be provided by the buyer may be in paper or electronic form as agreed or, where there is no agreement, as is customary.

**A2 Delivery**
The seller must deliver the goods by placing them at the disposal of the buyer at the agreed point, if any, at the named place of delivery, not loaded on any collecting vehicle. If no specific point has been agreed within the named place of delivery, and if there are several points available, the seller may select the point that best suits its purpose. The seller must deliver the goods on the agreed date or within the agreed period.

**B2 Taking delivery**
The buyer must take delivery of the goods when they have been delivered under A2 and notice given under A10.

**A3 Transfer of risks**
The seller bears all risks of loss of or damage to the goods until they have been delivered in accordance with A2, with the exception of loss or damage in the circumstance described in B3.

**B3 Transfer of risks**
The buyer bears all risks of loss of or damage to the goods from the time they have been delivered under A2. If the buyer fails to give notice in accordance with B10, then the buyer bears all risks of

---

[470] International Chamber of Commerce, 2019: *Incoterms® 2020*, English Edition, ICC Publication no. 723E, EXW.

293

loss of or damage to the goods from the agreed date or the end of the agreed period for delivery, provided that the goods have been clearly identified as the contract goods.

**A4 Carriage**
The seller has no obligation to the buyer to make a contract of carriage. However, the seller must provide the buyer, at the buyer's request, risk and cost, with any information in the possession of the seller, including transport-related security requirements, that the buyer needs for arranging carriage.

(…)

**A9 Allocation of costs**
The seller must pay all costs relating to the goods until they have been delivered in accordance with A2, other than those payable by the buyer under B9.

**B4 Carriage**
It is up to the buyer to contract or arrange at its own cost for the carriage of the goods from the named place of delivery.

(…)

**B9 Allocation of costs**

The buyer must:

**a)** pay all costs relating to the goods from the time they have been delivered under A2;

**b)** reimburse all costs and charges incurred by the seller in providing assistance or information under A4, A5, or A7;

**c)** pay, where applicable, all duties, taxes and other charges, as well as the costs of carrying out customs formalities payable upon export; and

**d)** pay any additional costs incurred by failing either to take delivery of the goods when they have been placed at its disposal or to give appropriate notice in accordance with B10, provided that the goods have been clearly identified as the contract goods.

(…)

(…)

Thanks to all the INCOTERMS clauses having the same structure, to visually opposing the sellers obligations (A) to the buyers obligations (B) and to the usage of simple wording and the provision of official translations into over 30 languages[471], orientation is relatively simple.

As mentioned, these clauses are preceded 1. *as a whole* by an introduction explaining the INCOTERMS and their usage and 2. *respectively* (before each clause's substantive content) by "Explanatory notes for users" referring to the corresponding clause. These include compact information on general characteristics and special features of the clause as well as "notes of caution" and good-to-knows.

By (decreasing) order of the buyer's obligations, after the "extreme" EXW clause with the buyer bearing all costs and risks of transport, the

> Free Carrier (FCA),
>
> Carriage Paid To (CPT),
>
> Carriage and Insurance Paid To (CIP),
>
> Delivered at Place (DAP) and
>
> Delivered at Place Unloaded (DPU)

clauses follow until reaching the other mentioned "extreme" DDP clause with the seller bearing all costs and risks of transport including import clearance.

Let us have a quick look at each of these clauses individually.

---

[471] https://2go.iccwbo.org/incoterms-2020-eng-config+book_version-Book.

**EXW**, as mentioned, is the least beneficial clause for the buyer.

"Delivery" and risk transfer, which are connected in all INCOTERMS[472], generally takes place at the seller's premises. However, EXW also provides for the option to *deliver* the goods to the buyer at a place not coinciding with the seller's premises (similarly to FCA/option B).
The seller is not obliged to load the goods on the means of transport used by the buyer for carriage. The contrary can be contractually agreed upon though, in which case it makes sense to also clarify who bears the risk during loading.[473]
The buyer assumes the risk of loss or damage of the good(s) during the whole process of transportation, which he/she also has to arrange and finance. Apart from that, in international sales, the buyer is obliged to organize and finance both export (!)[474] and import clearance. Where the buyer has no knowledge or experience with export procedures in the country of the seller, the FCA clause might be better suited, which provides for the seller to clear goods for export (and the buyer only for *import*).

**FCA** is the only one of *all modes of transport* INCOTERMS clauses whose explanatory notes (and graphs) explicitly mention two optional places of delivery, option A and option B.

Whereas in option A *delivery* (and risk transfer) takes place at the seller's premises, in option B *delivery* occurs at "another named place". There is another difference though: While option A (seller's premises) requires the seller to *load* the goods on the buyer's means of transport for *delivery*

---

[472] Due to the special meaning "delivery" has in the INCOTERMS being the act that causes risk passage (and – except for CPT, CIP, CFR and CIF – also a change in cost bearing), in the following it is displayed in *italics*.
[473] Although parties agree that the *seller* must load the good(s) on the buyer's vehicle(s) etc., EXW still differs from FCA because the latter provides for export clearance by the *seller* (and not the buyer as is the case with EXW).
[474] EXW is the only INCOTERMS clause that provides that the buyer has to carry out and pay for export clearance.

taking place, option B (other place) only requires the seller to have the goods "ready for unloading" by the buyer. In other words, for *delivery* and risk transfer taking place, the seller must load the good on the buyer's vehicles etc. *only if* the chosen place is his/her premises. Of course, the parties can modify these terms.

Therefore, risk transfer to the buyer occurs at the seller's premises or another named place and from that moment on transportation costs and import clearance are borne by the buyer. From that point on, the buyer also has to arrange carriage unless the parties have agreed that the seller should do so (in which case the transportation costs and risks must anyway be borne by the buyer). Export clearance, in contrast to EXW, is on the seller though.

Apart form the mentioned general characteristics of FCA, it is special because it is the only INCOTERMS clause that explicitly mentions *bills of lading* (B/L), i.e. the combination of **a)** a carriage contract, **b)** a receipt (and bailment contract) issued by the carrier and **c)** a document of title giving its owner the right to the possession of the goods. These bills of lading are of the utmost importance in documentary sales with a letter of credit (see *Documentary Letter of Credit Sales*).

Nevertheless, FCA does not set the issuing of bills of lading with an on-board notation as a default for the parties but only if they agree so contractually. Put differently, when parties choose FCA, the transport document provision of the clause remains ineffective except if the parties stipulate in their contract that such a bill of lading must be issued. In case the parties decide to do so, the buyer must instruct and pay for the carrier to issue a bill of lading (B/L) with an onboard notation to the seller. Then the seller must give this document to the buyer, an act which serves as proof by the seller of having "*delivered*" (and therefore risk passes to the buyer). In addition, when the goods arrive at the destination (e.g. the buyer's premises), the buyer regularly needs this document (of title) for rightfully getting them from the carrier. (FCA A6/B6)

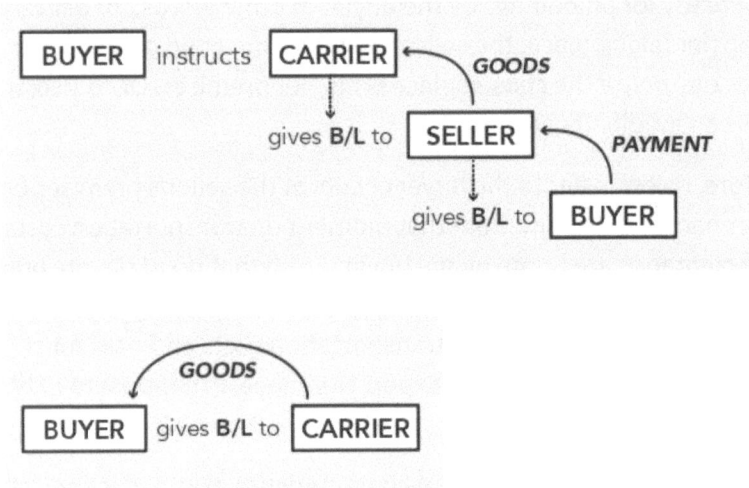

Image: © Karoline Schreiber. All rights reserved.

To give the seller additional security for receiving payment, often a bank is involved that – as an intermediary – receives the B/L from the seller and collects the payment from the buyer (in exchange for the B/L). See *Payment against documents*.

**CPT and CIP** are the only *all transport modes* INCOTERMS clauses where *delivery* and risk passage (these two go together in all INCOTERMS clauses) do not coincide with a change in cost bearing: Although *delivery* takes place and risk is passed to the buyer when the seller hands over the goods to the carrier (contracted by him/her), the seller *keeps bearing the costs* for transport. This obligation ceases once the carrier reaches the named *place* (or specific *point*) *of destination*, e.g. the buyer's premises. Unloading costs at *destination* must generally be borne by the buyer, but the parties can agree in their contract to transfer this obligation to the seller.

As with all the other INCOTERMS clauses except EXW and DDP, export formalities and costs are assumed by the seller while import clearance is on the buyer.

Concerning transport documents, CPT and CIP do not include a provision referring explicitly to bills of lading with an on-board notation (as FCA), but they also take account of the common practice of documentary sales/credits. They stipulate that the seller must provide the buyer with the usual transport document(s) and that "if agreed or customary, the document must also enable the buyer to claim the goods from the carrier". (CPT/CIP A6) For more information, see *Documentary Letter of Credit Sales*.

**CIP** provides for exactly the same obligations (and has the same phrasing) as CPT with one key difference: *insurance*. Even though (or because) the seller does not bear the risks for transport under CIP, he/she is obliged to provide insurance cover for the buyer:
He/she has to contract for insurance covering loss or damage of the goods from the point of delivery to the point of destination. The level of cover must be equivalent to the *Institute Cargo Clauses **A***, which is the highest level of coverage. The Institute Cargo Clauses are published by the International Underwriting Association of London and can be differentiated by their coverage in A (all risks covered), B (named peril covered) and C (limited named peril covered) clauses. As always, parties can agree on a lower level of coverage or further specify the insurance contract to be concluded by the seller.


**DAP, DPU and DDP** are the least "seller-friendly" INCOTERMS clauses. Since according to these clauses *delivery* takes place at the *place of destination* (commonly the buyer's premises), the seller assumes the risk for the *entire* transport. Apart from that, he/she has to arrange and finance the whole transport. The seller must also provide the necessary documents so the buyer can take over the goods (bill of lading etc.). The three clauses are very similar and only differ regarding **a)** unloading and **b)** import clearance:

> **DAP** is "best" of the three for the seller, obliging the *buyer* to both unload the goods from the seller's means of transport (and bear unloading risks) and clear the goods for import. Of course, the parties can agree in their contract that the seller must unload the goods, in which case DAP only differs from DPU any more in the risk bearing for unloading (which remains with the buyer).

> **DPU** obliges the *seller* to unload the goods and assume risks in this regard but the *buyer* to take care of import clearance.

> **DDP**, reversely, provides for an obligation of the *buyer* to unload the goods (including risk-bearing for it) and of the *seller* to carry out and pay for import clearance. It is, therefore, the only INCOTERMS clause where the seller (!) is responsible for import clearance (import duty, customs formalities, etc.). If it is specifically difficult for the seller to obtain import clearance or he/she is unable to do so, DAP might be the better choice.

 Please have a look at the Annex of this book where all any transport mode-INCOTERMS are visualized in color.

As mentioned, the INCOTERMS also include clauses suitable only for water transport, which was also their original focus when they were conceived: Free Alongside Ship (FAS), Free on Board (FOB), Cost and Feight (CFR) and Cost, Insurance and Freight (CIF). These clauses are relatively similar to the clauses for all modes of transport but tailored to sea and inland waterway transport.

300

Regardless of which INCOTERMS clause was chosen in their contract, parties do not only need a solid contractual basis where their mutual obligations are properly *specified*, but they also want to be sure that these obligations are actually *fulfilled*. Most importantly, of course, the obligation of the seller to deliver the goods and the obligation of the buyer to pay for them.

The seller generally has to perform in advance so the buyer can inspect the goods and pay afterwards (if everything is in order). This comes with the insecurity for the seller that – especially if he/she does not know the buyer well, which is common in international sales – he/she does not receive payment. Of course, he/she then could sue the buyer, which in international contracts potentially requires knowledge of another country's legal provisions (and local counsel), additional time and administrative efforts resulting often in considerable expenses for the seller. To avoid that, international commercial practice commonly opts for tools like documentary credits, which assure the seller getting paid in any case (without the necessity for lawsuits).

# II. Documentary Credits and securing performance

## 1. Uniform Customs and Practice (UCP)

No matter whether parties decide to incorporate an INCOTERMS clause (see above) or not in their international contract involving transportation, if the goods arrive correctly at their place of delivery/destination, the seller generally does not bear any risk of deterioration or loss anymore. But one risk of paramount importance remains: *the risk that the buyer does not pay*. If this happens, tedious and costly international litigation threatens.

To avoid this, many international sales contracts involve something called *documentary credits* or, synonymously, *documentary letters of credit*.

**Example**

A music shop chain based in the US (**A**) orders 500 *Rockhard* e-guitars for its guitar shops from a Japanese e-guitar producer (**B**) for 125 000 $ including transport. It is the first time **A** orders from **B** and **B** is therefore not 100% sure if it should accept the order including transportation of the guitars under a *DAP INCOTERMS 2020* clause. In the end it could happen that **B** packages the guitars, arranges and pays for carriage and, when they are at the disposal of **A** for inspection, he/she refuses to pay even though everything is in order.

In this case it makes sense for **B** to require a documentary credit, which obliges a bank to pay him/her the 125 000 $ as soon as he/she has handed over the "receipt" issued by the carrier, to the bank. This, of course, will cause additional (though usually relatively limited) expenses for **A**.

What is special is that documentary credits are regulated internationally generally not by a certain national law or an international convention concluded by several states but by an optional set of rules provided by a private organization: the *Uniform Customs and Principles for Documentary Credits* (UCP) by the ICC.

In their **nature** (but not content) the UCP are somewhat similar to the UNIDROIT Principles (PICC) we heard about, since both are an *optional* set of rules contracting parties can opt for. In this optionality the UCP also resemble the mentioned INCOTERMS parties can freely include in their contract. Nevertheless, the UCP are widely considered to be international commercial practice[475] and, thanks to that, it can generally be assumed that the application of the UCP is *implied* (tacitly agreed on) by the parties.[476] Finally, thanks also to this implicit *ex ante* acceptance, they in practice take effect not by express party agreement but by a *unilateral* express indication by the bank in the letter of credit that it is subject to the UCP.[477] (UCP Art. 1)

Regarding the **extent** of what they regulate and how they do so, they are in between the PICC and the INCOTERMS though:
The UCP are not *uniform law covering the most fundamental aspects* of a business contract (chosen mostly *instead* of otherwise applicable national private law) such as the PICC. At the same time, they are more (and something different) than individual clauses that are integrated in a

---

[475] For a differing view, see e.g. Schütze, Rolf A., 2016: *Das Dokumentenakkreditiv im internationalen Handelsverkehr*, R&W, Frankfurt am Main.
[476] This is especially valid if both parties are businesses and the international SWIFT System is used. See e.g. Kronke et al., 2017: 1157.
[477] See e.g. Folsom et al., 2016: 221.

contract to regulate certain matters (such as transport) like the INCOTERMS clauses.

Instead, they have elements of both: They are not *clauses* incorporated individually in a contract but a *united set of legal provisions* applied[478] to a contract (such as the PICC); they are not general uniform law intended to regulate most substantial contractual matters of a business contract but only one specific matter (the use of documentary credits[479], and that regularly in a *separate* contract with a bank).

The UCP were first published in 1933 by the ICC, which is the largest globally active private business organization (see *INCOTERMS and ICC*). Since then, they are regularly updated, last in 2007 ("UCP 600"), and supplemented by the *eUCP* for the area of electronic commerce.

According to the UCP 600's foreword, they "remain the most successful set of private rules for trade ever developed". What might seem a little overconfident (also in view of the INCOTERMS' importance), has its true core. While in a considerable approximately 15% of international business transactions letters of credit are used, nearly all of them are subjected to the UCP[480], which makes them *the* international standard for documentary credits (contracts).

Let us have a look in the next chapter what documentary letters of credit are and what the UCP substantively provide.

---

[478] Due to party *incorporation* / unilateral express indication by the bank in the letter of credit.

[479] But that not entirely either and excluding important matters such as fraud.

[480] https://www.iccgermany.de/standards-incoterms/handels-und-exportfinanzierung/dokumenten-akkreditive/.

304

## 2. Documentary Letter of Credit Sales

International documentary sales with a letter of credit are based on a structure where one or often two banks are involved to make sure the seller gets paid in any case. On the other hand, the buyer defines the conditions and documents the seller has to provide for the bank(s) to pay. This, in turn, reduces his/her risk of not being supplied (accordingly).

It is a rather simple construct that – due to the specific language used (in banking and specifically documentary credits) and the multiplicity of options of configuration of a documentary credit – often appears more complex than it actually is.

### *How does a documentary credit sale work?*

As mentioned, the considerable risks the parties incur in an international sales transaction can be distributed to third party intermediaries that can better bear and evaluate these risks: banks.

So – apart from the **a) sales contract** between the seller and the buyer and the **b) contract with the carrier** – also a **c) contract with the bank(s)** is concluded, the *letter of credit*.

### Contract between the buyer and the seller

The only (though essential) thing to mention regarding the sales contract is that, if the seller wants the transaction to be secured by a documentary credit, the parties should agree in the contract that the buyer has to arrange at his/her bank for an (irrevocable[481]) letter of credit with the seller as "beneficiary".

For additional security, the seller might want one of his/her *national* banks to promise payment.[482] In this case, parties include in their sales contract a provision according to which the buyer is obliged to request a "*confirmed* letter of credit" benefiting the seller.

Especially when parties agree on payment via letter of credit, which requires the presentation of documents (see below), they should specify in their contract what documents exactly (with which content) must be presented. The reason for that is simple: The buyer wants products with the needed characteristics. So they should be clearly specified in the documents since they serve as a guarantee[483] that the products (at least on the surface) match the information outlined in the documents. The seller, in turn, must know exactly which documents he/she must present to the bank to get paid.

These documents typically include

**1.** a negotiable bill of lading (see below) containing a description of the goods,

**2.** a commercial invoice that sets out the main terms of the sales contract, i.e. type, quantity and classification of goods, the amount owed for them, etc.,

**3.** a packing list, which confirms that the seller's shipping department has packed the goods for shipment,

---

[481] The UCP 600 presume the irrevocability of letters of credit, which is optional though. Parties can expressly agree to give the issuer or the applicant the right to cancel it. However, beneficiaries generally do not accept that for the risks involved of not getting paid.

[482] This way, the seller avoids economic risks in relation to the *foreign bank* itself as well as the economic and political risk of the buyer's bank's *country*. Obviously, the seller's confirming bank will charge a fee for taking over these risks (see below).

[483] The carrier is obliged (and liable) to deliver the goods as described in the bill of lading issued by him/her.

**4.** an export license confirming that the goods are cleared for export,

**5.** a certificate of origin displaying the origin of the goods, which is needed for correctly determining customs duties at importation.

In addition, parties can provide for additional security by incorporating insurance or third-party inspection (of the goods) obligations in their contract. Then, usually also **6.** an insurance policy and **7.** a certificate of inspection must be provided as well.

## Contract with the carrier (bill of lading)

In international sales the buyer and the seller are usually distant from each other, which regularly leads to the necessity of a carrier to transport the goods from the seller to the buyer.

The contract with the carrier is commonly concluded by the seller (but it can of course also be concluded by the buyer) and makes him/her the "shipper". The contract is the so-called *bill of lading* (B/L), which – apart from being **1.** contract of carriage – has two additional roles: It is also a **2.** receipt and bailment contract describing the goods received and **3.** a document of title embodying the legal rights to the goods and naming their legitimate owner (to who the goods must be delivered).

Bills of lading are regulated internationally by several conventions ("Hague", "Hague-Visby", "Hague-Visby/SDR", "Hamburg" and "Rotterdam"[the latter not being in force yet] Rules) with different state parties each. Unfortunately, this multiplicity of international treaties undermines the goal of having one internationally uniform set of rules regulating (this aspect of) carriage of goods.

Typically, international documentary sales transactions require a bill of lading to be "negotiable"[484] (transferable). *Negotiable* means that physical possession of the bill of lading (as document of title) confers the rights over the transported goods and, therefore, is necessary to obtain the goods from the carrier. Apart from the physical possession of the document, it is also usual that a "holder", i.e. the person to whose "order" the bill is issued, is named in the bill. Both things, physical possession *and* being the formal holder are then necessary to rightfully obtain the goods.

In these *order* bills of lading the person the bill is issued to (holder) regularly is the shipper (seller). In a next step, thanks to the bill being negotiable, the shipper can indorse (sign) the bill over to anybody he/she likes, who then becomes the new holder of the bill.
In documentary credit transactions this new holder is a bank (the seller's bank), which leads us to the third contract being concluded: the contract with the bank.


Contract with the bank(s) (letter of credit)


Before the seller concludes a contract of carriage and hands the goods over to a carrier, he/she wants to be sure to get paid by the buyer. At the same time, the buyer might not want to pay in advance because he/she does not trust the seller.

The seller prefers to have a solid promise by a bank to pay him (and the buyer prefers the bank to thoroughly revise the documentation accompanying the goods to be transported).

---

[484] Vs. "non-negotiable" bills of lading or "waybills", that oblige the carrier to deliver the goods only to the person named in the bill (without physical possession of the bill being necessary). Since this person regularly must be the *seller* (if it was the buyer, he/she could claim the goods without paying!), these non-transferable bills do not make sense in documentary letter of credit sales.

Therefore, the buyer ("applicant") usually asks one of his/her national banks ("buyer's/issuing bank") to issue a letter of credit to the seller. If the bank agrees, it contracts with the buyer and gives a *promise* to "honor a draft" later presented by the seller.

Of course, before expressing its promise of payment to the seller (as requested by the buyer) in the first place, the bank inquires about the buyer's creditworthiness and makes arrangements to make sure it gets reimbursed at the end.

① That means that the **bank obliges itself** to pay the contract price to the seller ("beneficiary"), *if* he/she provides the necessary documents, especially those confirming that the goods are shipped to the buyer. Among these documents, the *(negotiable) bill of lading* stands out, i.e. the document that will be issued by the carrier describing the goods received by the seller (see above).

Apart from that and other documents (see above), a so-called "draft" – a document in which the seller requires the bank to pay (see below) – is necessary. These documents must be in accordance with the requirements stipulated in the letter of credit based on the buyer's application.

If the seller does not trust the buyer's bank or just does not know about banks and/or banking regulations in the foreign country he/she is based in, he/she will most likely want a binding payment promise of a (national) bank known to it ("seller's/confirming bank").

In this case[485], as mentioned, the buyer applies at his/her bank for a *confirmed* letter of credit. Then his/her bank requests a bank at the seller's location to oblige itself to as well honor the seller's (future) draft, i.e. promise payment to the seller if the necessary documents (see above) are provided.

---

[485] If the parties have agreed in their sales contract that the buyer must initiate the issuance of a confirmed letter of credit.

② This is done through a **"confirmation" issued to the seller**.

Banks of course do not give their payment promises for free, but the fees – typically not more (and often less) than 2% of the letter of credit amount – are relatively limited compared with the security the banks provide. However, these fees may increase for confirmed letters of credit if the buyer's bank is e.g. located in an (economically and politically) high-risk country. It may also happen that no bank at all is willing to cover the country risk of the buyer and his/her bank, respectively.

③ Then, well equipped with both the promises from the buyer's and seller's bank, the **seller hands the goods over to the carrier** for transportation to the agreed destination, from who he/she receives the bill of lading.

Afterwards, the **seller presents the necessary documents**[486] including a commercial invoice and the negotiable bill of lading (see *Contract between the buyer and the seller*), **to his/her bank**.
Along with these documents, the seller also presents a so-called "draft" (legal basis for demanding payment) to his/her (seller's) bank.
A *draft* is necessary because up until now the banks only gave payment *promises*, which constitute the (letter of) credit. However, a legal means to draw on this credit (demand payment) has been missing so far. That is what the seller's draft is – the legal vehicle to instruct a bank to make payment. This instructed bank is usually the *buyer's* bank and the person designated to be paid is, at this point, the seller[487].

---

[486] These documents can be presented electronically, as equivalent "electronic records", if the *eUCP* are expressly included in the letter of credit. For that, commonly the *Society for Worldwide Interbank Financial Telecommunication* (SWIFT) *System* is used, which provides a uniform format and standardized elements for electronically transmitted messages.
[487] This changes later with the *seller's bank* becoming the payee instead of the seller, see ⑤.

④ The seller's bank then carefully[488] **revises** if the documents are in conformity with the requirements in the letter of credit (since the bank is liable for mistakes). For that, the bank has no longer than five (!) banking days according to the UCP 600 (Art. 14).

 About one half (!) of all presentations of documents are rejected by the bank in that context. However, the bank can consult the buyer for waiving the discrepancies, which is done in around 90% of all cases.[489] It is nevertheless recommended for sellers to be as precise as possible and make sure that the provided documents fulfil the requirements in the letter of credit by 100%.

If the seller's bank finds the documents in conformity with the letter of credit, it "honors" the presentation, i.e. pays the promised sum to the seller.

⑤ For that to happen, the seller **indorses the draft and the negotiable bill of landing over to his/her bank** (which is already in possession of the documents), which becomes **a)** the new *payee* of the draft (the buyer's bank must honor) and **b)** *holder* of the bill.
Thanks to the seller's bank's physical possession of the bill and being its formal holder, it now controls access to the goods. Due to now being the payee of the draft, the seller's bank can demand payment by the buyer's bank, for which the latter will require becoming holder and physical possessor of the bill (and other documents).

⑥ Then, as announced, the **seller's bank indorses the draft and the bill of lading over to the buyer's bank** and forwards the provided documents to it

---

[488] There is a *strict compliance* standard in documentary credits that, apart from minor misspellings or typos, does not leave much room for deviations between the presented documents and the requirements stipulated in the letter of credit.
[489] Folsom et al., 2016: 226, 228.

311

⑦ In turn, the **buyer's bank** – if it also **determines that the documents conform to the letter of credit requirements** – honors the draft presented now by the seller's bank, i.e. **reimburses** it.

⑧ Finally, the **buyer** is requested by his/her bank to **pay the contractually agreed sum against the documents including the bill of lading** (B/L), which is indorsed over to him/her by his/her bank.

If the buyer's bank is unsure about the buyer's creditworthiness and trustworthiness, before expressing its payment promise to the seller (as requested by the buyer) at the very beginning of the just explained process, it regularly makes arrangements to make sure it gets reimbursed at the end.
For that, it often prepones the moment of payment by the buyer to the moment of *application* for the letter of credit, either by direct payment by the buyer or by granting a loan secured with sufficient collateral for the meantime.
In most cases, however, an ongoing relationship exists between the buyer and his/her bank with credit lines in place to facilitate the customer's business and make such purchases possible without the bank having to check every transaction individually.

⑨ After payment by the **buyer** and his/her reception of the documents, he/she can **get the goods from the carrier.**

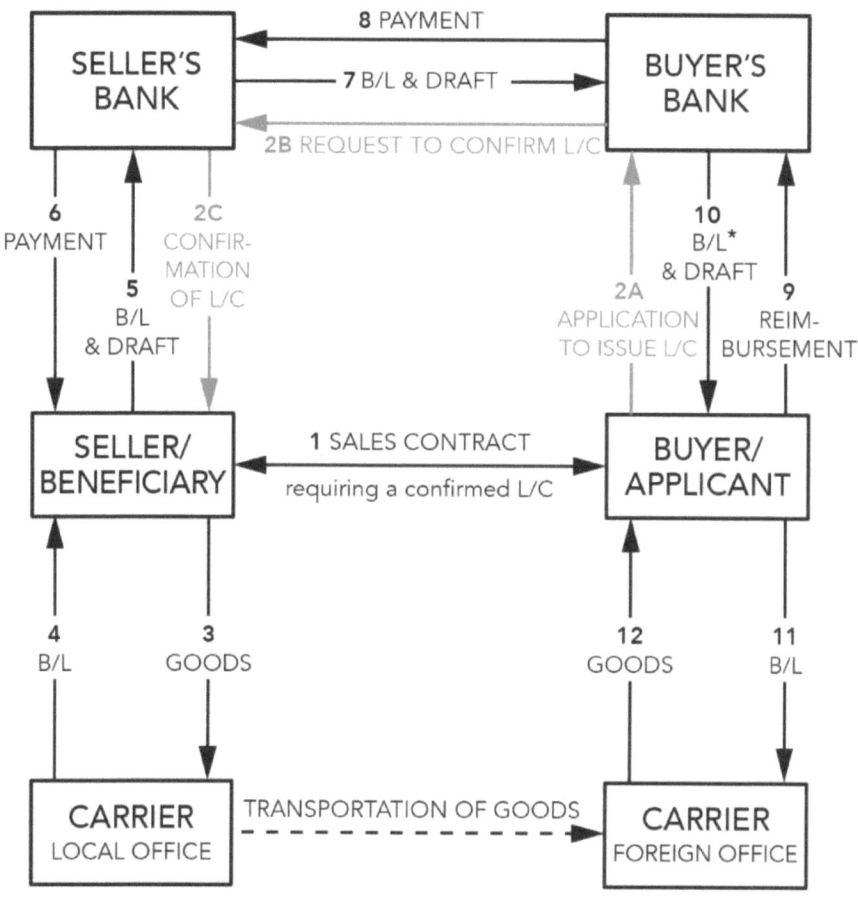

*shown to buyer *before* payment but formally handed over normally *after* payment

Diagram based on Folsom et al., 2016: 211

The risks to be borne by the different parties are limited because

- the seller has up to three payment promises: from the buyer, from the buyer's bank, in case of a *confirmation*, and from his/her own bank,
- the buyer, thanks to the careful revision of the bank(s), will get the documentation of the goods exactly as agreed in the sales contract and the letter of credit; if the goods finally do not correspond to the documents, the carrier and/or the seller are liable,

- the seller's bank is entitled to reimbursement by both the buyer's bank and the buyer,
- the buyer's bank initially had the chance to properly evaluate the buyer's creditworthiness and likeliness of payment and, even in case of non-payment by the buyer, it theoretically[490] has control over the shipped goods thanks to the bill of lading in its possession.

---

[490] Selling/auctioning the shipped goods is very seldom necessary because the credit line of the buyer regularly is collateralized. This means that, if the buyer can/does not pay, the collateral (e.g. mortgage, pledge of assets) is normally used by the bank to satisfy its claim.

## 3. Standby Letters of Credit

There are several types of documentary letters of credit ("transferable", "back-to-back", "revolving" letters of credit, etc.) and different possible roles of e.g. the seller's bank (as "advising/notifying" or "nominated" bank) parties can arrange for.[491]

One of these types of letters of credit is shortly explained here for its relevance in securing performance in international business, the so-called "**standby letter of credit**".

The standby letter of credit can be understood as something like an "inverted" classical/commercial documentary letter of credit. This is due to the fact that its primary goal is not to provide the seller with additional security but the *buyer*: The main objective is not that the buyer pays but that the seller performs its obligations, i.e. delivery of goods, provision of (related) services such as construction, etc.

This assurance of performance is often required not by small companies or for sales/projects of limited scope but by large project developers or governments tasking major international corporations with bigger projects.

Here **1.** the *seller*/contractor ("applicant") applies for an irrevocable letter of credit at his/her bank ("seller's bank") – with the possible involvement of a local bank of the buyer ("buyer's bank") – in favor of the *buyer*/orderer ("beneficiary").

Regarding classical documentary credits, the condition for payment by the bank(s) to the seller is the presentation of documents by the seller indicating that the goods are in order and carriage ongoing according to the letter of credit's requirements.
As for standby letters of credit though, **2.** the bank(s) must pay the *buyer/orderer* not in case everything is in order but if **3.** the obligations of

_____

[491] See e.g. Folsom et al., 2016: 261-265.

315

the seller/contractor are *not* performed according to the contract. Documents play only a secondary role here[492] and the question if the seller/contractor has performed accordingly is not primarily based on provided documents but on a simple written statement by the buyer/orderer that the seller/contractor has *not* duly carried out his/her contractual obligations. This statement must, of course, fulfil basic conditions such as good faith and reasonable discretion in determining non-compliance with the contract. Therefore, at least some kind of explanation or proof must be provided.

Therefore, there is an essential difference between classical letters of credit and standby letters of credit. Regarding the former, the beneficiary (seller) gets paid by his/her bank *as the regular case* whereas regarding the latter the beneficiary (buyer) only gets paid by his/her bank in *the exceptional case* of the other party's performance being *not* correct.

Having understood the functioning of a regular/commercial letter of credit (see *Contract with the bank(s) (letter of credit)*) and in view of the fact that the procedure in standby letters of credit works similar (but "backwards" with limited importance of documents), this diagram should be enough of an explanation:

---

[492] They are regularly *no* documents of title giving control over the goods.

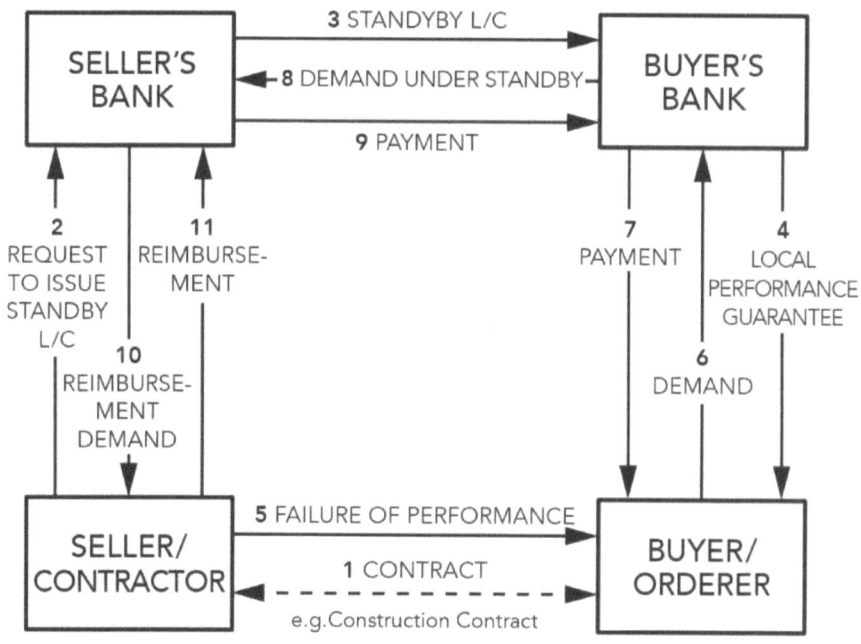

Diagram based on Folsom et al., 2016: 241

As for the rules governing standby letters of credit, the UCP apply if they are expressly incorporated in the standby letter. Nonetheless, the UCP are not ideal for their application to standby letters of credit since they are designed primarily for documentary letters of credit and, therefore, impose some document-related requirements which are rather unnecessary for standbys.

Therefore, the ICC has introduced the *International Standby Practices* (ISP 98), which are tailored specifically to *standby* letters of credit. As with the UCP, the ISP must be explicitly incorporated in the letter of credit to be applied to it. Since the ISP are heavily influenced by US legal practice in their conception (which can cause complications with other legal orders), European parties tend to be hesitant to subject their standby letter of credit to them entirely. A reasonable compromise can e.g. be the general application of the UCP and the incorporation of suitable *individual* articles of the ISP 98 by the parties.

317

# 4. Payment against documents

Apart from that, parties can also agree on a simple "**payment against documents**" or "documents against payment" sale, where the banks have the mere function of *collecting* the necessary documents (but not revising the documents nor giving payment promises) and releasing them against payment by the buyer.

Also for these transactions the ICC provides optional rules, the *Uniform Rules for Collections* (URC 522 and eURC). These are widely accepted among most banks and banking associations and are often considered to be, such as the UCP, codified international business practices.

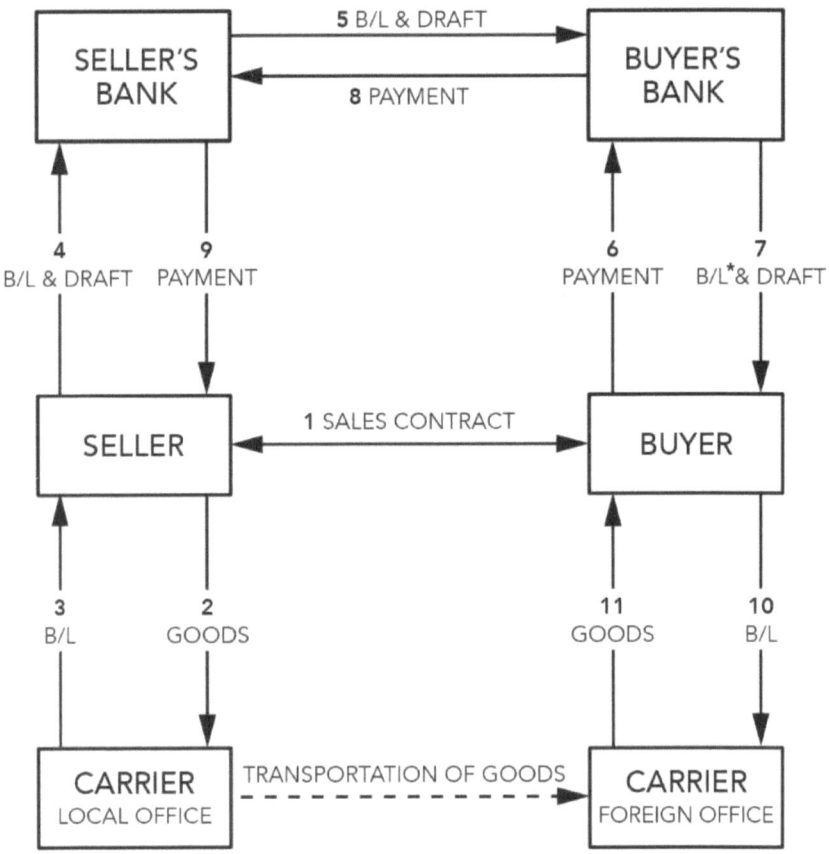

*shown to buyer *before* payment but formally handed over normally *after* payment

Diagram based on Folsom et al., 2016: 165

In this kind of transaction, however, important risks remain:

Thanks to the documents (and resulting goods possession) being only released to the buyer if and when he/she pays, the seller will not lose its property and control of the goods up to then. If the buyer – for whatever reason – refuses to pay the collecting bank, he/she will not receive the goods, **but** the seller has already shipped them to the buyer's (foreign) location. There, the seller might not be able to re-sell them (at a profitable price) and might have to ship them back to his/her premises. This, in addition to the costs already incurred by the carriage to the buyer's location, again generates shipment costs. In the end, the total carriage and administrative costs may exceed the value of the goods themselves and, finally, the seller may have lost time and money.

This risk of the buyer not paying can be avoided if the bank makes sure the seller gets paid even though the buyer does not pay. In such arrangements, the bank usually pays the seller upfront, i.e. before the buyer pays (the bank gives the seller a "credit"[493] arranged by the buyer).

This is called *documentary credit* (see above).

---

[493] Instead of the seller to repay the credit, the buyer must repay the credit paid to the seller in exchange for the transport documents (→ products).

# Literature

Balassa, Bela, 1962: *The Theory of Economic Integration*, George Allen&Unwin, London.

Balassa, Bela, 1976: "Types of Economic Integration", in Machlup, Fritz (ed.), 1976: *Economic Integration: Worldwide, Regional, Sectoral*, Macmillan, London, p. 16-31.

Beham, Markus et al., 2019: *Völkerrecht verstehen²*, Facultas, Vienna.

Bernstorff, Graf von, 2020: INCOTERMS® 2020: *Kommentierung für die Praxis inklusive offiziellem Regelwerk*, Linde, Vienna.

Binder, Christina et al., 2015: *Einführung in die Internationalen Grundlagen des Rechts: Einführung in das Völkerrecht*, University of Vienna, Vienna.

Dolan, John. F., Baker, Walter, 2008: *Users' Handbook for Documentary Credit under UCP 600*, 2008 Edition; ICC Publication no. 694E.

Doralt, Werner, Cap, Verena (eds.), 2023: *Internationales Privatrecht⁹*, Lexis Nexis, Vienna.

Fernández Rozas, José Carlos et al., 2013: *Derecho de los negocios internacionales⁴*, Iustel, Madrid.

Ferrari, Franco et al. , 2023: *Recognition and Enforcement of Foreign Arbitral Awards*, Elgar, Cheltenham/Northampton.

Folsom, Ralph H., Gordon, Michael W. et al., 2016: *International Business Transactions in a nutshell*, West Academic, St. Paul.

Henricksen, Anders, 2019: *International Law²*, Oxford University Press, Oxford.

Henricksen, Anders, 2023: *International Law⁴*, Oxford University Press, Oxford.

International Chamber of Commerce, 2007: *UCP 600: Uniform Rules for Documentary Credits*, ICC Publication no. 822E.

International Chamber of Commerce, 2019: *Incoterms® 2020*, English Edition, ICC Publication no. 723E.

Jaeger, Thomas, 2017: *Materielles Europarecht*, LexisNexis, Vienna.

Jaeger, Thomas, 2024: *Materielles Europarecht*[3], LexisNexis, Vienna.

Jaeger, Thomas, 2021: *Introduction to European Union Law*, Facultas, Vienna.

Jauk, Harald J., 2023: "Zur „Ordnungskapazität" des Völker- und Unionsrechts", in *Pro Scientia Reader: Chaos & Ordnung*, Facultas, Vienna, 22-26.

Karas, Othmar, 2018: *Die europäische Demokratie: Grenzen und Möglichkeiten des Europäischen Parlaments*, Verlag Österreich, Vienna.

Klauser, Alexander, Kodek, Georg, 2018: *Jurisdiktionsnorm und Zivilprozessordnung (JN-ZPO) – Österreichisches und Europäisches Zivilprozessrecht*[18], commentary, Manz, Vienna.

Krejci, Heinz, 2013: *Unternehmensrecht*[5], Manz, Vienna.

Kronke, Herbert et al., 2017: *Handbuch Internationales Wirtschaftsrecht*[2], Linde, Vienna.

Krugman, Paul, 1997: "What Should Trade Negotiators Negotiate About?", in *Journal of Economic Literature*, vol. XXXV, 113-120.

Lester, Simon et al., 2018: *World Trade Law: Text, Materials and Commentary*[3], Bloomsbury, Oxford.

Lowenfeld, Andreas F., 2008: *International Economic Law*[2], Oxford University Press, New York.

Lurger, Brigitta, Melcher, Martina, 2020: *Internationales Privatrecht*[3], vol. VII / Bürgerliches Recht, Verlag Österreich, Vienna.

OECD, EU (Eurostat), WHO, 2017: *System of Health Accounts 2011: Revised edition*, OECD Publishing, Paris.

Reinisch, August (Ed.), 2021: *Österreichisches Handbuch des Völkerrechts*[6], vol. 1, Manz, Vienna.

Riedl, Eckhard et al., 2020: *Die Europäische Union*, Skriptum, Federal Academy of Public Administration, Vienna.

Rummel, Peter et al. (Eds.), 2023: *ABGB*[4], Manz / RDB online.

Smith, Adam, 2005 (1776): *The Wealth of Nations*, Electronic Classics Series, Pennsylvania State University.

Trebilcock, Michael, Trachtman, Joel, 2020: *Advanced Introduction to International Trade Law*$^2$, Elgar, Cheltenham/Northhampton.

UNIDROIT, 2016: *Official Comment to the UNIDROIT Principles of International Commercial Contracts*, UNIDROIT, Rome.

Van den Bossche, Peter, Prévost, Denise, 2021: *Essentials of WTO Law*$^2$, Cambridge University Press, Cambridge.

Van den Bossche, Peter, Zdouc, Werner, 2022: *The Law and Policy of the World Trade Organization*$^5$, Cambridge University Press, Cambridge.

Welser, Rudolf, Zöchling-Jud, Brigitta, 2015: *Grundriss des bürgerlichen Rechts*$^{14}$, vol. 2, Manz, Vienna.

WTO, 1995: *Analytical Index of the GATT 1994*, WTO, Geneva.

Zöchling-Jud, Brigitta, Aspöck, Florian, 2015: *Internationales Privatrecht*$^3$, Lexis Nexis, Vienna.

# Annex

## WTO Organigram

**Secretariat**

**Committees on**
Trade and Environment
Trade and Development
Regional Trade Agreements
Budget, Finance and
Administration
etc.

**Working parties on**
Accession

**Working groups on**
Trade, debt and finance
Trade and technology transfer

**Council for Trade
in Goods**

**Committees on**
Agriculture
Anti-Dumping Practices
Customs Valuation
Import Licensing
etc.

**Working party on**
State Trading Enterprises

**Ministerial Conference**

**General Council**

**Council for
Trade-Related
Aspects of Intellectual
Property Rights**

**Council for Trade
in Services**

**Committees on**
Trade in
Financial Services
Specific Commitments
bodies

**Working parties on**
Domestic Regulation
GATS Rules

**Plurilaterais**
Trade in Civil Aircraft Committee
Government Procurement Committee
Information Technology Agreement Committee

**General Council
meeting as Trade Policy
Review Body**

**General Council
meeting as Dispute
Settlement Body**

**Appellate Body Dispute
Settlement Panels**

**Trade Negotiations
Committee**

**Doha Development
Agenda Negotiations:**
Trade Negotiations
Committee and its
bodies

**Special Sessions of**
Services Council/
TRIPS Council/
Dispute Settlement
Body
+ certain Committees

**Negotiation groups on**
Market Access
Rules

——— Reporting to General Council or a subsidiary
– – – Reporting to Dispute Settlement Body
– · – · Informing the General Council or Goods Council of their activities
·········· Reporting to General Council

© Karoline Schreiber, based on WTO. All rights reserved.

# WTO Panel Proceedings – Basic Working Procedures[494]

## APPENDIX 3

### WORKING PROCEDURES

1.  In its proceedings the panel shall follow the relevant provisions of this Understanding. In addition, the following working procedures shall apply.

2.  The panel shall meet in closed session. The parties to the dispute, and interested parties, shall be present at the meetings only when invited by the panel to appear before it.

3.  The deliberations of the panel and the documents submitted to it shall be kept confidential. Nothing in this Understanding shall preclude a party to a dispute from disclosing statements of its own positions to the public. Members shall treat as confidential information submitted by another Member to the panel which that Member has designated as confidential. Where a party to a dispute submits a confidential version of its written submissions to the panel, it shall also, upon request of a Member, provide a non-confidential summary of the information contained in its submissions that could be disclosed to the public.

4.  Before the first substantive meeting of the panel with the parties, the parties to the dispute shall transmit to the panel written submissions in which they present the facts of the case and their arguments.

5.  At its first substantive meeting with the parties, the panel shall ask the party which has brought the complaint to present its case. Subsequently, and still at the same meeting, the party against which the complaint has been brought shall be asked to present its point of view.

6.  All third parties which have notified their interest in the dispute to the DSB shall be invited in writing to present their views during a session of the first substantive meeting of the panel set aside for that purpose. All such third parties may be present during the entirety of this session.

7.  Formal rebuttals shall be made at a second substantive meeting of the panel. The party complained against shall have the right to take the floor first to be followed by the complaining party. The parties shall submit, prior to that meeting, written rebuttals to the panel.

8.  The panel may at any time put questions to the parties and ask them for explanations either in the course of a meeting with the parties or in writing.

9.  The parties to the dispute and any third party invited to present its views in accordance with Article 10 shall make available to the panel a written version of their oral statements.

10.  In the interest of full transparency, the presentations, rebuttals and statements referred to in paragraphs 5 to 9 shall be made in the presence of the parties. Moreover, each party's written submissions, including any comments on the descriptive part of the report and responses to questions put by the panel, shall be made available to the other party or parties.

11.  Any additional procedures specific to the panel.

[494] WTO, 1994: *Understanding on Rules and Procedures Governing the Settlement of Disputes – Appendix 3*, WTO, Geneva, 375, 376.

12. Proposed timetable for panel work:

    (a)    Receipt of first written submissions of the parties:

            (1)    complaining Party: _____ 3-6 weeks
            (2)    Party complained against: _____ 2-3 weeks

    (b)    Date, time and place of first substantive meeting
           with the parties; third party session: _____ 1-2 weeks

    (c)    Receipt of written rebuttals of the parties: _____ 2-3 weeks

    (d)    Date, time and place of second substantive
           meeting with the parties: _____ 1-2 weeks

    (e)    Issuance of descriptive part of the report to the parties: _____ 2-4 weeks

    (f)    Receipt of comments by the parties on the
           descriptive part of the report: _____ 2 weeks

    (g)    Issuance of the interim report, including the
           findings and conclusions, to the parties: _____ 2-4 weeks

    (h)    Deadline for party to request review of part(s) of report: _____ 1 week

    (i)    Period of review by panel, including possible
           additional meeting with parties: _____ 2 weeks

    (j)    Issuance of final report to parties to dispute: _____ 2 weeks

    (k)    Circulation of the final report to the Members: _____ 3 weeks

The above calendar may be changed in the light of unforeseen developments. Additional meetings with the parties shall be scheduled if required.

**ICC Force Majeure Clause** (short form)[495]

1. "Force Majeure" means the occurrence of an event or circumstance that prevents or impedes a party from performing one or more of its contractual obligations under the contract, if and to the extent that that party proves: [a] that such impediment is beyond its reasonable control; and [b] that it could not reasonably have been foreseen at the time of the conclusion of the contract; and [c] that the effects of the impediment could not reasonably have been avoided or overcome by the affected party.

2. In the absence of proof to the contrary, the following events affecting a party shall be presumed to fulfil conditions (a) and (b) under paragraph 1 of this Clause: (i) war (whether declared or not), hostilities, invasion, act of foreign enemies, extensive military mobilisation; (ii) civil war, riot, rebellion and revolution, military or usurped power, insurrection, act of terrorism, sabotage or piracy; (iii) currency and trade restriction, embargo, sanction; (iv) act of authority whether lawful or unlawful, compliance with any law or governmental order, expropriation, seizure of works, requisition, nationalisation; (v) plague, epidemic, natural disaster or extreme natural event; (vi) explosion, fire, destruction of equipment, prolonged break-down of transport, telecommunication, information system or energy; (vii) general labour disturbance such as boycott, strike and lock-out, go-slow, occupation of factories and premises.

3. A party successfully invoking this Clause is relieved from its duty to perform its obligations under the contract and from any liability in damages or from any other contractual remedy for breach of contract, from the time at which the impediment causes inability to perform, provided that the notice thereof is given without delay. If notice thereof is not given without delay, the relief is effective from the time at which notice thereof reaches the other party. Where the effect of the impediment or event invoked is temporary, the above consequences

---

[495] International Chamber of Commerce, 2020: *ICC Force Majeure and Hardship Clauses*, March 2020. There is also a long form of this clause available on the ICC webpage.

shall apply only as long as the impediment invoked impedes performance by the affected party. Where the duration of the impediment invoked has the effect of substantially depriving the contracting parties of what they were reasonably entitled to expect under the contract, either party has the right to terminate the contract by notification within a reasonable period to the other party. Unless otherwise agreed, the parties expressly agree that the contract may be terminated by either party if the duration of the impediment exceeds 120 days.

**ICC Hardship Clause**[496]

1. A party to a contract is bound to perform its contractual duties even if events have rendered performance more onerous than could reasonably have been anticipated at the time of the conclusion of the contract.

2. Notwithstanding paragraph 1 of this Clause, where a party to a contract proves that:

a) the continued performance of its contractual duties has become excessively onerous due to an event beyond its reasonable control which it could not reasonably have been expected to have taken into account at the time of the conclusion of the contract; and that

b) it could not reasonably have avoided or overcome the event or its consequences, the parties are bound, within a reasonable time of the invocation of this Clause, to negotiate alternative contractual terms which reasonably allow to overcome the consequences of the event.

3A Party to terminate
Where paragraph 2 of this Clause applies, but where the parties have been unable to agree alternative contractual terms as provided in that paragraph, the party invoking this Clause is entitled to terminate the

---

[496] International Chamber of Commerce, 2020: *ICC Force Majeure and Hardship Clauses*, March 2020.

contract, but cannot request adaptation by the judge or arbitrator without the agreement of the other party.

3B Judge adapt or terminate
Where paragraph 2 of this Clause applies, but where the parties have been unable to agree alternative contractual terms as provided for in that paragraph, either party is entitled to request the judge or arbitrator to adapt the contract with a view to restoring its equilibrium, or to terminate the contract, as appropriate.

3C Judge to terminate
Where paragraph 2 of this Clause applies, but where the parties have been unable to agree alternative contractual terms as provided in that paragraph, either party is entitled to request the judge or arbitrator to declare the termination of the contract

# INCOTERMS[497] for all modes of transport

## OBLIGATIONS, COSTS AND RISKS

**BLUE** indicates seller's

**RED** indicates buyer's

**GREEN** indicates shared

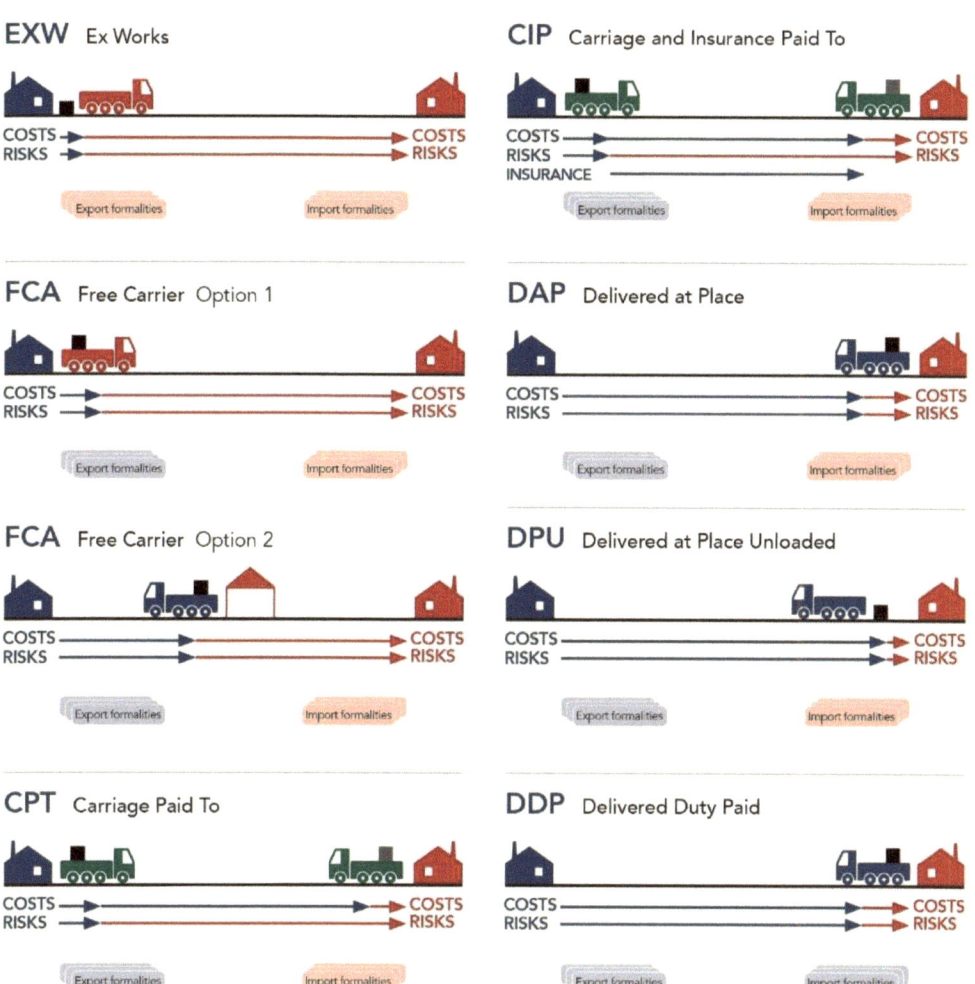

© Karoline Schreiber. All rights reserved. No part of this diagram may be reproduced, copied, distributed, translated or adapted in any form or by any means (whether graphic, electronic or mechanical, and including without limitation photocopying and scanning, or by use of computer, the internet or information retrieval systems) without written permission of the copyright owner.

---

[497] Diagram based on Bernstorff, Graf von, 2020: INCOTERMS® 2020: *Kommentierung für die Praxis inklusive offiziellem Regelwerk*, Linde, Vienna.

Thank you for having read this book.